Fodor's InFocus

ST. MAARTEN,
ST. MARTIN,
ST. BARTH &
ANGUILLA

D0006001

Excerpted from *Fodor's Caribbean*

15
TOP EXPERIENCES

St. Maarten/St. Martin, St. Barth &
Anguilla offer terrific experiences
that should be on every traveler's
list. Here are Fodor's top picks for
a memorable trip.

1 Shoal Bay, Anguilla

This 2-mile-long beach is covered with sand as fine and white as powdered
sugar, making it one of the best of many excellent beaches on this tiny
island. *(Ch. 4)*

2 Loterie Farm, St. Martin

On the slopes of Pic du Paradis, the highest mountain on the island, Loterie Farm is a wonderful family-friendly, family-run private nature reserve. *(Ch. 2)*

3 Shopping, St. Barth

Whatever you're shopping for, you will find no better place in all the Caribbean than St. Barth, especially the shops along Gustavia's Quai de la République. *(Ch. 3)*

4 Eden Rock, St. Barth

Since the Eden Rock's construction in the 1950s, extensive renovations and recent expansions have raised it into the top category of St. Barth properties, where it has remained. *(Ch. 3)*

5 Golf at CuisinArt, Anguilla

At this wonderful $50-million course designed by Greg Norman, 13 of the 18 holes are directly on the water. The island's only golf course is a winner. *(Ch. 4)*

6 Lunch at the "lolos," St. Martin

Some of the best dining bargains in St. Martin can be found at one of several roadside barbecue stands in Grand Case, the island's culinary capital. *(Ch. 2)*

7 Elvis' Beach Bar, Anguilla

You can have one of the best rum punches in the Caribbean at this bar (which is made from a beached boat) at Sandy Ground every day but Tuesday, when it's closed. *(Ch. 4)*

8 Anse de Grande Saline, St. Barth

Secluded, with a sandy ocean bottom, this is just about everyone's favorite St. Barth beach, and it's great for swimmers, too. Best of all, there's no major development here. *(Ch. 3)*

9 Marigot, St. Martin

St. Martin's lovely seaside French capital, with its bustling harbor, shopping stalls, open-air cafés, and boutiques, is a must-see destination. *(Ch. 2)*

10 Butterfly Farm, St. Martin

This quiet, shady haven will mesmerize you with hundreds of beautiful tropical butterflies flitting about in a large, screened enclosure. *(Ch. 2)*

11 La Samanna Spa, St. Martin

One of the best places on the island to relax and rejuvenate is this spa in one of St. Martin's toniest resorts. *(Ch. 2)*

12 Dune Preserve, Anguilla

A trip to Anguilla is not complete without a visit to this funky wooden beach bar, where famous reggae star Bankie Banx performs on weekends. *(Ch. 4)*

13 Le Gaïac, St. Barth

Chef Stéphane Mazières' restaurant at Le Toiny showcases his gastronomic art on a dramatic, tasteful cliff-side dining porch. *(Ch. 3)*

14 Baie Orientale, St. Martin

Many consider this 2-mile-long wonder the island's most beautiful beach, and it buzzes with lively water-sports outfitters, beach clubs, and hotels. *(Ch. 2)*

15 Yellow Submarine, St. Barth

A trip aboard this air-conditioned submarine shows you what's going on under the sea without requiring you to get your head or feet wet. *(Ch. 3)*

CONTENTS

ABOUT THIS GUIDE

Fodor's Ratings

Everything in this guide is worth doing—we don't cover what isn't—but exceptional sights, hotels, and restaurants are recognized with additional accolades. Fodor's Choice★ indicates our top recommendations. Care to nominate a new place? Visit Fodors.com/contact-us.

Trip Costs

We list prices wherever possible to help you budget well. Hotel and restaurant price categories from **$** to **$$$$** are noted alongside each recommendation. For hotels, we include the lowest cost of a standard double room in high season. For restaurants, we cite the average price of a main course at dinner or, if dinner isn't served, at lunch. For attractions, we always list adult admission fees; discounts are usually available for children, students, and senior citizens.

Hotels

Our local writers vet every hotel to recommend the best overnights in each price category, from budget to expensive. Unless otherwise specified, you can expect private bath, phone, and TV in your room. For expanded hotel reviews, facilities, and deals visit Fodors.com.

Restaurants

Unless we state otherwise, restaurants are open for lunch and dinner daily. We mention dress code only when there's a specific requirement and reservations only when they're essential or not accepted. To make restaurant reservations, visit Fodors.com.

Credit Cards

The hotels and restaurants in this guide typically accept credit cards. If not, we'll say so.

Top Picks

★ Fodor's Choice

Listings

✉ Address
✉ Branch address
📫 Mailing address
☎ Telephone
📠 Fax
🌐 Website
📧 E-mail
🎟 Admission fee
🕒 Open/closed times
[M] Subway
✣ Directions or Map coordinates

Hotels & Restaurants

🏨 Hotel
🛏 Number of rooms
🍽 Meal plans
✕ Restaurant
✍ Reservations
👔 Dress code
▭ No credit cards
[$] Price

Other

⇨ See also
☞ Take note
⛳ Golf facilities

EXPERIENCE ST. MAARTEN, ST. BARTH, AND ANGUILLA

WHAT'S WHERE

Anguilla

Island Harbour

The Valley O   **3**
                O The Quarter
North Hill O   ✈

Blowing Point
O Harbour
West End
O

St. Maarten/ St. Martin

Grand Case O ✈

Colombier O
Marigot O   O Orléans
Sandy Ground O   **1**
                    O Beneden
                    Prinsen
✈
Koolbaai O
        ✪ PHILIPSBURG

Caribbean Sea

1 St. Maarten/St. Martin.
Two nations (Dutch and French),
many nationalities, one small island,
a lot of development. But there are
also more white, sandy beaches
than days in a month. Go for
the awesome restaurants,
extensive shopping, and wide
range of activities. Don't go if
you're not willing to get out and
search for the really good stuff.

2 St. Barthélemy. If you come to
St. Barth for a taste of European village life, not for a conventional full-
service resort experience, you will
be richly rewarded. Go for excellent
dining and wine, great boutiques
with the latest hip fashions, world-
class people-watching, and an active, on-the-go vacation. Don't go
for big resorts, and make sure your
credit card is platinum-plated.

3 Anguilla. With miles of brilliant
white sand and accommodations
that range from funky guest houses
to elegant super-luxury resorts,
Anguilla is a laid-back beach lover's
heaven. Go for fine cuisine in elegant surroundings, great snorkeling,
family-friendliness, and the funky
late-night music scene. This island is
all about relaxing and reviving. Don't
go for shopping and sightseeing.

Scrub
Island

The Bahamas

ATLANTIC OCEAN

Cuba

Dominican
Republic

Haiti

Jamaica

Puerto
Rico

Caribbean   Sea

COLOMBIA   VENEZUELA

Caribbean

0   5 mi

0   5 km

ATLANTIC

OCEAN

St. Barthélemy

Colombier   Lorient   Anse de
Petit Cul de Sac

Gustavia   Lurin

PLANNER

Island Activities	Logistics
All three islands have beautiful **beaches**, but Anguilla's are probably the best. Baie Orientale on St. Martin is one of the Caribbean's most beautiful beaches. St. Barth has a wide range of lovely beaches.	**Getting to the Islands:** Only Princess Juliana International Airport (SXM) in St. Maarten has nonstop flights from the U.S. But you can get a small plane or ferry to Anguilla (AXA) or St. Barth (SBH) from St. Maarten; there are also connecting flights to Anguilla and St. Barth through San Juan.

All three islands have beautiful **beaches**, but Anguilla's are probably the best. Baie Orientale on St. Martin is one of the Caribbean's most beautiful beaches. St. Barth has a wide range of lovely beaches.

Anguilla has a good **golf course**, but these islands are not a major golfing destination.

Water sports, including windsurfing, and sailing are popular, especially on St. Barth and St. Maarten/St. Martin. **Diving** is good but not great in the area. St. Maarten in particular also has many **land activities** and attractions.

Shopping is great on both St. Barth and St. Maarten/St. Martin.

Great restaurants and the "foodie" vibe on the three islands is unique. Grand Case in St. Martin is renowned for its great restaurants, St. Barth attracts chefs from around the world.

Gambling in St. Maarten's lively casinos is a popular attraction.

Getting to the Islands: Only Princess Juliana International Airport (SXM) in St. Maarten has nonstop flights from the U.S. But you can get a small plane or ferry to Anguilla (AXA) or St. Barth (SBH) from St. Maarten; there are also connecting flights to Anguilla and St. Barth through San Juan.

Hassle Factor: Low for St. Maarten, medium to high for Anguilla or St. Barth

Nonstops: There are nonstop flights from Atlanta (Delta, seasonal), Boston (JetBlue), Charlotte (US Airways), Miami (American), New York–JFK (American, Delta, JetBlue), New York–Newark (United), and Philadelphia (US Airways).There are also some nonstop charter flights (including GWV/Apple Vacations from Boston). You can also connect in San Juan on JetBlue, LIAT or Air Sunshine. Many smaller Caribbean-based airlines, including Air Caraïbes, Anguilla Air Services, Caribbean Airlines, Copa, Dutch Antilles Express, Insel, LIAT, and Winair (Windward Islands Airways) offer service from other islands in the Caribbean.

On the Ground: Taxis are available on all three islands, but many hotels in St. Barth offer free airport transfers since they own and rent out cars themselves.

Renting a Car: Most visitors to all three islands rent cars (taxis are particularly expensive on St. Barth). Driving is on the right on both St. Maarten/St. Martin and St. Barth. Driving is on the left in Anguilla. Gas is more expensive than in the U.S.

1

Where to Stay

Time-Shares: Only Dutch St. Maarten has a large number of time-share resorts. When the units are not being used by participants in the various points systems, they are often available to rent to anyone, but rarely are they available during the busiest parts of the high season. Try to talk your way into a recently refurbished unit.

Large Resorts: Both St. Maarten/St. Martin and Anguilla have several fairly large resorts. On Anguilla they are quite luxurious and expensive. Some resorts in St. Maarten offer all-inclusive (AI) plans. There are no large resorts on St. Barth.

Small Hotels: All three islands have their share of small hotels (all hotels and resorts on St. Barth are quite small, and most are rather expensive). On French St. Martin in particular, small hotels predominate, but there are a few larger resorts.

Villas: Many St. Barth visitors stay in villas. Anguilla and St. Maarten/St. Martin also have many private villas of all sizes and prices for rent.

Hotel and Restaurant Costs

Restaurant prices are the average cost of a main course at dinner or, if dinner is not served, at lunch. Hotel prices are the lowest cost of a standard double room in high season. Prices for rentals are the lowest per-night cost for a one-bedroom unit in high season.

Tips for Travelers

English is widely understood by most people involved in the tourism industry on all three islands; French is spoken in St. Barth and French St. Martin.

The minimum legal drinking ages: 18 in St. Maarten/St. Martin and St. Barth, 16 in Anguilla.

Electricity is 110 volts, just as in the U.S., on both St. Maarten and Anguilla; the standard in French St. Martin and St. Barth is the European, at 220 volts AC (60-cycle), requiring a plug adaptor and, for some appliances, a voltage converter.

U.S. currency is accepted almost everywhere in the islands, though the standard currency in French St. Martin and St. Barth is the euro.

Regardless of which island you choose, you'll need a valid passport and a round-trip ticket.

There's a $20 departure tax in Anguilla when you are departing by ferry; it must be paid in cash.

IF YOU LIKE

A Romantic Rendezvous

Anguilla, St. Barth, and St. Maarten/St. Martin are all popular destinations for weddings, honeymoons, second honeymoons, and other intimate getaways. Here are some of our favorites:

Hotel St-Barth Isle de France, St. Barth. Hide away with the rich and famous in this elegant classic with a white-sand beach and a magnificent spa with Natura Bissé products.

Karibuni Lodge, St. Martin. Eco-sensitive private suites with pools are new and surprisingly reasonable. Simple décor in a tropical garden setting offers amazing views over Pinel Island. Suites have kitchenettes, but breakfast is delivered.

La Samanna, St. Martin. Recent renovations and redecoration are on the mark, and the huge beachfront suites feel like private villas. The resort also has the best breakfast buffet on the island.

Le Sereno, St. Barth. The name says it all. Serene, comfortable, tasteful, with delicious food, and right on the beach. Don't miss a massage in the private spa cabins on the beach.

Malliouhana, Anguilla. This classic and beautifully sited property, taken over and luxuriously renovated by the Auberge Resorts group, will reopen in late 2014.

Viceroy Anguilla. Design freaks swoon for the luxury; service is equally detailed.

Great Eating

You can find absolutely any cuisine you fancy, but you can't go wrong with these choices:

Bacchus, St. Martin. The best local chefs cook lunch (only) in this unique wine shop/restaurant in the warehouse area (think SoHo) of Grand Case. You can also buy gourmet provisions.

La Cigale, St. Martin. Innovative French cuisine, candlelight, and friendly service make a great formula for a pleasant dinner.

Le Pressoir, St. Martin. French cuisine is beautifully and creatively presented in a carefully restored traditional house.

Le Ti St. Barth Caribbean Tavern, St. Barth. It's how you imagine St. Barth: with sexy-cool, chic beauties dancing on the tables. Don't even think about a reservation before 10 pm if you want to be part of the real fun.

Straw Hat, Anguilla. Come for breakfast, lunch, or dinner on an airy terrace with a friendly crowd (and a big TV for sports) over gorgeous views of Mead's Bay.

Veya, Anguilla. A treehouselike verandah with a lively jazz lounge and sophisticated food to match the surroundings.

The Water

All three islands offer a number of ways to enjoy the beautiful Caribbean Sea with very little or a whole lot of exertion, but always plenty of fun. Here are some suggestions:

Wind Adventures St. Martin. Learn kiteboarding or windsurfing from the experts. They even have a five-day intensive package of instruction and practice.

Aqua Mania Adventures, St. Maarten. Great snorkeling trips or a "Rock 'n' Roll Safari" are conducted on a motorized raft

St. Maarten 12-Metre Challenge. Compete on actual America's Cup racing yachts or just enjoy the day on the water. (This is also one of the most popular cruise-ship excursions in the Caribbean, so book ahead.)

TriSport, St. Maarten. Try sea-kayaking, or join one of their bike trips.

Jet Ski Tour of St. Barth. Guided tours around the island are tons of fun for the young.

Scuba Diving, Anguilla. There is a great wreck dive off the north coast, or hunt stingrays in the coral of Ram's Head.

Shopping

It's fun to bring home a memento for yourself and souvenirs for your friends and family. Here are some things you might like to enjoy on the island or take home:

Cuban Cigars. St. Barth's tobacconists stock the best Cubans to enjoy before you return stateside.

Natural Body and Beauty Products. Products from Ligne de St. Barth are crafted from tropical plants.

Island Arts and Crafts. Anguilla's Arts and Crafts Center in the Valley has charming local crafts, and there are several galleries showing work by a range of artists. Hibernia sells amazing pieces collected by its owners on their annual explorations in exotic parts of the world in a gallery beside its excellent restaurant.

The Perfect Bikini. The hunt can be disheartening, but the prize makes it worthwhile. Look for labels like Pain de Sucre, Banana Moon, and HipUp where the tops and bottoms are bought separately, and for men, colorful Vilebrequin—all available both in St. Martin and St. Barth.

WHEN TO GO

The Caribbean high season runs about December 15 through April 15—great for escaping winter. The Christmas holiday season is an especially expensive time to visit Anguilla and St. Barth, and you may very well pay double during this period, with minimum rental requirements for some villas and hotels. After April prices may be 20% to 50% less, and you can often book on short notice. Some hotels and restaurants close for all or part of September and October.

Climate

The Caribbean climate is fairly consistent, with slightly higher temperatures and more humidity when summer trade winds blow. But the warm ocean temperatures are a delight for swimmers. Hurricanes are most likely August through October, although heavy rain can occur in any season. Major hurricanes are a relatively rare occurrence, and in recent years building standards have been raised to a much higher level to avoid some of the devastating damage of past storms.

Festivals and Events

St. Maarten: The **Heineken Regatta** in early March brings sailors and partygoers from all over the world. **Carnival** follows Easter with parades, great food, and music for all. November is foodie paradise during **Culinary Month** events.

St. Barth: Carnival celebrations begin in late January, leading up to **Mardi Gras,** which falls on March 3, 2015, but the festivities begin as of February 25 with a parade for school children to get the party started. The **St. Barth Music Festival** brings jazz and chamber music for the first three weeks of January. April brings the **Cinéma Caraïbe Film Festival,** and an International Regatta, **Les Voiles de Saint Barth.** Everyone loves shopping during the first two weeks of August during the **Shopping Festival.** On **New Year's Eve** locals join visiting boats for a round-the-island regatta, and a fantastic fireworks display over Gustavia Harbour.

Anguilla: Bankie Banx hosts **Moonsplash,** an annual full-moon music festival that brings reggae acts and fans from all over; it's in early March in 2015. The **Boat Races** start the first Monday in August, with 10 days of beauty pageants, nonstop partying, and the races themselves, in old-fashioned wooden boats. The "landracers" following onshore have as much fun as the boats. May 30 is **Anguilla Day,** and there is a round-the-island race.

GREAT ITINERARIES

Here are some suggestions for how to make the most of your trip to the islands, whichever one you choose.

A Perfect Day in St. Maarten/St. Martin

In the morning head out to the Butterfly Farm and watch the beauties emerge, before heading to Loterie Farm on the slopes of Pic du Paradis to take advantage of the hiking trails or try the zip line. You can stay and have lunch in the Hidden Forest Café, and lounge around the beautiful spring-fed swimming pool. If you are hot, head right to Baie Orientale, where you can rent some chairs and umbrellas from one of the beach clubs and take advantage of the lovely surf. If you get hungry, you can have snacks or lunch there, too. The afternoon is a good time to stroll along Front Street in Philipsburg, because you can duck into one of the many air-conditioned stores to escape the heat. In the late afternoon, a nap is in order, but you have to be awake before sunset. For a splurge, have your sunset cocktail at the bar of La Samanna before heading to one of the restaurants in Grand Case for a perfect dinner. Dance the whole night away in Maho. The party starts at Sky Beach then moves on to Tantra.

A Perfect Day in St. Barth

Have your café au lait and croissant in a harborside café in Gustavia, and explore some of the many boutiques on Quai de la République. If you tire of the hubbub, have lunch in quieter St-Jean and then shop and stroll some more. If you're not a shopper, tie on your sneakers and hike for half an hour down the path to the secluded cove at Colombier, take a snorkeling excursion or go deep-sea fishing. Be sure to get a late-afternoon nap, because the nightlife in St. Barth doesn't get going until late. After a sunset cocktail in Gustavia, have dinner at one of the island's many great restaurants. Perhaps you'll choose Le Ti St. Barth Caribbean Tavern, which is as much a gathering spot as a restaurant. By the time dessert comes, someone is sure to be dancing on the tables. Late-night partying really gets going after midnight.

A Perfect Day in Anguilla

The perfect day in Anguilla often involves the least activity. After breakfast, head to powdery Shoal Bay. If you get tired of sunning and dozing, take a ride on Junior's Glass Bottom Boat, or arrange a wreck dive at Shoal Bay Scuba. Have lunch at one of the beachside restaurants and relax a little more. In the late afternoon, head back to your hotel room to shower and change before going to Elvis' Beach Bar to watch the sunset with a cold rum punch. Have dinner at one of the island's great restaurants.

WEDDINGS AND HONEYMOONS

There's no question that St. Maarten/St. Martin, St. Barth, and Anguilla are three of the Caribbean's foremost honeymoon destinations. Romance is in the air here, and the white, sandy beaches and turquoise water, swaying palm trees, balmy tropical breezes, and perpetual summer sunshine put people in the mood for love. Destination weddings—no longer exclusive to celebrities and the super rich—are also popular on Anguilla and Dutch St. Maarten, but French residency requirements make getting married in French St. Martin or St. Barth too difficult. All the larger resorts in Anguilla and St. Maarten have wedding planners to help you with the paperwork and details.

The Big Day

Choosing the Perfect Place. When choosing a location, remember that you really have two choices to make: the ceremony location and where to have the reception, if you're having one. For the former, there are beaches, bluffs overlooking beaches, gardens, private residences, resort lawns, and, of course, places of worship. As for the reception, there are these same choices, as well as restaurants. If you decide to go outdoors, remember the seasons (yes, the Caribbean has seasons). If you're planning a wedding outdoors, be sure you have a backup plan in case it rains.

If your heart is set on an outdoor wedding at sunset, match the time of your ceremony to the time the sun sets at that time of year.

Finding a Wedding Planner. If you're planning to invite more than an officiant and your loved one to your wedding ceremony, seriously consider on-island wedding planners who can help with selecting a location, designing the floral décor, and recommending a reliable photographer. They can plan the menu, and suggest local traditions to incorporate into your ceremony. Of course, all the larger resorts have their own wedding planners. If you're planning a resort wedding, work with the on-site wedding coordinator to prepare a detailed list of the exact services they'll provide. If your idea of your wedding doesn't match their services, try a different resort. Or look for an independent wedding planner. Both Anguilla and St. Maarten have independent wedding planners who are not employed by resorts.

Legal Requirements. There are minimal residency requirements on Anguilla and St. Maarten, and no blood tests or shots are required on either island. On Anguilla, you can get a wedding license in two working days; paperwork in St. Maarten has to be submitted 14 days in advance, but there is no

residency requirement there. You need to supply proof of identity (a passport or certified copy of your birth certificate signed by a notary public, though in Anguilla even a driver's license with a photo will do). You must provide proof of divorce with the original or certified copy of the divorce decree if you are divorced, or copy of the death certificate if you are a widow or widower.

Wedding Attire. In the Caribbean, basically anything goes, from long, formal dresses with trains to white bikinis. Floral sundresses are fine, too. Men can wear tuxedos or a simple pair of solid-color slacks with a nice white linen shirt. If you want formal dress and a tuxedo, it's usually better to bring your formal attire with you.

Photographs. Deciding whether to use the photographer supplied by your resort or an independent photographer is an important choice. Resorts that host a lot of weddings usually have their own photographers, but you can also find independent, professional island-based photographers, and an independent wedding planner will know the best in the area. Look at the portfolio (many photographers now have websites), and decide whether this person can give you the kind of memories you are looking for. If you're satis-fied with the photographer that your resort uses, then make sure you see proofs and order prints before you leave the island. In any case, arrange to take a CD home with you of HD photos, because uploading them via the Internet is a time-consuming frustration what with (typically slow) Caribbean connections.

The Honeymoon

Do you want champagne and strawberries delivered to your room each morning? An infinity pool in which to float? A five-star restaurant in which to dine? Then a resort is the way to go, and both Anguilla and St. Maarten have options in different price ranges (though Anguilla resorts are more luxurious and more expensive as a rule). Whether you want a luxurious experience or a more modest one, you'll certainly find someplace romantic to which you can escape. You can usually stay on at the resort where your wedding was held. On the other hand, maybe you want your own private home in which to romp naked—or your own kitchen in which to whip up a gourmet meal for your loved one. In that case, a private vacation-rental home or condo is the answer.

KIDS AND FAMILIES

All three islands have plenty of activities and attractions that will keep children of all ages (and their parents) busy and interested. Children are generally welcome at restaurants, especially earlier in the evenings.

St. Maarten/St. Martin

The Hotel Riu Palace St. Martin (formerly the Radisson Blu) is perfect for families, with an all-inclusive option, a huge pool, gentle surf, and activities for all. **The Westin** is another option with a great spa and a huge pool but the beach can be windy and the water rougher. **Le Petit Hotel,** a boutique property in Grand Case, has full apartment units and a caring management team. Don't miss the zip line at **Loterie Farm** or a visit to the **Butterfly Farm;** ride the **Carousel,** try kiteboarding on **Orient Beach,** wade in surf gentle enough for babies at **Le Galion Beach,** and enjoy incredible water sports all over the island. **Pineapple Pete's** suits for easy meals all day long, or try the creole specials in Marigot's **Enoch's Place,** and the jerk chicken and salads at **Taloula Mango's** in Phillipsburg. Vegetarians flock to **Top Carrot.**

St. Barth

Children are welcome at most resorts. **Hotel Guanahani & Spa** offers programs for children ages 2–12, a good list of local babysitters, and activities galore. **Hotel Le Village St. Jean** makes is an easy to walk to beaches or shopping. Only in St. Barth would you find a **Yellow Submarine** from which to observe undersea life in air-conditioned comfort. Don't leave without a visit to the **Inter Oceans (Shell) Museum.** Casual dining options include Gustavia's **La Crêperie,** and **Gloriette's** beachy **picnic tables and hammocks,** and the loads of local-style grills and pizzerias for take-out.

Anguilla

CuisinArt Golf Resort and Spa offers children's programs, babysitting, and a great beach. Many activities are included at **Cap Juluca,** and **Viceroy** has programs for little kids and a media room and club for teens. Anacaona Beach Resort has some great family-size villas at a budget-friendly price.

Family dining options include **Smokey's at the Cove, Blanchard's Beach Shack,** and **Picante.** Don't miss a family excursion to gorgeous **Scilly Cay;** wave from the dock and a boat will take you out to the island for a day of snorkeling and fresh grilled fish and lobster. Thursday night head to **Fire Fly** at Anacaona for the Anguillian buffet and folkloric dance performance. Even nonswimmers can enjoy an excursion on **Jonno's Glass Bottom Boat.**

ST. MAARTEN/
ST. MARTIN

Updated
by Elise
Meyer

ST. MAARTEN/ST. MARTIN IS VIRTUALLY UNIQUE among Caribbean destinations. The 37-square-mile (96-square-km) island is a seamless place (there are no border gates), but it is governed by two nations—the Netherlands and France—and has residents from 70-some different countries. A call from the Dutch side to the French is an international call, currencies are different, and even the vibe is different. In the Caribbean, only the island of Hispaniola is remotely in a similar position, ecompassing two distinct countries: Haiti and the Dominican Republic.

Happily for Americans, who make up the majority of visitors to St. Maarten/St. Martin, English works in both nations. Dutch St. Maarten might feel particularly comfortable for Americans: the prices are lower (not to mention in U.S. dollars), the big hotels have casinos, and there is more nightlife. Huge cruise ships disgorge masses of shoppers into the Philipsburg shopping area at midmorning, when roads can quickly become overly congested. But once you pass the meandering, unmarked border into the French side, you will find a bit of the ambience of the south of France: quiet countryside, fine cuisine, and in Marigot, a walkable harbor area with outdoor cafés, outdoor markets, and plenty of shopping and cultural activities.

Almost 4,000 years ago, it was salt and not tourism that drove the little island's economy. Arawak Indians, the island's first known inhabitants, prospered until the warring Caribs invaded, adding the peaceful Arawaks to their list of conquests. Columbus spotted the isle on November 11, 1493, and named it after St. Martin (whose feast day is November 11), but it wasn't populated by Europeans until the 17th century, when it was claimed by the Dutch, French, and Spanish. The Dutch and French finally joined forces to claim the island in 1644, and the Treaty of Concordia partitioned the territory in 1648. According to legend, the border was drawn along the line where a French man and a Dutch man, running from opposite coasts, met.

Both sides of the island offer a touch of European culture along with a lot of laid-back Caribbean ambience. Water sports abound—diving, snorkeling, sailing, windsurfing, and in early March, the Heineken Regatta. With soft trade winds cooling the subtropical climate, it's easy to while away the day relaxing on one of the 37 beaches, strolling Philipsburg's boardwalk, and perusing the shops on Philipsburg's Front Street or the *rues* (streets) of the very

Oyster Pond, St. Maarten

French town of Marigot. Although luck is an important commodity at St. Maarten's 13 casinos, chance plays no part in finding a good meal at the excellent eateries or after-dark fun in the subtle to sizzling nightlife. Heavy development—especially on the Dutch side—has stressed the island's infrastructure, but slowly some of the more dilapidated roads are showing signs of improvement. A series of large roundabouts, with the beginnings of some decent signposting, and attractive monumental sculptures, has improved traffic flow (remember, the cars already in the roundabout have right-of-way). At long last, the eyesore of hurricane-wrecked buildings that line the golf course at Mullet Bay has been demolished, and most welcome is the new swing bridge that crosses Simpson Bay Lagoon, connecting the airport and Cole Bay.

When cruise ships are in port (and there can be as many as seven at once), shopping areas are crowded and traffic moves at a snail's pace. We suggest spending these days on the beach or the water, and planning shopping excursions for the early morning or at cocktail hour, after "rush hour" traffic calms down. Still, these are minor inconveniences compared with the feel of the sand between your toes or the breeze through your hair, gourmet food sating your appetite, and having the ability to crisscross between two nations on one island.

PLANNING

WHEN TO GO

The high season begins in December and runs through the middle of April. During the off-season, hotel rooms can be had for as little as half the high-season rates.

The French side's **Carnival** is a pre-Lenten bash of costume parades, music competitions, and feasts. Carnival takes place after Easter on the Dutch side—the last two weeks of April—with a parade and music competition.

On the French side, parades, ceremonies, and celebrations commemorate **Bastille Day** on July 14, and there's more revelry later in the month on **Grand Case Day.**

The Dutch side hosts the **Heineken Regatta** in early March, with as many as 300 sailboats competing from around the world. (For the experience of a lifetime, you can sometimes purchase a working berth aboard a regatta vessel.) Other local holidays include November 11 (St. Martin's Day), and April 30, the birthday of Queen Juliana.

ACCOMMODATIONS

The island, though small, is well developed—some say over-developed—and offers a wide range of lodging. The larger resorts and time-shares are mostly on the Dutch side; the French side has more intimate properties. Just keep in mind that the popular restaurants around Grand Case, on the French side, are a long drive from most Dutch-side hotels. French-side hotels often charge in euros. Be wary of some of the very lowest-price alternatives, as some of these can be very run-down time-shares, or properties that function as short-term housing for temporary workers or tourists with very low-end tour companies. Additionally, make note of locations of properties very close to the airport, to avoid unpleasant surprises related to noise. In general, the newer a property, the better off you will be.

Resorts and Time-Shares: In general, many of the older properties, especially the time-shares, are suffering from the wear-and-tear of multiple owners, and it is hard to recommend many of them because of great variances from unit to unit.

Small Inns: Small guesthouses and inns can be found on both sides of the island. It is worth exploring these, especially if you are not the big-resort type.

Villas and Condos: Both sides of the island have a wide variety of villas and condos for every conceivable budget.

LOGISTICS

Getting to St. Maarten/St. Martin: There are nonstop flights to St. Maarten from the United States, as well as connecting service through San Juan. Further, St. Maarten is a hub for smaller, regional airlines. The island's main airport is Princess Juliana International Airport (SXM), on the Dutch side. Aeroport de L'Espérance (SFG), on the French side, is small and handles only small planes.

Hassle Factor: Low to medium.

On the Ground: Most visitors rent a car upon arrival, but taxi service is available at the airport with fixed fares to all hotels on the island, and you'll be able to pay the fare in U.S. dollars. Although the island is small, it's still a long drive to many hotels on the French side, and the fares will add up.

Getting Around the Island: Most visitors rent a car because rates are fairly cheap and the island is easy to navigate. It's possible to get by with taxis if you are staying in a major hub such as Philipsburg or Baie Orientale, but you may spend more money than if you rented a car.

Some of the resorts offer villa alternatives, which make for a good compromise, and perhaps better security. In addition, some of the high-end condo developments are offering unsold units as rentals, and some are brand-new and terrific bargains.

HOTEL AND RESTAURANT PRICES

Prices in the restaurant reviews are the average cost of a main course at dinner or, if dinner is not served, at lunch; taxes and service charges are generally included. Prices in the hotel reviews are the lowest cost of a standard double room in high season, excluding taxes, service charges, and meal plans (except at all-inclusives). Prices for rentals are the lowest per-night cost for a one-bedroom unit in high season.

For expanded lodging reviews and current deals, visit Fodors.com.

WHAT IT COSTS IN U.S. DOLLARS				
	$	**$$**	**$$$**	**$$$$**
Restaurants	under $12	$12–$20	$21–$30	over $30
Hotels	under $275	$276–$375	$376–$475	over $475

Restaurant prices are the average cost of a main course at dinner or, if dinner is not served, at lunch. Hotel prices are the lowest cost of a standard double room in high season.

EXPLORING ST. MAARTEN/ ST. MARTIN

The best way to explore St. Maarten/St. Martin is by car. Though often congested, especially around Philipsburg and Marigot, the roads are fairly good, though narrow and winding, with some speed bumps, potholes, roundabouts, and an occasional wandering goat herd. Few roads are marked with their names, but destination signs are common. Besides, the island is so small that it's hard to get really lost—at least that is what locals tell you.

If you're spending a few days, get to know the area with a scenic "loop" around the island. Be sure to pack a towel and some water shoes, a hat, sunglasses, and sunblock. Head up the east shoreline from Philipsburg, and follow the signs to Dawn Beach and Oyster Pond. The road winds past soaring hills, turquoise waters, quaint West Indian houses, and wonderful views of St. Barth. As you cross over to the French side, turn into Le Galion for a stop at the calm sheltered beach, the stables, the butterflies, or the windsurfing school, then keep following the road toward Orient Bay, the "St-Tropez of the Caribbean." Continue to Anse Marcel, Grand Case, Marigot, and Sandy Ground. From Marigot, the flat island of Anguilla is visible. Completing the loop brings you past Cupecoy Beach, through Maho and Simpson Bay, where Saba looms in the horizon, and back over the mountain road into Philipsburg.

DUTCH SIDE

TOP ATTRACTIONS

PHILIPSBURG

The capital of Dutch St. Maarten stretches about a mile (1½ km) along an isthmus between Great Bay and the Salt Pond and has five parallel streets. Most of the village's dozens

TOP ATTRACTIONS

Great Food: The island has so many good places to dine that you could eat out for a month and never repeat a restaurant visit.

Lots of Shops: Philipsburg is one of the top shopping spots in the Caribbean, and Marigot brings a touch of France.

Beaches Large and Small: Thirty-seven picture-perfect beaches are spread out all over the island.

Water Sports Galore: The wide range of water sports will satisfy almost any need and give you the perfect excuse to finally try stand-up paddle-boarding or kiteboarding.

Nightlife Every Night: There is a wide variety of nightlife: shows, discos, beach bars, and casinos.

of shops and restaurants are on Front Street, narrow and cobblestone, closest to Great Bay. It's generally congested when cruise ships are in port, because of its many duty-free shops and several casinos. Little lanes called *steegjes* connect Front Street with Back Street, which has fewer shops and considerably less congestion. Along the beach is a ½ mile-long (1-km-long) boardwalk with restaurants and several Wi-Fi hot spots.

St. Maarten Museum. The Sint Maarten Museum hosts rotating cultural exhibits addressing the history, industry, geology, and archaeology of the island. Artifacts range from Arawak pottery shards to objects salvaged from the wreck of the HMS *Proselyte*. An interesting exhibit about hurricanes focuses on Hurricane Luis, which devastated the island in 1995. There is a good reference and video library as well. ⊠ *7 Front St., Philipsburg* ☎ *721/542–4917* ⊕ *www. museumsintmaarten.org* ☜ *$1* ⊙ *Weekdays 10–4.*

Wathey Square (pronounced *watty*) is in the heart of the village. Directly across from the square are the town hall and the courthouse, in the striking white building with the cupola. The structure was built in 1793 and has served as the commander's home, a fire station, a jail, and a post office. The streets surrounding the square are lined with hotels, duty-free shops, restaurants, and cafés. The **Captain Hodge Pier,** just off the square, is a good spot to view Great Bay and the beach that stretches alongside.

CLOSE UP

St. Maarten/St. Martin Top Reasons to Go

A two-nation vacation is what you get with St. Maarten/St. Martin. But the island has much more going for it than that.

■ Philipsburg is one of the best shopping spots in the Caribbean; though it has fewer bargains (and fewer stores) these days with competetive Internet pricing, the growing strength of the euro, and worldwide economic woe. Marigot (the capital of French St. Martin) is fun to explore, especially on Wednesday or Saturday when the market is open, and if beachwear is on your shopping list, everybody can find the perfect one before or after a terrific lunch in the boutiques around Marina Royale. Nonshoppers can watch the boats or sample some of the great fruit-infused rums proudly made by nearly every restaurateur.

■ Grand Case is the gastronomic capital of the French side, and Maho-Coupecoy of the Dutch, but there are great restaurants all over the Island. We suggest spending an evening in each of the Islands' different areas, checking out restaurants, nightlife, and the general vibe. Taking taxis is a great way to get around in the evening, no worries about routing, parking, or designated drivers. At the end of the night any restaurant or club will call for a cab. (Rates are regulated—only use taxis with official stickers, and don't fall for any attempts at added charges.) You'll find plenty of great restaurants in Philipsburg and Simpson Bay as well.

■ Thirty-seven perfect beaches are spread out all over the island (and most of the island's hotels are not on the best beaches, one reason so many people choose to rent a car). Whether you are looking for the busy scene at Baie Orientale or the deserted stretches of sand at Simpson Bay, each is unique.

■ The wide range of water sports—from sailing to waterskiing, snorkeling to deep-sea fishing—will meet almost any need.

ELSEWHERE IN ST. MAARTEN

FAMILY **The Carousel.** Ride a beautiful restored Italian carousel and enjoy dozens of flavors of homemade Italian gelato and French pastries. Adults will love the espresso bar with great coffee drinks, and there is even a small cocktail bar. It's a perfect attraction for kids of all ages. ⊠ *60 Welfare Rd., Cole Bay* ☎ *721/544–3112* ⊡ *$2* ⊙ *Tues.–Sun. 2–10.*

Yoda Guy Movie Exhibit. This odd-sounding exhibit is actually a nonprofit museum run by Nick Maley, a movie industry artist who was involved in the creation of Yoda and other movie icons. Learn how the artist worked while you enjoy the models and memorabilia on display. While it's certainly a must-see for any *Star Wars* fan, Maley's work should interest every movie buff out there. There are also souvenirs for sale that Maley is happy to autograph. ✉ *19a Front St., Philipsburg* ☎ *721/542–4009* ⊕ *www.netdwellers. com/mz/planetp/home.html.*

FRENCH SIDE

TOP ATTRACTIONS

MARIGOT

It is great fun to spend a few hours exploring the bustling harbor, shopping stalls, open-air cafés, and boutiques of St. Martin's biggest town, especially on Wednesday and Saturday, when the daily open-air crafts markets expand to include fresh fruits and vegetables, spices, and all manner of seafood. The market might remind you of Provence, especially when aromas of delicious cooking waft by. Be sure to climb up to the fort for the panoramic view, stopping at the museum for an overview of the island. **Marina Port La Royale** is the shopping–lunch spot central to the port, but rue de la République and rue de la Liberté, which border the bay, have duty-free shops, boutiques, and bistros. The West Indies Mall offers a deluxe (and air-conditioned) shopping experience, with such shops as Lacoste. There's less bustle here than in Philipsburg, but the open-air cafés are still tempting places to sit and people-watch. From the harborfront you can catch ferries for Anguilla and St. Barth. Parking can be a real challenge during the business day, and even at night during the high season.

Fort Louis. Though not much remains of the structure itself, Fort Louis, which was completed by the French in 1789, is great fun if you want to climb the 92 steps to the top for the wonderful views of the island and neighboring Anguilla. On Wednesday and Saturday there is a market in the square at the bottom. ✉ *Marigot.*

FAMILY **Saint Martin Museum.** At the southern end of Marigot, next to the Marina Port La Royale, is a museum dedicated to preserving St. Martin's history and culture. A new building houses a variety of pre-Columbian treasures unearthed by the Hope Estate Archaeological Society. ✉ *Terre Basse Rd.,*

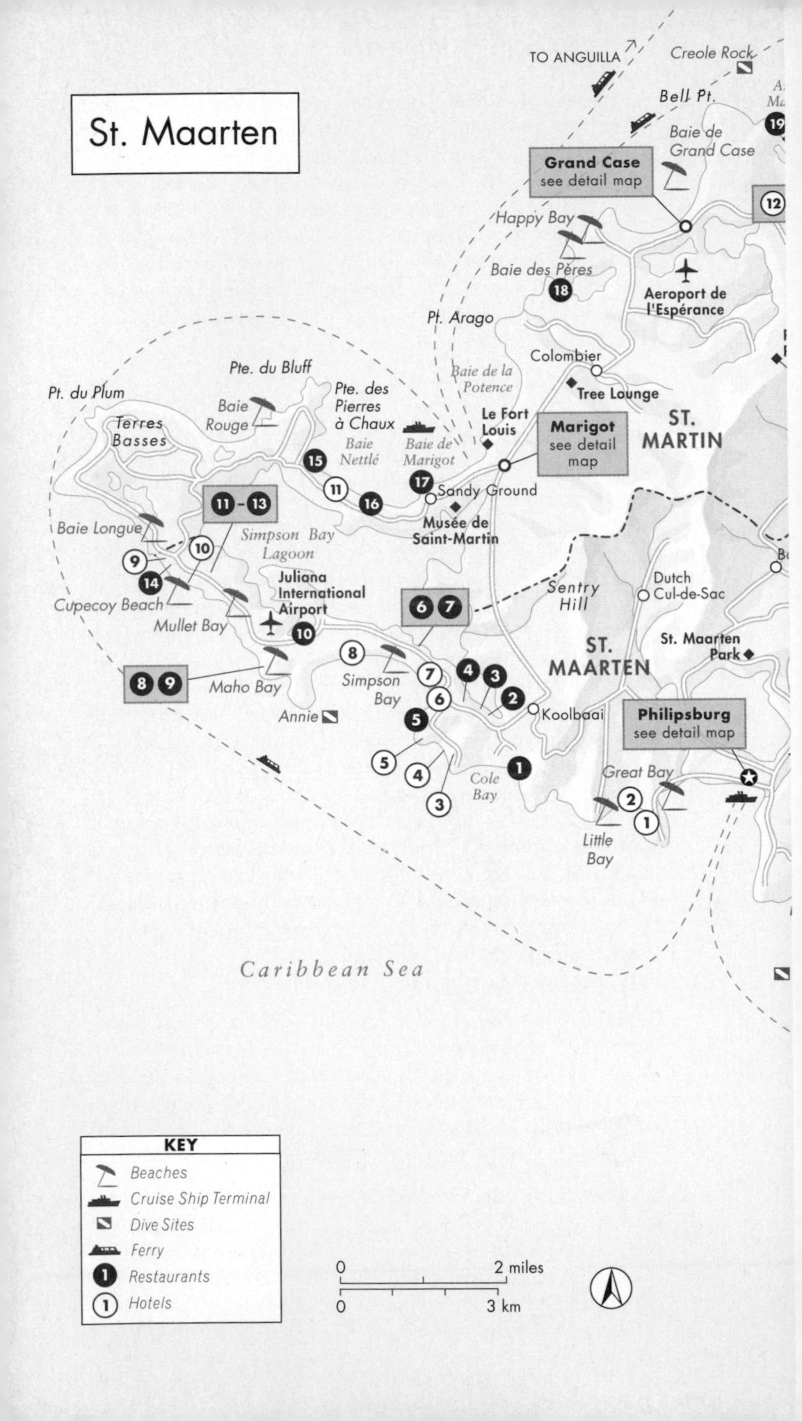

St. Maarten
TO ANGUILLA
Creole Rock
Bell Pt.
Baie de Grand Case
Grand Case see detail map
Happy Bay
Baie des Pères
18
19
12
Aeroport de l'Espérance
Pt. Arago
Colombier
Tree Lounge
Pte. du Bluff
Pt. du Plum
Baie Rouge
Terres Basses
Pte. des Pierres à Chaux
Baie de la Potence
Le Fort Louis
Marigot see detail map
ST. MARTIN
Baie Nettlé
Baie de Marigot
15
11
16
17
Sandy Ground
Musée de Saint-Martin
11 - 13
Baie Longue
Simpson Bay Lagoon
10
9
14
Cupecoy Beach
Mullet Bay
Juliana International Airport
10
6 7
Sentry Hill
Dutch Cul-de-Sac
ST. MAARTEN
St. Maarten Park
8 9
Maho Bay
8
Simpson Bay
7
4
3
2
6
5
Koolbaai
Annie
Philipsburg see detail map
5
4
3
1
Cole Bay
Great Bay
2
1
Little Bay
Caribbean Sea
KEY
Beaches
Cruise Ship Terminal
Dive Sites
Ferry
Restaurants
Hotels
0
2 miles
0
3 km

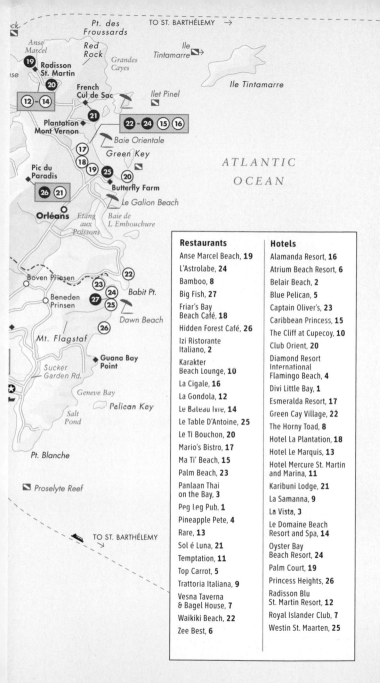

Pt. des Froussards

TO ST. BARTHÉLEMY →

Anse Marcel
Red Rock
Grandes Cayes
Ile Tintamarre

19 Radisson St. Martin
20

12 – 14

French Cul de Sac

Ile Tintamarre

21

Plantation Mont Vernon

22 – 24 15 16

Baie Orientale

Ilet Pinel

Green Key

ATLANTIC OCEAN

17
18
19 25
20

Pic du Paradis

26 21

Butterfly Farm

Le Galion Beach

Orléans

Etang aux Poissons

Baie de L'Embouchure

Boven Prinsen

22
23
24
27 25

Babit Pt.

Beneden Prinsen

Dawn Beach

26

Mt. Flagstaf

Guana Bay Point

Sucker Garden Rd.

Geneve Bay

Pelican Key

Salt Pond

Pt. Blanche

Proselyte Reef

TO ST. BARTHÉLEMY

Restaurants

Anse Marcel Beach, **19**
L'Astrolabe, **24**
Bamboo, **8**
Big Fish, **27**
Friar's Bay Beach Café, **18**
Hidden Forest Café, **26**
Izi Ristorante Italiano, **2**
Karakter Beach Lounge, **10**
La Cigale, **16**
La Gondola, **12**
Le Bateau Ivre, **14**
Le Table D'Antoine, **25**
Le Ti Bouchon, **20**
Mario's Bistro, **17**
Ma Ti' Beach, **15**
Palm Beach, **23**
Panlaan Thai on the Bay, **3**
Peg Leg Pub, **1**
Pineapple Pete, **4**
Rare, **13**
Sol é Luna, **21**
Temptation, **11**
Top Carrot, **5**
Trattoria Italiana, **9**
Vesna Taverna & Bagel House, **7**
Waikiki Beach, **22**
Zee Best, **6**

Hotels

Alamanda Resort, **16**
Atrium Beach Resort, **6**
Belair Beach, **2**
Blue Pelican, **5**
Captain Oliver's, **23**
Caribbean Princess, **15**
The Cliff at Cupecoy, **10**
Club Orient, **20**
Diamond Resort International Flamingo Beach, **4**
Divi Little Bay, **1**
Esmeralda Resort, **17**
Green Cay Village, **22**
The Horny Toad, **8**
Hotel La Plantation, **18**
Hotel Le Marquis, **13**
Hotel Mercure St. Martin and Marina, **11**
Karibuni Lodge, **21**
La Samanna, **9**
La Vista, **3**
Le Domaine Beach Resort and Spa, **14**
Oyster Bay Beach Resort, **24**
Palm Court, **19**
Princess Heights, **26**
Radisson Blu St. Martin Resort, **12**
Royal Islander Club, **7**
Westin St. Maarten, **25**

Concordia

The smallest island in the world to be shared between two different countries, St. Maarten/St. Martin has existed peacefully in its subdivided state for more than 360 years. The Treaty of Concordia, which subdivided the island, was signed in 1648 and was really inspired by the two resident colonies of French and Dutch settlers (not to mention their respective governments) joining forces to repel a common enemy, the Spanish, in 1644. Although the French were promised the side of the island facing Anguilla and the Dutch the south side of the island, the boundary itself wasn't firmly established until 1817 and only then after multiple disputes (16 of them, to be exact).

Visitors to the island will likely not be able to tell that they have passed from the Dutch to the French side unless they notice that the roads on the French side feel a little smoother. In 2003 the population of St. Martin (and St. Barthélemy) voted to secede from Guadeloupe, the administrative capital of the French West Indies. That detachment became official in 2007, and St. Martin is now officially known as the Collectivité de Saint-Martin.

Marigot ☎ *0690/29–48–36* ⊕ *museesaintmartin.e-monsite. com* 🎫 *$5* ☉ *Weekdays 9–1 and 3–5.*

FRENCH CUL DE SAC
North of Orient Bay Beach, the French colonial mansion of St. Martin's mayor is nestled in the hills. Little red-roof houses look like open umbrellas tumbling down the green hillside. The area is peaceful and good for hiking. From the beach here, shuttle boats make the five-minute trip to **Ilet Pinel,** an uninhabited island that's fine for picnicking, sunning, and swimming. There are full-service beach clubs there, so just pack the sunscreen and head over.

GRAND CASE
The Caribbean's own Restaurant Row is the heart of this French-side town, a 10-minute drive from either Orient Bay or Marigot, stretching along a narrow beach overlooking Anguilla. You'll find a first-rate restaurant for every palate, mood, and wallet. At lunchtime, or with kids, head to the casual *lolos* (open-air barbecue stands) and feet-in-the-sand beach bars. Twilight drinks and tapas are fun. At night, stroll the strip and preview the sophisticated

offerings on the menus posted outside before you settle in for a long and sumptuous meal. If you still have the energy, there are lounges with music (usually a DJ) that get going after 11 pm.

ORLÉANS
North of Oyster Pond and the Étang aux Poissons (Fish Lake) is the island's oldest settlement, also known as the French Quarter. You can still find a few classic, vibrantly painted West Indian–style homes with the original ginger-bread fretwork. There are also large areas of the nature and marine preserve that is working to save the fragile ecosystem of the island.

★ **Fodor's** Choice **PIC DU PARADIS**
Between Marigot and Grand Case, "Paradise Peak," at 1,492 feet, is the island's highest point. There are two observation areas. From them, the tropical forest unfolds below, and the vistas are breathtaking. The road is quite isolated and steep, best suited to a four-wheel-drive vehicle, so don't head up here unless you are prepared for the climb. There have also been some problems with crime in this area, so it might be best to go with an experienced local guide.

★ **Fodor's** Choice **Loterie Farm.** Halfway up the road to Pic du Paradis is Loterie Farm, a peaceful 150-acre private nature preserve opened to the public in 1999 by American expat B. J. Welch. There are hiking trails and maps, so you can go on your own (€5) or arrange a guide for a group (€25 for six people). Along the marked trails you will see native forest with tamarind, gum, mango, and mahogany trees, and wild-life including greenback monkeys if you are lucky. In 2011 Loterie opened a lovely spring-fed pool and Jacuzzi area with lounge chairs, great music, and chic tented cabanas called L'Eau Lounge; if you're with a group, consider the VIP package there. Don't miss a treetop lunch or dinner at **Hidden Forest Café** (⇨ *Where to Eat, below*), Loterie Farm's restaurant, where Julie Perkis cooks delicious, healthy meals and snacks. If you are brave—and over 4 feet 5 inches tall—try soaring over trees on one of the longest zip lines in the Western Hemisphere. ⊠ *Rte. de Pic du Paradis 103, Rambaud* ☎ *0590/87–86–16, 0590/57–28–55* ⊕ *www. loteriefarm.com* ⊠ *€35–€55* ⊙ *Tues.–Sun. 9–4.*

DID YOU KNOW?

Not counting Trinidad, the Caribbean has about 300 native species of butterflies, far fewer than Central America, which has more than 2,000.

ELSEWHERE IN ST. MARTIN

★ Fodor'sChoice **Butterfly Farm.** If you arrive early in the morn-
FAMILY ing when the butterflies first break out of their chrysalis,
you'll be able to marvel at the absolute wonder of dozens
of butterflies and moths from around the world and the
particular host plants with which each evolved. At any
given time, some 40 species of butterflies—numbering
as many as 600 individual insects—flutter inside the lush
screened garden and hatch on the plants housed there. Butterfly art and knickknacks are for sale in the gift shop. In
case you want to come back, your ticket, which includes
a guided tour, is good for your entire stay. ⊠ *Le Galion
Beach Rd., Quartier d'Orléans* ☏ *0590/87–31–21* ⊕ *www.
thebutterflyfarm.com* ⊠ *$12* ⊘ *Daily 9–3:30.*

Plantation Mont Vernon. Wander past indigenous flora, a
renovated 1786 cotton plantation, and an old-fashioned
rum distillery at a unique outdoor history and eco-museum.
Along the rambling paths of this former wooded estate,
with beautiful views of Orient Bay, bilingual signs give
detailed explanations of the island's agricultural history
when its economy was dependent on salt, rum, coffee,
sugar, and indigo. There's a complimentary coffee bar along
the way and a delightful gift shop at the entrance. ⊠ *Rte.
d'Orient-Baie* ☏ *0590/29–50–62* ⊕ *www.plantationmont-
vernon.com* ⊠ *€12* ⊘ *Daily 9–5.*

BEACHES

For such a small island, St. Maarten/St. Martin has a wide
array of beaches, from the long expanse of Baie Orientale
on the French side to powdery-soft Mullet Bay on the
Dutch side.

Warm surf and a gentle breeze can be found at the island's
37 beaches, and every one of them is open to the public.
What could be better? Each is unique: some bustling and
some bare, some refined and some rocky, some good for
snorkeling and some for sunning. Whatever you fancy
in the beach landscape department, it's here, including a
clothing-optional one at the south end of Baie Orientale,
one of the Caribbean's most beautiful beaches. The key to
enjoying beach life on St. Maarten and St. Martin is to try
out several beaches; one quickly discovers that several of
the island's gems don't have big hotels lining their shores.
⚠ Petty theft from cars in beach parking lots is an unfortunate fact

Cupecoy Beach, St. Maarten

of life in St. Maarten and St. Martin. Leave nothing in your parked car, not even in the glove compartment or the trunk.

DUTCH SIDE

Several of the best Dutch-side beaches are developed and have large-scale resorts. But others, including Simpson Bay and Cupecoy, have little development. You'll sometimes find vendors or beach bars to rent chairs and umbrellas (but not always).

Cupecoy Beach. Near the Dutch-French border, this picturesque area of sandstone cliffs, white sand, and shoreline caves is a necklace of small beaches that come and go according to the whims of the sea. Even though the western part is more developed, the surf can be rough. It's popular with gay locals and visitors. Break-ins have been reported in cars, so don't leave anything at all in your vehicle. **Amenities:** food and drink. **Best for:** solitude; sunset. ⊠ *Between Baie Longue and Mullet Bay, St. Maarten.*

Dawn Beach. True to its name, Dawn Beach is the place to be at sunrise. On the Atlantic side of Oyster Pond, just south of the French border, this is a first-class beach for sunning and snorkeling, but the winds and rough water mean only strong swimmers should attempt to take a dip. It's not usually crowded, and there are several good restaurants nearby. To find it, follow the signs to the Westin or Mr.

Busby's restaurant. **Amenities:** food and drink. **Best for:** snorkeling; sunrise. ⊠ *South of Oyster Pond, St. Maarten.*

Great Bay. A bustling, white-sand beach, Great Bay is just behind Front Street and curves around Philipsburg, making it very easy to find. Here you'll find boutiques, eateries, a pleasant boardwalk, and even Segway tours. Busy with cruise-ship passengers, the beach is best west of Captain Hodge Pier or around Antoine Restaurant. **Amenities:** food and drink. **Best for:** swimming; walking ⊠ *Philipsburg, St. Maarten.*

Guana Bay. If you're looking for seclusion, you'll find it here. There are no umbrellas and no lounge chairs; even the beach shack has no regular service. What this bay does have is a long expanse of soft sand. The surf is strong, making this beach a popular surfer hangout, but it's definitely not recommended for kids because of the rough surf. It's five minutes northeast of Philipsburg. Turn on Guana Bay Road, which is behind Great Bay Salt Pond. **Amenities:** none. **Best for:** solitude; surfing; walking. ⊠ *Upper Prince's Quarter, St. Maarten.*

Little Bay. Despite its popularity with snorkelers and divers as well as kayakers and boating enthusiasts, Little Bay isn't usually crowded, perhaps due to its gravelly sand. But, it does boast panoramic views of St. Eustatius, Philipsburg, the cruise-ship terminal, Saba, and St. Kitts. The beach is west of Fort Amsterdam and accessible via the Divi Little Bay Beach Resort. **Amenities:** food and drink; parking; toilets. **Best for:** snorkeling; swimming; walking. ⊠ *Little Bay Rd., St. Maarten.*

Mullet Beach. Many believe that this mile-long, powdery white-sand beach behind the Mullet Bay Golf Course is the island's best. Swimmers like it because the water is usually calm, but when the swell is up, the surfers take over the beach. It's also the place to listen for the "whispering pebbles" as the waves wash up. **Amenities:** none. **Best for:** surfing; swimming. ⊠ *South of Cupecoy, Mullet Bay, St. Maarten.*

Simpson Bay Beach. This secluded, half-moon stretch of white-sand beach on the island's Caribbean side is a hidden gem. It's mostly surrounded by private residences, with no big resorts, no Jet Skiers, and no crowds. It's just you, the sand, and the water (along with one funky beach bar to provide some nourishment). Southeast of the airport, follow the signs to Mary's Boon and the Horny Toad guesthouses. **Amenities:** food and drink; showers; toilets. **Best for:** solitude; swimming; walking. ⊠ *St. Maarten*.

FRENCH SIDE

Almost all the French-side beaches, whether busy Baie Orientale or less busy Baie des Pères (Friar's Bay), have beach clubs and restaurants. For about $25 a couple you get two chaises (*transats*) and an umbrella (*parasol*) for the day, not to mention chairside service for drinks and food. Only some beaches have bathrooms and showers, so if that is your preference, inquire.

Anse Heureuse (*Happy Bay*). Not many people know about this romantic, hidden gem. Happy Bay has powdery sand, gorgeous luxury villas, and stunning views of Anguilla. The snorkeling is also good. To get here, turn left on the rather rutted dead-end road to Baie des Péres (Friars Bay). The beach itself is a 10- to 15-minute walk from the last beach bar. **Amenities:** food and drink; toilets. **Best for:** solitude; walking; swimming; snorkeling. ⊠ *St. Martin*.

Baie de Grand Case. Along this skinny stripe of a beach bordering the culinary capital of Grand Case, the old-style gingerbread architecture sometimes peeps out between the bustling restaurants. The sea is calm, and there are tons of fun lunch options from bistros to beachside *lolos*. Several of the restaurants rent chairs and umbrellas; some include their use for lunch patrons. In between there is a bit of shopping—for beach necessities but also for the same kinds of handicrafts found in the Marigot market. **Amenities:** food and drink; toilets. **Best for:** swimming; walking. ⊠ *St. Martin*.

FAMILY **Baie des Pères** (*Friar's Bay*). This quiet cove close to Marigot has beach grills and bars, with chaises and umbrellas, calm waters, and a lovely view of Anguilla. Kali's Beach Bar, open daily for lunch and (weather permitting) dinner, has a Rasta vibe and color scheme—it's the best place to be on the full moon, with music, dancing, and a huge bonfire, but you can get lunch, beach chairs, and umbrellas any time. Friar's Bay Beach Café is a French Bistro on the sand, open from breakfast to sunset. To get to the beach, take National Road 7 from Marigot, go toward Grand Case to the Morne Valois hill, and turn left on the dead-end road at the sign. **Amenities:** food and drink; toilets. **Best for:** partiers; swimming; walking. ⊠ *St. Martin*.

Baie Orientale, widely considered St. Martin's best beach

Baie Longue (*Long Bay*). Though it extends over the French Lowlands, from the cliff at La Samanna to La Pointe des Canniers, the island's longest beach has no facilities or vendors. It's the perfect place for a romantic walk, but be warned that car break-ins are a particular problem here. To get here, take National Road 7 south of Marigot. Rue de Baie Longue is the first entrance to the beach. It's worth it to splurge for lunch or a sunset cocktail at the elegant La Samanna. **Amenities:** none. **Best for:** solitude; walking. ⊠ *St. Martin.*

★ **Fodor'sChoice Baie Orientale** (*Orient Bay*). Many consider this the island's most beautiful beach, but its 2 miles (3 km) of satiny white sand, underwater marine reserve, variety of water sports, beach clubs, and hotels also make it one of the most crowded. Lots of "naturists" take advantage of the clothing-optional policy, so don't be shocked. Early-morning nude beach walking is de rigueur for the guests at Club Orient, at the southeastern end of the beach. Plan to spend the day at one of the clubs; each bar has different color umbrellas, and all boast terrific restaurants and lively bars. You can have an open-air massage, try any sea toy you fancy, and stay until dark. To get to Baie Orientale from Marigot, take National Road 7 past Grand Case, past the Aéroport de L'Espérance, and watch for the left turn. **Amenities:** food and drink; parking; toilets; water sports.

Best for: nudists; partiers; swimming; walking; windsurfing. ⊠ *St. Martin.*

Baie Rouge (*Red Bay*). Here you can bask with the millionaires renting the big-ticket villas in the "neighborhood," joining them on the gorgeous Baie Rouge. The beach and its salt ponds make up a nature preserve, the location of the oldest habitations in the Caribbean. This area is widely thought to have the best snorkeling beaches on the island. You can swim the crystal waters along the point and explore a swim-through cave. The beach is fairly popular with gay men in the mornings and early afternoons. There are two restaurants here; only Chez Raymond is open every day, and cocktail hour starts when the conch shell blows, so keep your ears open. There is a sign and a right turn after you leave Baie Nettlé. **Amenities:** food and drink; toilets. **Best for:** snorkeling; swimming; walking. ⊠ *St. Martin.*

Ilet Pinel. A protected nature reserve, this kid-friendly island is a five-minute ferry ride from French Cul de Sac ($7 per person round-trip). The ferry runs every half hour from midmorning until dusk. The water is clear and shallow, and the shore is sheltered. If you like snorkeling, don your gear and paddle along both coasts of this pencil-shaped speck in the ocean. You can rent equipment on the island or in the parking lot before you board the ferry for about $10. Plan for lunch any day of the week at a palm-shaded beach hut, Karibuni (except in September, when it's closed) for the freshest fish, great salads, tapas, and drinks—try the frozen mojito for a treat. **Amenities:** food and drink; parking. **Best for:** snorkeling; swimming. ⊠ *St. Martin.*

FAMILY **Le Galion.** A coral reef borders this quiet beach, part of the island's nature preserve, which is paradise if you are traveling with children. The water is calm, clear, and quite shallow, so it's a perfect place for families with young kids. It's a full-service place, with chair rentals, restaurants, and water-sports operators. Kiteboarders and windsurfers like the trade winds at the far end of the beach. On Sunday there are always groups picnicking and partying. To get to Le Galion, follow the signs to the unmissable Butterfly Farm and continue toward the water. **Amenities:** food and drink; parking; toilets; water sports. **Best for:** partiers; swimming; windsurfing. ⊠ *Quartier d'Orléans, St. Martin.*

BEST BETS FOR DINING

Fodor's Choice★

Bacchus, Bamboo, L'Effet Mer,
La Cigale, Le Pressoir,
Mario's Bistro, Sky's The Limit,
Top Carrot

MOST ROMANTIC
La Samanna, Le Marrakech,
Le Pressoir, Sol é Luna,
Temptation

BEST VIEW
La Samanna, La Cigale,
Sol é Luna, Taloula Mango's

BEST LOCAL FOOD
Chesterfield's

BEST FOR FAMILIES
Taloula Mango's, Top Carrot

BEST FOR A SPECIAL OCCASION
Le Pressoir, La Samanna
(especially the wine dinner
in the cellar)

HIP AND YOUNG
Bamboo, Calmos Café,
Karakter Beach Lounge,
Palm Beach, Temptation,
Hidden Forest Café

WHERE TO EAT

Although most people come to St. Maarten/St. Martin for sun and fun, they leave praising the cuisine. On an island that covers only 37 square miles (96 square km), there are more than 400 restaurants from which to choose. You can sample the best dishes from France, Thailand, Italy, Vietnam, India, Japan, and, of course, the Caribbean.

Many of the best restaurants are in Grand Case (on the French side), but you should not limit your culinary adventures to that village. Great dining thrives throughout the island, from the bistros of Marigot to the hopping restaurants of Cupecoy to the low-key eateries of Simpson Bay. Whether you enjoy dining on fine china in one of the upscale restaurants or off a paper plate at the island's many lolos (roadside barbecue stands), St. Maarten/St. Martin's culinary options are sure to appeal to every palate. Loyalists on both "sides" will cheerfully try to steer you to their own favorites, and it's common to cite high euro prices to deter exploration, but quite a few restaurants still offer a one-to-one exchange rate between dollars and euros if you use cash, and main-course portions are often large enough to be shared.

During high season, it's essential to make reservations, and making them a month in advance is advisable for some of the best places. Dutch-side restaurants sometimes include a 15% service charge, so check your bill before tipping. On the French side, service is always included, but it is customary to leave 5% to 10% extra in cash for the server. Don't count on leaving tips on your credit card—it's customary to tip in cash. A taxi is probably the easiest solution to the parking problems in Grand Case, Marigot, and Philipsburg. Grand Case has two lots—each costs $4—at each end of the main boulevard, but they're often packed by 8 pm.

What to Wear: Although appropriate dining attire ranges from swimsuits to sport jackets, casual dress is usually appropriate throughout restaurants on the island. For men, a jacket and khakis or jeans will take you anywhere; for women, dressy pants, a skirt, or even fancy shorts are usually acceptable. Jeans are fine in the less formal eateries.

DUTCH SIDE

COLE BAY

$$$ 🍴 **Peg Leg Pub.** *Steakhouse.* This place is a cross between your typical beach bar and an English pub, albeit one where steaks make up the heart of the menu. Lunch options include deli-style sandwich platters at much more moderate prices than what you'll find at dinner (most options are under $10). By night, red meat rules the menu, though seafood, kebabs, and pastas shouldn't be overlooked. Good news for beer lovers: Peg Leg Pub serves more than 35 different brews. Best of all, appetizers are half price during happy hour; try the bacon-wrapped shrimp, jalapeño poppers, or the coconut shrimp. There's entertainment on Wednesday and Friday nights as well as a Sunday buffet that starts at 4 pm. [$] *Average main: $30* ✉ *Port de Plaisance, Cole Bay* ☎ *721/544–5859* 🌐 *www.peglegpub.com* ⏲ *No lunch Sun.*

CUPECOY

$$$ 🍴 **La Gondola.** *Italian.* Under new management, but still in the hands of chef Matteo Puccini, the kitchen rolls out the dough for the dozens of pasta dishes on the encyclopedic Italian menu, which also includes favorites like veal parmesan, chicken piccata in marsala sauce, and osso buco milanese. Save room for desserts like the *fantasia di dessert del Carnevale di Venezia* (a warm chocolate tart and frozen nougat served with raspberry sauce) or tiramisù. The service is professional and high-tech—the waiters take orders with earpieces and handheld computers. [$] *Average main:*

$29 ✉ Atlantis World Casino, 106 Rhine Rd., Cupecoy ☎ 721/544–3938 🌐 www.lagondola-sxm.com ⏲ No lunch.

$$$$ ✕ **Rare.** *Steakhouse.* Within an intimate, clubby setting, a guitarist provides background music while carnivores delight in chef Dino Jagtiani's creative menu. The focus is steak: certified Angus prime cuts topped with chimichurri, béarnaise, horseradish, peppercorn, or mushroom sauce. Not into red meat? You can also choose from seafood, pork, lamb, or veal. Sample some delicious sides like truffled mashed potatoes or cultivated mushroom sauté (a tasty fungi variety). Luscious desserts will make you forget that you will want to look good in your bathing suit tomorrow morning. Check the restaurant's website for specials. [$] *Average main: $54 ✉ Atlantis World Casino, 106 Rhine Rd., Cupecoy ☎ 721/545–5714 🌐 www.rareandtemptation.com ✍ Reservations essential ⏲ Closed Sept. and Mon. June–Oct. No lunch.*

$$$$ ✕ **Temptation.** *Eclectic.* Supercreative chef Dino Jagtiani, who trained at the Culinary Institute of America, is the mastermind behind dishes like seared foie gras PB&J (melted foie gras accented with peanut butter and homemade port wine and fig jam) and lump crab-stuffed jumbo shrimp wrapped in salmon bacon with pasta pearls primavera. The chef, who compares dessert to lovemaking ("both intimate, and not to be indulged in lightly"), offers a crème brûlée tasting, as well as tempura apple pie with cinnamon ice cream and caramel sauce. The wine list is extensive, and features a number of reasonably priced selections.The dining room is pretty and intimate, in spite of its location behind the casino. There's outdoor seating as well. [$] *Average main: $36 ✉ Atlantis Casino Courtyard, 106 Rhine Rd., Cupecoy ☎ 721/545–2254 🌐 www.rareandtemptation.com ✍ Reservations essential ⏲ Closed Sun. June–Oct. No lunch.*

MAHO

★ **Fodor's Choice** ✕ **Bamboo.** *Asian.* This dramatic and hip addition to the top level of the Maho central shopping area features red lacquer walls, lounging tables, Indonesian art, a first-rate bar, and electro-house tunes. You can get terrific sushi and sashimi, both the classic Japanese varieties and the Americanized ones (California roll, for example). All are good, as are the Asian hot appetizers and exotic cocktails like the Tranquillity (citrus vodka and smoky oolong tea). If you're not into Asian fare, try the salmon, ribs, or beef. The young crowd keeps this place hopping way past midnight. If you're solo, you will have a great

$$

time hanging and even dining at the bar. There is a sake and sushi happy hour from 5 to 7 nightly. [$] *Average main: $20* ✉ *Sonesta Maho Beach Resort & Casino, 1 Rhine Rd., Maho* ☎ *721/545–3622* 🌐 *www.bamboo-sxm.com* ⏲ *No lunch weekends.*

$$$ FAMILY 🍴 **Big Fish.** *Seafood.* A chic, white interior, fresh-caught fish, and friendly, if sometimes relaxed, service, are the draw at this Oyster Pond restaurant. The location is convenient whether you are staying in Oyster Pond or Dawn Beach. Stick with whatever was most recently in the sea, and you will be happy with your food. If offered, grouper in curry-coconut is a yummy option, and the hurricane shrimp is a local favorite. Light eaters will love the huge fresh salads. The owners also run a fishing-charter outfit, and they will happily cook up your daily catch here, too. [$] *Average main: $28* ✉ *14 Emerald Merrit Rd., Oyster Pond* ☎ *721/586–1961.*

$$$ FAMILY 🍴 **Le Bateau Ivre.** *Mediterranean.* Located in the middle of an anonymous-looking plaza in the new-ish Porto Cupecoy Marina complex, the big salads, American-style sandwiches, and varied crêpes make this place a good choice for an easy lunch around the marina. At night there are all the French bistro classics, plus seafood specials; all are frequently accompanied by a singer performing Edith Piaf. You can sit outdoors and admire the yachts, or indoors for a lounge-ier feel. [$] *Average main: $26* ✉ *Marina Porto Cupecoy, Maho* ☎ *721/526–2157.*

$$$ FAMILY 🍴 **Trattoria Italiana.** *Italian.* Tucked behind Casino Royale, this plain Italian eatery is extremely popular with locals. The menu includes favorites like penne Bolognese and eggplant Parmesan, but the real winners are the thin-crust pizzas. The freshly brewed iced tea is great on a hot day. With its laid-back atmosphere and friendly staff, this is a cozy spot for families with small children or a place where you just run in and grab a quick bite. [$] *Average main: $22* ✉ *Maho Shopping Plaza, Maho* ☎ *721/545–4034* ⏲ *No lunch Sun.*

PHILIPSBURG

$$$$ 🍴 **Antoine by the Sea.** *French.* Owner Jean Pierre Pomarico greets guests and ushers them into this comfy seaside restaurant. Low-key, blue-accented décor, white bamboo chairs, watercolors lining the walls, and candles—along with the sound of the nearby surf—create a relaxing atmosphere. The lobster thermidor (a succulent tail oozing with cream and Swiss cheese) is a favorite, but other special-

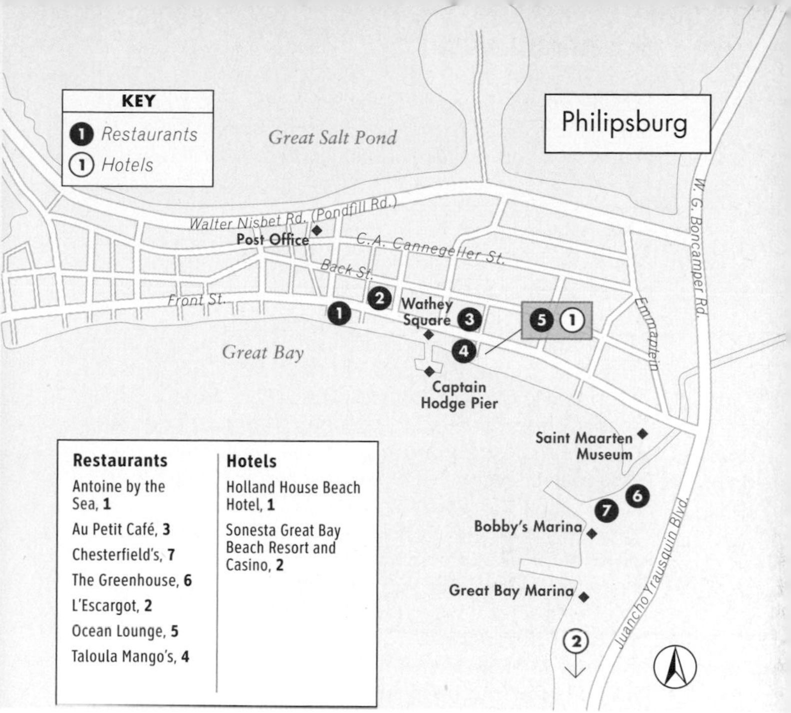
KEY
Restaurants
Hotels
Philipsburg
Great Salt Pond
Walter Nisbet Rd. (Pondfill Rd.)
Post Office
C.A. Cannegeller St.
Back St.
Front St.
Wathey Square
Great Bay
Captain Hodge Pier
W. G. Boncamper Rd.
Emmaplein
Saint Maarten Museum
Bobby's Marina
Great Bay Marina
Juancho Yrausquin Blvd.
Restaurants
Antoine by the Sea, 1
Au Petit Café, 3
Chesterfield's, 7
The Greenhouse, 6
L'Escargot, 2
Ocean Lounge, 5
Taloula Mango's, 4
Hotels
Holland House Beach Hotel, 1
Sonesta Great Bay Beach Resort and Casino, 2

ties include lobster bisque, seafood linguine, and a beef filet with béarnaise sauce. The $36 prix-fixe menu is a great deal. Open every day for lunch and dinner, it gets packed for lunch when there are a lot of cruise ships in the harbor. $ *Average main: $32* ✉ *119 Front St., Philipsburg* ☎ *721/542–2964* 🌐 *www.antoinerestaurant.com* ✍ *Reservations essential.*

$ 🍴 **Au Petit Café.** *Café.* This tiny bistro is found in the quaint shopping arcade just off Front Street. Although there are only a small number of tables (both indoor and out), you should still stop by for a quick, inexpensive snack or for a freshly ground cup of coffee. Watching employees make crepes is half the fun; eating them is the other half. You can also order hearty salads, pizza, and hot or cold sandwiches on fresh bread. It is open from 8 am to 4:30 pm. $ *Average main: $9* ✉ *120 Old St., Philipsburg* ☎ *721/552–8788* 💳 *No credit cards* ⏲ *Closed Sun. No dinner.*

$$ 🍴 **Chesterfield's.** *Caribbean.* Both locals and tourists seem
FAMILY to love this restaurant at Great Bay Marina. Seafood is the main focus, but steaks, burgers, pasta, and poultry are all on the dinner menu, and you can also get breakfast and lunch. If you love sophisticated cuisine, look

elsewhere, but the portions are big and the prices reasonable. Happy hour is every night from 5 to 7. Delivery is available if you're staying in a condo or timeshare in the area. [$] *Average main: $19* ✉ *Great Bay Marina, Philipsburg* ☎ *721/542–3484.*

$$$ FAMILY 🍴 **The Greenhouse.** *Eclectic.* The famous happy hour with two-for-one drinks is just one of the reasons people flock to the Greenhouse. This waterfront restaurant balances a relaxed atmosphere, reasonable prices, and popular favorites like burgers, prime rib, and steaks. If you're seeking something spicy, try the creole shrimp. The daily specials, like the Friday-night Lobster Mania, are widely popular. [$] *Average main: $21* ✉ *Bobby's Marina, Philipsburg* ☎ *721/542–2941* 🌐 *www.thegreenhouserestaurant.com.*

$$$ 🍴 **L'Escargot.** *French.* The wraparound verandah, the bunches of grapes hanging from the chandeliers, and the Toulouse-Lautrec–style murals add to the colorful atmosphere of this restaurant in a 150-year-old gingerbread Creole house. As the name suggests, snails are a specialty, and are offered several ways. But the menu also includes many other French standards like onion soup, crispy duck, and veal cordon bleu. There's a cabaret show, complete with cancan in the tradition of *La Cage aux Folles.* [$] *Average main: $28* ✉ *96 Front St., Philipsburg* ☎ *721/542–2483* 🌐 *www.lescargotrestaurant.com* 🕒 *Closed Sun. June–Oct. No lunch weekends.*

$$$ FAMILY 🍴 **Ocean Lounge.** *Eclectic.* An airy modern verandah perched on the Philipsburg boardwalk gives Ocean Lounge its distinct South Beach vibe. You'll want to linger over fresh fish and steaks as you watch the scene with tourists passing by on romantic strolls by night or determined cruise-ship passengers surveying the surrounding shops by day. The $45 daily three-course tasting menu is a great deal. There is also a fun menu of bar snacks and martinis. It's a bit hard to park here so consider taking a taxi at night. [$] *Average main: $29* ✉ *Holland House Beach Hotel, 43 Front St., Philipsburg* ☎ *721/542–2572* 🌐 *www.hhbh.com.*

$$ FAMILY 🍴 **Taloula Mango's.** *Eclectic.* Ribs are the specialty at this casual beachfront restaurant, but the jerk chicken and thin-crust pizza, not to mention a few vegetarian options like the tasty falafel, are not to be ignored. On weekdays lunch is accompanied by live music (warning: loud); every Friday during happy hour a DJ spins tunes. In case you're wondering, the restaurant got its name from the owner's golden retriever. [$] *Average main: $17* ✉ *Sint Rose Shop-*

ping Mall, off Front St. on beach boardwalk, Philipsburg ☎ *721/542–1645* 🌐 *www.taloulamango.com.*

SIMPSON BAY

$$$ FAMILY 🍴 **Izi Ristorante Italiano.** *Italian.* The former chef of La Gondola serves up huge, shareable portions of more than 400 different dishes in this cheerful, centrally located space. For something fun and different, diners are invited to create their own menu: pick a pasta and a sauce, then add in your choice of meat, fish, and veggies. [$] *Average main: $23* ✉ *Paradise Mall, 67 Welfare Rd., Simpson Bay* ☎ *721/544–3079* 🌐 *www.iziristoranteitaliano.com* ✍ *Reservations essential* ⏲ *Closed Tues. May–Nov.*

★ $$ FAMILY **Fodor's Choice** 🍴 **Karakter Beach Lounge.** *Eclectic.* Karakter, a funky and charming modern beach bar, is right behind the airport, serving up fun, great music, relaxation, and a lot of style. The vibe is more like St-Tropez than St. Maarten. Open from 9 am till 10 pm, the restaurant serves up healthy and tasty choices for any appetite: fresh fruit smoothies, tropical cocktails, fresh fruit salads, healthy sandwiches, and tapas. A sign near the shower/bathhouse invites guest to "come hang out here and shower before you go to the airport." So this is a place to keep in mind in case your flight is delayed or if you have a layover between flights, or even if you just want to spend every last second of your vacation on the sand. [$] *Average main: $14* ✉ *121 Simpson Bay Rd., Simpson Bay* ☎ *721/523–9983* 🌐 *www.karakterbeach.com.*

$$$ FAMILY 🍴 **Panlaan Thai on the Bay.** *Thai.* This new Thai restaurant serves up big portions of fresh-tasting and nicely presented classic Thai dishes like curries and satays in a pretty, centrally located waterfront deck on Simpson Bay. There's delivery and take-out if you don't have time for a sit-down meal. Happy hour in high season (November–June) features $4 martinis served with $5 appetizers, and there is live music on Sunday night. ■ **TIP→** It can be breezy at night, so bring a light sweater. [$] *Average main: $22* ✉ *Welfare Rd., Simpson Bay* ☎ *721/559–2811* 🌐 *www.panlaansxm.com.*

$$ FAMILY 🍴 **Pineapple Pete.** *Seafood.* This popular, casual, and fun (if slightly touristy) place is well located, with a game room that includes seven pool tables, four dart boards, an arcade, and flat-screen TVs tuned to sports. A friendly, efficient staff will serve you burgers, seafood, and ribs, but for a real treat try one of the specialties like the tasty crab-stuffed shrimp appetizer. Follow it up with succulent, herb-crusted rack of lamb. There's free Wi-Fi and

live entertainment Tuesday through Sunday. It's an easy choice for a bite near the airport, and is open from 11 am through closing. Note the 15% service charge included in the check. There's also a little shop for with T-shirts and local crafts for sale. [$] *Average main: $20* ✉ *56 Welfare Rd., Simpson Bay* ☎ *721/544–6030* 🌐 *www.pineapplepete.com* ✍ *Reservations essential.*

★ **Fodor's Choice** 🍴 **Top Carrot.** *Vegetarian.* Open from 7:30 am
$ to 6 pm, this friendly café and juice bar is a popular break-
FAMILY fast and lunch stop. It features fresh and tasty vegetarian entrées, sandwiches, salads, homemade pastries, and fresh fish. Favorites include a pastry stuffed with pesto, avocado, red pepper, and feta cheese, or a cauliflower, spinach, and tomato quiche. The house-made granola and yogurt are local favorites, but folks also drop in just for espresso and the large selection of teas. Many also come for the free Wi-Fi. Adjacent to the restaurant is a gift shop with Asian-inspired items, spiritual books, and half-price cotton beach cover-ups. [$] *Average main: $8* ✉ *Airport Rd., near Simpson Bay Yacht Club, Simpson Bay* ☎ *721/544–3381* ⏲ *Closed Sun. No dinner.*

$ 🍴 **Vesna Taverna and Bagel House.** *Deli.* Centrally located near
FAMILY the Simpson Bay Bridge, this casual eatery is open all day long, with tasty but healthy options like smoothies, bagel sandwiches, omelets, crêpes, pancakes, and salads (burgers are available for dinner). The patio makes for great outdoor eating, plus there's free Wi-Fi. [$] *Average main: $10* ✉ *15 Airport Rd., Unit 1, Simpson Bay* ☎ *721/524–5283.*

$ 🍴 **Zee Best.** *Café.* This friendly bistro serves one of the best breakfasts on the island. There's a huge selection of fresh-baked pastries—try the almond croissants—plus sweet and savory crêpes, omelets, quiches, and other treats from the oven. When you sit down a basket of assorted pastries arrives, and you are charged for the ones you select. Specialties include the St. Martin omelet, filled with ham, cheese, mushrooms, onions, green peppers, and tomatoes. Best of all, breakfast is served from 7:30 am until 2 pm. Lunch includes sandwiches, salads, and the chef's famous spaghetti Bolognese. ■ **TIP→** There are also locations near the Airport, and at Port de Plaisance. [$] *Average main: $8* ✉ *Pl. del Lago, Simpson Bay* ☎ *721/544–2477* 💳 *No credit cards.*

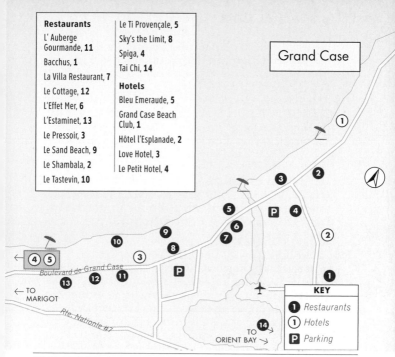

Restaurants

L' Auberge Gourmande, **11**

Bacchus, **1**

La Villa Restaurant, **7**

Le Cottage, **12**

L'Effet Mer, **6**

L'Estaminet, **13**

Le Pressoir, **3**

Le Sand Beach, **9**

Le Shambala, **2**

Le Tastevin, **10**

Le Ti Provençale, **5**

Sky's the Limit, **8**

Spiga, **4**

Tai Chi, **14**

Hotels

Bleu Emeraude, **5**

Grand Case Beach Club, **1**

Hôtel l'Esplanade, **2**

Love Hotel, **3**

Le Petit Hotel, **4**

Grand Case

← TO MARIGOT

Boulevard de Grand Case

Rte. Nationle #7

TO ORIENT BAY →

KEY

1 *Restaurants*

① *Hotels*

P *Parking*

FRENCH SIDE

BAIE NETTLÉ

★ Fodor'sChoice ✕ **La Cigale.** *French.* On the edge of Baie Nettlé,
$$$$ La Cigale has wonderful views of the lagoon from its dining
room and its open-air patio, but the charm of the restaurant comes from the devoted attention of adorable owner
Olivier, helped by his mother and brother, and various
cousins, too. Stephane Istel's delicious food is edible sculpture: ravioli of lobster with wild mushrooms and foie gras
is poached in an intense lobster bisque, and house-smoked
swordfish and salmon is garnished with goat cheese and
seaweed salad drizzled with dill-lime vinaigrette. For dessert, the raspberry macaron is a favorite. ⑤ *Average main:*
€43 ⊠ *101 Laguna Beach, Baie Nettlé* ☎ *599/87–90–23*
⊕ *www.restaurant-lacigale.com* ⩫ *Reservations essential*
☾ *Closed Sun. No lunch.*

$$$$ ✕ **Le Sand Beach.** *French.* A stylish St. Barth vibe and a
FAMILY beachfront location make Le Sand Beach a great choice
for any meal. Relax on the terrace and enjoy cocktails and
snacks, or park yourself on a lounge chair on the beach
with an umbrella (no charge if you're dining), and enjoy the
music and ambience. The refined food is fresh and nicely

presented; the snapper and fish tartares are stand-outs, but real credit is due to the management and staff who are friendly and attentive. $ *Average main: $35* ⊠ *Sandy Bay, Baie Nettlé* ☎ *690/73–14–38* ⊕ *www.whereisstmartin.com.*

$$$ ✕ **Ma Ti' Beach.** *French.* Here's a great choice for a casual
FAMILY beach bar with better-than-average food, right across from the Hotel Mercure on the road to Marigot. Open for lunch and dinner, it offers great views across the turquoise water to Anguilla. You can always get fresh lobster from the tank, and don't forget the excellent traditional French onion soup with a cheesy crust. If the *moules frites* (fresh mussels with fries) are a special, snap them up. $ *Average main: €23* ⊠ *Anse Margot, across the road from the Mercure Resort, Baie Nettlé* ☎ *0590/87–01–30* ⊗ *Closed Tues.*

BAIE ORIENTALE

$$$ ✕ **L'Astrolabe.** *French.* Chef Maxime Orea gets raves for his modern interpretations of classic French cuisine served around the pool at this cozy, relaxed restaurant in the Esmeralda Resort. Corn soup; foie gras terrine with apricot and quince jam; an amazing roast duck with pineapple-ginger sauce; and deliciously fresh fish dishes are just some of the offerings. There are lots of choices for vegetarians, a three-course prix fixe, a children's menu, and a lobster party with live music every Friday night. $ *Average main: $26* ⊠ *Esmeralda Resort, Baie Orientale* ☎ *0590/87–11–20* ⊕ *www.esmeralda-resort.com* ⚱ *Reservations essential* ⊗ *No lunch; no dinner Wed.*

$$$$ ✕ **La Table d'Antoine.** *French.* Settle in here for an evening
FAMILY of attentive, friendly service and hearty French-country food with a side dish of lively people-watching. The varied menu features slightly unfamiliar dishes that are worth a try, like the *tartiflette* (a kind of cheese and potato gratin), beef baked in a salt crust, and duck magret with foie gras. Desserts are delicious, as is the selection of house-made infused rums. $ *Average main: €35* ⊠ *Place de la Baie Orientale, Baie Orientale* ☎ *0590/62–82–28.*

$$$ ✕ **Palm Beach.** *French Fusion.* Just as stylish as its Florida namesake, this Baie Orientale beach club sets the stage with Balinese art and furniture, big comfy chaises on the beach, and an active bar. There are three big treehouse-like lounges for lunch or if you are looking for a place to spend the afternoon, plus a spa for beachside massages. The menu of salads, tartares, and Thai-influenced salads and noodle specialties is served in a pavilion shaded by sail-like awnings. The Sunday night beach party is the place to be for locals and guests alike. [$] *Average main: €21* ✉ *Baie Orientale* ☎ *690/35–99–06* 🌐 *www.palmbeachsxm.net* 🕒 *No dinner.*

$$$ 🍴 **Waikiki Beach.** *Eclectic.* Sit at a picnic table, or on a lounge–bed and enjoy the food and great people-watching. If there's a big cruise-ship group, however, you may just want to head down to the beach. During the Christmas holiday season, top DJs are brought in for partying into the night, and there is a lobster buffet lunch on Saturday. [$] *Average main: $25* ✉ *5 Baie Orientale* ☎ *0590/87–43–19* 🌐 *www.waikikibeachsxm.com.*

FRIAR'S BAY

$$ 🍴 **Friar's Bay Beach Café.** *Bistro.* There is a sophisticated vibe at this quiet, rather elegant beach club that may make patrons feel as if they are on a private beach. The décor is not as funky as some of the other beach-club restaurants, but look out for the red and black signs on the road between Grand Case and Marigot so you'll know where to turn. Drive slow because the road is rough. You can rent lounge chairs and umbrellas and spend the whole day relaxing, drinking, and dining. The restaurant is open from breakfast through the spectacular sunset, offering a menu reminiscent of a French bistro. Be sure to look at the specials on the blackboard, but carpaccios of meat and fish are sparklingly fresh, and the salads are terrific. Plus, you'll also find French standbys such as tomato and goat cheese tartlets, as well as "international" ones like burgers and sandwiches. On Sunday evening there is live music until 9 pm. [$] *Average main: $18* ✉ *Friar's Bay Rd., Friar's Bay* ☎ *0590/49–16–87* 💳 *No credit cards.*

FRENCH CUL DE SAC

$$$ 🍴 **Anse Marcel Beach.** *Modern French.* Beachside calm with a side order of chic is on the menu at this lovely and private cove, where the restaurant/beach club is a perfect choice for couples or families looking for a beach day, a sunset cocktail, or a great swimming spot. You can dine and lounge all day long, either in the tented pavilion or right on the beach. The food changes according to market availability but there are always salads, tasty mussels, fresh grilled fish and lobster, steaks, and sandwiches; try the smoked salmon and bagel combo if it's offered. The desserts are amazing, especially the crêpes. There is safe, private parking for your car and moorings available for boats. [$] *Average main: €24* ✉ *Anse Marcel* ☎ *690/26–38–50.*

$$$ ✕ **Le Ti Bouchon.** *French.* This tiny restaurant, close to Anse Marcel hotels, captures the spirit of Lyon, the capitol of French gastronomy, where casual small restaurants serve hearty traditional cuisine, wine comes by the pitcher, and the patron is very much part of the party. The eight tables are set on the porch of a traditional cottage and the menu (written on a chalkboard) changes frequently, assuring that each visit will be unique. Chances are you will become fast friends with the owner Momo, join in conversations with the next table, and linger over your chocolate mousse. Dietary restrictions are handled with grace and accuracy. [$] *Average main: €30* ✉ *110 Rte. de Cul de Sac, French Cul de Sac* ☎ *690/64–84–64* 🌐 *www.tibouchonrestaurant.com* ✍ *Reservations essential.*

$$$ ✕ **Sol é Luna.** *Caribbean.* Charming and romantic, with modern décor, this restaurant puts its best tables on the balcony, from which you can best appreciate the great views. Begin your meal with an appetizer like curry tuna carpaccio, monkfish spring rolls, or roasted vegetables with goat cheese; then move on to an entree such as fresh pasta with mixed seafood or beef tenderloin flamed with Cognac. Try the chocolate soufflé for dessert. Don't be surprised if you see a proposal or two during your meal, as this is one of the most romantic restaurants on the island. ■ **TIP→** Before ordering one of the "specials" ask about the prices; sometimes they can be surprisingly high compared to regular menu items. [$] *Average main: €28* ✉ *61 Rte. de Mont Vernon, French Cul de Sac* ☎ *0590/29–08–56* 🌐 *www.solelunarestaurant.com* ✍ *Reservations essential* ⏲ *Closed mid-June–early July and Sept.–early Oct.*

GRAND CASE

★ **Fodor's Choice** ✕ **Bacchus.** *French.* If you want to lunch with

$$ the savviest locals, you have to scrape yourself from the beach and head into the industrial park outside Grand Case, where Benjamin Laurent, the best wine importer in the Caribbean, has built this lively, deliciously air-conditioned reconstruction of a wine cellar. He serves up first-rate starters, salads, and main courses made from top ingredients brought in from France, lovingly prepared by top chefs. Shop here for gourmet groceries for your villa, or order from the extensive take-out menu. Smokers love to hang in the new cigar/rum lounge. The wines are sublime, and you will get an amazing education along with a great lunch. You won't mind eating indoors here—just think of it as the perfect sunblock. Enter at the "Hope Estate" sign in the roundabout across from the road that leads to the Grand Case Airport. $ *Average main: $20* ✉ *18–19 Hope Estate, Grand Case Rd., Grand Case* ☎ *0590/87–15–70* ⊕ *www. bacchussxm.com* ⊗ *Closed Sun. No dinner.*

$$$ ✕ **L'Auberge Gourmande.** *French.* A fixture of Boulevard Grand Case, L'Auberge Gourmande is in one of the oldest Creole houses in St. Maarten/St. Martin. The formal dining room is framed by elegant arches. The light Provençal cuisine includes menu choices like roasted rack of lamb with an herb crust over olive mashed potatoes, Dover sole in lemon butter, and pork filet mignon stuffed with apricots and walnuts. There are vegetarian options, a kids' menu, and a good selection of wines. Ask for an outside table. $ *Average main: $21* ✉ *89 Bd. de Grand Case* ☎ *0590/87–73–37* ⊕ *www.laubergegourmande.com* ⊗ *Closed Sept. No lunch.*

$$$ ✕ **La Villa.** *Caribbean.* Visitors continually flock here for the friendly management, the varied French-Caribbean menu, and the fun location in the middle of Grand Case. The €49 three-course menu also helps, plus they accept one-dollar-per-euro for cash. $ *Average main: $28* ✉ *93 Bd. de Grand Case* ☎ *0590/52–36–59* ⊕ *www.lavillasxm. com* ⊗ *No lunch.*

$$$ ✕ **Le Cottage.** *French.* The inventive French cuisine is prepared with a light touch and presented with flair, and perhaps a bit of humor here. On the "fooding-tasting" menus, you can create your own selection from a tempting list of beautifully plated mini-servings. Or try a prix-fixe meal. Huge portions of hearty French food are served by a genial staff to a lively community gathered on the streetfront porch. Don't miss the caramel dessert tasting, which features a perfect soufflé, or the house-made salted caramel meringues. $ *Average main: $27* ✉ *97 Bd. de Grand Case* ☎ *0590/29–03–30* ⊕ *www.lecottagesxm.com* ⌕ *Reservations essential.*

★ **Fodor's**Choice ✕ **L'Effet Mer.** *Modern French.* Longtime visitors
$$$$ to St. Martin are sure to remember the award-winning cuisine prepared by chef Stephane Decluseau at L'Astrolabe. Now, along with his partner Damien Pointeau, he's opened this Grand Case waterfront restaurant. You can hang out on beach chairs outside if you'd like, but the real action is inside, where creative and first-rate cooking is served with charm, precision, and panache. A tasting-plate of foie gras, or the incomparable foamy "lobster cappuccino" soup makes a fine starter, mains are lively and unique, and the desserts are gorgeous edible art (try the crème brûlée tast-

ing, with three variations on the theme). The €29 prix-fixe is a good deal. [$] *Average main: €34* ✉ *48 Bd. de Grand Case* ☎ *0590/87–05–65* 🌐 *www.effetmer.net* ✍ *Reservations essential* ⏲ *Closed Sun.*

★ Fodor's Choice ✕ **L'Estaminet.** *French.* The name of this restaurant is an old-fashioned word for "tavern" in French, but the food is anything but archaic. The creative, upscale cuisine served in this modern, clean space is fun and surprising, utilizing plenty of molecular gastronomy. This means that intense liquid garnishes might be inserted into your goat cheese appetizer or perhaps given to you in a tiny toothpaste tube, or even a plastic syringe. The bright flavors, artistic plating, and novelty make for a lively meal that will be remembered fondly. Under no circumstances should you pass up the chocolate tasting for dessert. [$] *Average main: €23* ✉ *139 Bd. de Grand Case* ☎ *0590/29–00–25* 🌐 *www.estaminet-sxm.com* ⏲ *Closed Mon. June–Nov.*
$$$

★ Fodor's Choice ✕ **Le Pressoir.** *French.* In a carefully restored West Indian house painted in brilliant reds and blues, Le Pressoir has charm to spare. The name comes from the historic salt press that sits opposite the restaurant, but the thrill comes from the culinary creations of chef Franc Mear and the hospitality of his beautiful wife Melanie. If you are indecisive, or just plain smart, try any (or all) of the *degustations* (tastings) of four soups, four foie gras preparations, or four fruit desserts, each showcasing sophisticated preparations with adorable presentations. Foie gras is served in a dollhouse-size terrine, with a teensy glass of Sauternes. [$] *Average main: $30* ✉ *30 Bd. de Grand Case* ☎ *0590/87–76–62* 🌐 *www.lepressoir-sxm.com* ✍ *Reservations essential* ⏲ *Closed mid-Sept.–mid-Oct., and Sun. May–Dec. No lunch.*
$$$

$$$$ ✕ **Le Shambala.** *French Fusion.* Romantic and beachy-chic, this waterfront restaurant has a lavish south-of-France vibe, with prices to match. Come for the sunset and start out with an interesting cocktail, before moving on to grilled ribeye steaks, veal T-bone, or simply prepared fish garnished with fresh veggies. All the sophisticated desserts are made in-house; try pairing yours with a glass of champagne (there are more than a dozen types to choose from). [$] *Average main: €31* ✉ *28 Bd. de Grand Case* ☎ *0590/29–17–09* 🌐 *www.leshambala.com* ✍ *Reservations essential.*

$$$ ✕ **Le Tastevin.** *French.* In the heart of Grand Case, Le Tastevin is on everyone's list of favorites. The attractive wood-beamed room is the "real" St. Martin style, and the tasty food is enhanced by Joseph, the amiable owner, who serves

up lunch and dinner every day on a breezy porch over a glittering blue sea. Salads and simple grills rule for lunch; at dinner, try one of the two tasting menus, either a "brasserie" style menu or a more expensive "gourmet" menu that includes excellent wines. [$] *Average main: $29* ✉ *86 Bd. de Grand Case* ☎ *0590/87–55–45* 🌐 *www.letastevin-restaurant.com* ✍ *Reservations essential* ⏲ *Closed mid-Aug.–Sept.*

$$$ ✕ **Le Ti Provençale.** *French.* Its always a good idea to follow the French locals for the best food in St. Martin; chef Hervé Sageot has won the gold medal as the chef of the year in the local Taste of St. Martin festival several times. Now located right on the water, you'll find a full blackboard of daily specials, which invariably focus on seafood. The day's catch is brought to your table for you to "meet" and for you to discuss its preparation. This offers a great opportunity to learn about local seafood. The fish soup is made from *rouget* (red mullet) and served with the traditional garlicky *rouille.* But the restaurant does serve more than just fish; there are good pastas and lamb and steaks if your preferences aren't fishy. The restaurant is open for both lunch and dinner, and there is a little beach club too. [$] *Average main: $27* ✉ *140 Bd. de Grand Case* ☎ *0590/87–02–31* 🌐 *www.letiprovencal.com* ⏲ *Closed Sun.*

★ **Fodor's Choice** ✕ **Sky's the Limit.** *Caribbean.* Although St. Martin
$ is known for its upscale dining, each town has its roadside lolos, including the island's culinary capital of Grand Case. They are open from lunchtime until evening, but earlier in the day you'll find fresher offerings. Locals flock to the square of a half-dozen stands in the middle of Grand Case, on the waterside. Not to say that these stands offer haute or fine cuisine, but they are fun, relatively cheap, and offer an iconic St. Martin meal. With plastic utensils and paper plates, Sky's the Limit couldn't be more informal. The menu includes everything from succulent grilled ribs to stewed conch, fresh snapper, and grilled lobster at the most reasonable price on the island. Don't miss the johnnycakes and side dishes like plantains, curried rice, beans, and coleslaw that come with your choice. The service is friendly, if a bit slow, but sit back with a $1.50 beer and enjoy the experience. On weekends there is often live music. At this writing the lolos are still offering a one-to-one exchange between euros and dollars. [$] *Average main: €10* ✉ *Bd. de Grand Case* ☎ *0590/35–67–84* ✍ *Reservations not accepted* 💳 *No credit cards.*

$$$ ✕ **Spiga.** *Italian.* In a beautifully restored Creole house, Spiga's tasty cuisine fuses Italian and Caribbean ingredients and

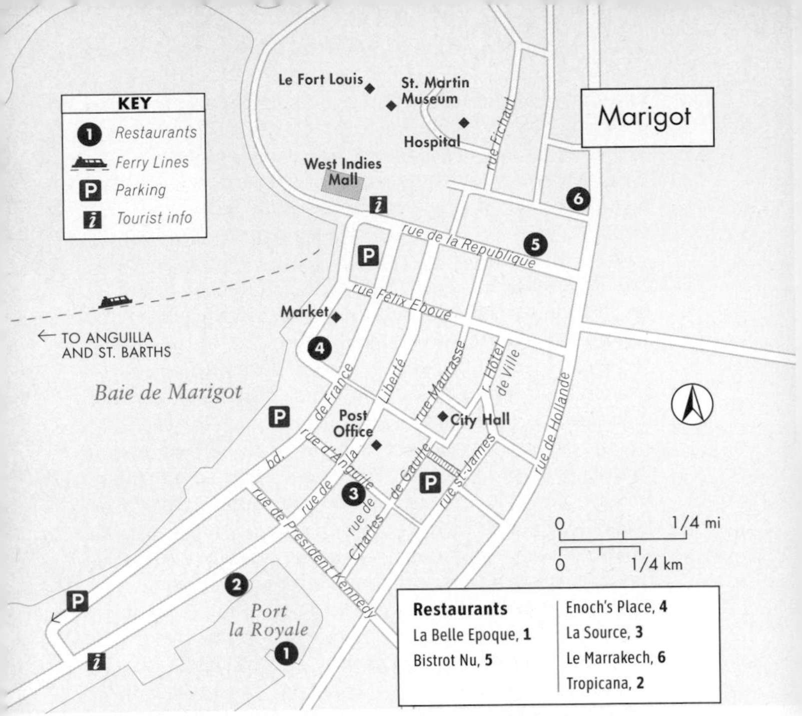
Marigot
KEY
Restaurants
Ferry Lines
Parking
Tourist info
Le Fort Louis
St. Martin Museum
Hospital
West Indies Mall
rue Fichaut
rue de la Republique
rue Félix Eboué
Market
← TO ANGUILLA AND ST. BARTHS
Baie de Marigot
bd. de France
Liberté
rue Maurasse
r. Hôtel de Ville
rue de Hollande
City Hall
Post Office
rue d'Anguille
rue de la
rue de Charles de Gaulle
rue St-James
rue de President Kennedy
Port la Royale
0 1/4 mi
0 1/4 km
Restaurants
La Belle Epoque, 1
Bistrot Nu, 5
Enoch's Place, 4
La Source, 3
Le Marrakech, 6
Tropicana, 2

cooking techniques. Appetizers are tasty and ample. Follow with one of the excellent pasta dishes or a main course featuring fresh fish or meat such as the delicious pesto-crusted rack of lamb. Save room for the lemon-ricotta cake, and try the selection of grappas. [$] *Average main: $28* ✉ *4 Rte. de L'Esperance, Grand Case* ☎ *0590/52–47–83* 🌐 *www.spiga-sxm.com* ✍ *Reservations essential* ⏲ *Closed mid-Sept.–late Oct., and Tues. June–mid-Sept. No lunch Sun.*

$$$ ✕ **Tai Chi.** *Asian.* Sushi and Thai-fusion dishes are served with flashy cocktails at the end of the Orient Bay Plaza on the way from the beach. There are innovative sushi rolls, lots of choices for vegetarians and vegans, and congenial happy hours. [$] *Average main: $23* ✉ *Pl. du Parc de la Baie Orientale, Grand Case* ☎ *0590/87–73–98*.

MARIGOT

$$$ ✕ **Bistro Nu.** *French.* It's hard to top the authentic French fare and reasonable prices you can find at this intimate restaurant tucked in a Marigot alley. Traditional French dishes like steak au poivre, sweetbreads with mushroom sauce, and sole meuniere are served in a friendly, intimate dining room, which is now air-conditioned. The prix-fixe menu is a very good value. The place is popular, and the tables are routinely packed until it closes at midnight. It can be difficult to park here, so take your chances at finding a spot on the street—or try a taxi. [$] *Average main: €24* ✉ *Allée de l'Ancienne Geôle, Marigot* ☎ *0590/87–97–09* 🌐 *www.bistronu.com* ✍ *Reservations essential* ⏲ *Closed Sun.*

2

$$ 🍴 **Enoch's Place.** *Caribbean.* The blue-and-white-striped awning on a corner of the Marigot Market makes this place hard to miss. But Enoch's lolo-style cooking is what draws the crowds. Specialties include garlic shrimp, fresh lobster, and rice and beans like your St. Martin mother used to make. Try the saltfish and fried johnnycake—a great breakfast option. The food more than makes up for the lack of décor, and chances are you'll be counting the days until you can return. [$] *Average main: €13* ✉ *Marigot Market, Front de Mer, Marigot* ☎ *0590/29–29–88* ✍ *Reservations not accepted* 💳 *No credit cards* ⏲ *Closed Sun. No dinner.*

$$ 🍴 **La Belle Epoque.** *Eclectic.* A favorite among locals, this
FAMILY brasserie is a good choice at the Marigot marina. Whether you stop for a drink or a meal, you'll soon discover that it's a great spot for boat- and people-watching. The menu has a bit of everything: big salads, thin-crust pizza, and seafood are always good bets. There's also a good wine list. And it's open nonstop seven days a week for breakfast through late dinner. [$] *Average main: €20* ✉ *Marina Port la Royale, Marigot* ☎ *0590/87–87–70* 🌐 *www.belle-epoque-sxm.com.*

$$ 🍴 **La Source.** *Contemporary.* Somewhat hidden behind the boutiques in Marina La Royale (look near Vilbrequin), this tiny "healthy" restaurant features a French seasonal menu as well as sandwiches, salads, soups, fair-trade coffee and teas, and organic pastries. A bargain lunch special includes the special of the day and a drink, and the organic pasta dishes are delicious and inventive. The light choices, which include crab tartare with seaweed and organic-chicken salad, are terrific. Even the pastries are organic. [$] *Average main: $14* ✉ *Marina Port la Royale, Marigot* ☎ *0590/27–17–27.*

$$$ 🍴 **Le Marrakech.** *Moroccan.* Some twenty years ago, the charming owners renovated this beautifully historic St. Martin *case.* After several other restaurant ventures, they have returned to the original cottage to serve up delicious, authentic Moroccan cuisine in a beautiful and romantic space with an open garden that feels just like Morocco. The food is fragrant and delicious, with portions so huge you will have enough lunch for the next day. The couscous and tagines are authentically spiced and served with profes-

sional friendliness by an affable staff in Moroccan serving pieces. The mixed appetizers (*mezes*) are delectable, and the royal couscous is justly popular. Kabobs and tajines are a great change of pace from the usual Caribbean and French fare. Lounge in the tented courtyard after dinner—and don't be surprised to be entertained by a talented belly-dancer. The restaurant is on Marigot's main road across from the stadium. $ *Average main: $24* ✉ *169 Rue de Hollande, Marigot* ☎ *0590/27–54–48* ✍ *Reservations essential* ⊗ *Closed Sun.*

$$$ 🍴 **Tropicana.** *French.* This bustling bistro at the Marina Port la Royale is busy all day long, thanks to a varied menu, (relatively) reasonable prices, and friendly staff. Salads are a must for lunch, especially the salad niçoise with medallions of crusted goat cheese. Dinner includes some exceptional steak and seafood dishes. The wine list is quite extensive. Desserts are tasty, and you'll never be disappointed with old standbys like the crème brûlée. You can dine outside or inside along the yacht-filled waterfront, which is busy with shoppers during the day. $ *Average main: $21* ✉ *Marina Port la Royale, Marigot* ☎ *0590/87–79–07.*

PIC DU PARADIS

★ $$ FAMILY **Fodor's Choice** 🍴 **Hidden Forest Café.** *Caribbean.* Schedule your trip to Loterie Farm to take advantage of the lovely treehouse pavilions where lunch or dinner has a safari vibe the hip clientele can appreciate and the yummy, locally sourced food is inventive and fresh. You can also enjoy the L'Eau Lounge, a giant spring-fed pool with jacuzzis, lounge-cabanas, and a St. Barth–meets–Wet 'n' Wild atmosphere. Curry-spinach chicken with banana fritters is a popular pick, but there are great choices for vegetarians too, including cumin lentil balls; those with stouter appetites dig into the massive black Angus tenderloin. Loterie Farm's other eatery, Treelounge, features great cocktails and tapas, is open Monday through Saturday, and stays open late with frequent live music. $ *Average main: $20* ✉ *Loterie Farm, Pic Paradis 103, Rambaud* ☎ *0590/87–86–16* 🌐 *www.loteriefarm.com* ⊗ *Closed Mon.*

SANDY GROUND

★ $$$$ **Fodor's Choice** 🍴 **Mario's Bistro.** *French Fusion.* Don't miss dinner at this romantic eatery, a perennial favorite for its ravishing cuisine, romantic ambience, and most of all the marvelously friendly owners. Didier Gonnon and Martyne Tardif are out front, while chef Mario Tardif is in the kitchen creating ravishing dishes such as bouillabaisse

CLOSE UP

St. Maarten vs. St. Martin

If this is your first trip to St. Maarten/St. Martin, you're probably wondering which side will better suit your needs. That's hard to say, because in some ways the difference between the two can seem as subtle as the hazy boundary line dividing them. But there are some major distinctions.

St. Maarten, the Dutch side, has casinos, more nightlife, smaller price tags, and bigger hotels. St. Martin, the French side, has no casinos, less nightlife, and hotels that are smaller and more intimate. Many have kitchenettes, and most include breakfast. There are many good restaurants on the Dutch side, but if fine dining makes your vacation, the French side rules.

The biggest difference might be currency—the Netherlands Antilles guilder (also called the florin) on the Dutch side, the euro on the French side. And the relative strength of the euro can translate to some expensive surprises. Many establishments on both sides (even the French) accept U.S. dollars.

with green Thai curry, a duet of grilled lamb chops and braised lamb shank shepherd pie, and sautéed jumbo scallops with crab mashed potatoes and leek tempura. Leave room for the heavenly upside-down banana coconut tart with caramel sauce and coconut ice cream. The restaurant is rather strict about reservations for large groups, so be sure to call and get the details. They don't take American Express. [$] *Average main: $31* ✉ *48 Rue Morne, at the Sandy Ground Bridge, Sandy Ground* ☎ *0590/87–06–36* 🌐 *www.mariosbistro.com* ✍ *Reservations essential* 🕒 *Closed Sun., Aug., and Sept. No lunch.*

WHERE TO STAY

St. Maarten/St. Martin accommodations range from modern megaresorts such as the Radisson and the Westin St. Maarten to condos and small inns. On the Dutch side many hotels cater to groups, and although that's also true to some extent on the French side, you can find a larger collection of intimate accommodations there. ■ **TIP→** Off-season rates (April through the beginning of December) can be as little as half the high-season rates.

TIME-SHARE RENTALS

Time-share properties are scattered around the island, mostly on the Dutch side. There's no reason to buy a share, as these condos are rented out whenever the owners are not in residence. If you stay in one, be prepared for a sales pitch. Most rent by the night, but there's often substantial savings if you secure a weekly rate. Not all offer daily maid service, so make sure to ask before you book. As some properties are undergoing renovations at this writing, be sure to ask about construction conditions, and in any case, ask for a recently renovated unit.

PRIVATE VILLAS

Villas are a great lodging option, especially for families who don't need to keep the kids occupied, or groups of friends who just like hanging out together. Since these are for the most part freestanding houses, their greatest advantage is privacy. These properties are scattered throughout the island, often in gated communities or on secluded roads. Some have bare-bones furnishings, whereas others are over-the-top luxurious, with gyms, theaters, game rooms, and several different pools. There are private chefs, gardeners, maids, and other staffers to care for both the villa and its occupants.

Villas are secured through rental companies. They offer properties with weekly prices that range from reasonable to more than many people make in a year. Check around, as prices for the same property vary from agent to agent. Because of the economy, many villas are now offered by the night rather than by the week, so it's often possible to book for less than a full week's stay. Rental companies usually provide airport transfers and concierge service, and for an extra fee will even stock your refrigerator.

RENTAL CONTACTS

French Caribbean International. This company offers rental properties on the French side of the island. ☎ *800/322–2223 in the U.S.* ⊕ *www.frenchcaribbean.com.*

Island Hideaways. The island's oldest rental company rents villas on both sides. ☎ *800/832–2302 in the U.S., 703/378–7840* ⊕ *www.islandhideaways.com.*

Island Properties. This company's properties are scattered around the island. ✉ *62 Welfare Rd., Simpson Bay, St. Maarten* ☎ *599/544–4580, 866/978–5852 in the U.S.* ⊕ *www.remaxislandproperties.com.*

BEST BETS FOR LODGING

Fodor's Choice★

Blue Pelican, The Horny Toad, Hôtel L'Esplanade, La Samanna, Le Petit Hotel, Palm Court, Radisson Blu St. Martin, Westin St. Maarten Dawn Beach Resort & Spa

BEST FOR ROMANCE

Hotel le Marquis, La Samanna, Le Domaine, Palm Court

BEST BEACHFRONT

Esmeralda, The Horny Toad, La Samanna, Le Domaine, Le

Petit Hotel, Radisson Blu St. Martin

BEST POOL

Radisson Blu St. Martin, Westin St. Maarten Dawn Beach Resort & Spa

BEST SERVICE

La Samanna, Radisson Blu St. Martin

BEST FOR KIDS

Alamanda Resort, Divi Little Bay Beach Resort, Hotel Mercure, Radisson Blu St. Martin

Jennifer's Vacation Villas. You can rents villas on both sides of the island from this company. ⊠ *Pl. del Lago, Simpson Bay Yacht Club, Simpson Bay, St. Maarten* ☎ *631/546–7345 in New York, 721/544–3107 in St. Maarten* ⊕ *www.jennifersvacationvillas.com.*

Pierres Caraïbes. Owned by American Leslie Reed, Pierres Caraïbes has been renting and selling upscale St. Martin villas to satisfied clients for more than a decade. The company's well-designed website makes it easy to get a sense of the first-rate properties available in all sizes and prices. The company is associated with Christies Great Estates. ⊠ *Pl. Caraïbes, Rue Kennedy, Bldg. A, Marigot, St. Martin* ☎ *0590/51–02–85 in St. Martin* ⊕ *www.pierrescaraibes.com.*

Villas of Distinction. This company is one of the oldest villa-rental companies on both the French and Dutch sides of the island. Check their website for special deals. ☎ *800/289–0900 in the U.S.* ⊕ *www.villasofdistinction.com.*

WIMCO. Go here for more hotel, villa, apartment, and condo listings in the Caribbean than just about any other company. ☎ *401/849–8012 in Rhode Island, 800/449–1553 in the U.S.* ⊕ *www.wimco.com.*

DUTCH SIDE

CUPECOY

$$$ **The Cliff at Cupecoy Beach.** *Rental.* These luxurious, high-rise condos are rented out when the owners are not in residence and depending on the owner's personal style, they can be downright fabulous. **Pros:** great views; good for families; close to Maho casinos and restaurants; tight security. **Cons:** it's apartment living, so if you're looking for resort-y or beachy, this is not your place; there is a concierge, but no other hotel services. [$] *Rooms from: $425* ✉ *Rhine Rd., Cupecoy* ☎ *866/978–5839, 721/546–6633* 🌐 *www.cliffsxm.com* ⇨ *72 apartments* 🍴 *No meals.*

LITTLE BAY

$$$ **Belair Beach.** *Rental.* This time-share complex has an unbeatable location on Little Bay Beach, one of St. Maarten's nicest and least crowded stretches of sand. **Pros:** close to Philipsburg; away from the crowds. **Cons:** no full-service restaurant; some rooms are dated. [$] *Rooms from: $429* ✉ *Little Bay Beach Rd., Little Bay* ☎ *599/542–3366* 🌐 *www.belairbeach.com* ⇨ *72 suites* 🍴 *Multiple meal plans.*

$$ FAMILY **Divi Little Bay Beach Resort.** *Resort.* Bordering the lovely but sparsely populated Little Bay, this semirenovated property is well located and is awash with water sports. **Pros:** good location; lovely beach; kids stay and eat free. **Cons:** ongoing renovations; pool areas not great. [$] *Rooms from: $299* ✉ *Little Bay Rd., Little Bay* ☎ *721/542–2333, 800/367–3484 in the U.S.* 🌐 *www.divilittlebay.com* ⇨ *218 rooms* 🍴 *No meals.*

MAHO

$$ FAMILY **Royal Islander Club La Terrasse.** *Rental.* This smaller and somewhat nicer sister time-share resort to the Royal Island Club La Plage is right across the street and shares many of the same amenities, including the larger resort's beach. **Pros:** in a hip area, near restaurants and bars. **Cons:** not on the beach; because this is a time-share, rooms can be hard to book during peak periods. [$] *Rooms from: $309* ✉ *1 Rhine Rd., Maho* ☎ *721/545–2388* 🌐 *www.royalislander.com* ⇨ *76 units* ⏲ *Closed early Sept.* 🍴 *No meals.*

OYSTER POND

$ FAMILY **Oyster Bay Beach Resort.** *Resort.* Jutting out into Oyster Bay, this happening condo/time-share resort sits on Dawn Beach. **Pros:** lots of activities; nightly entertainment; comfortable accommodations. **Cons:** isolated location; need a car to get around; older units are plain. [$] *Rooms from: $275* ✉ *10*

Emerald Merit Rd., Oyster Pond ☎ *721/543–6040* 🌐 *www.oysterbaybeachresort.com* ⇨ *157 units* 🍴 *No meals.*

$ 🏨 **Princess Heights.** *Rental.* Perched on a hill 900 feet above Oyster Bay, newly renovated, spacious suites offer privacy, luxury, and white-balustrade balconies with a smashing view of St. Barth. **Pros:** away from the crowds; friendly staff; lovely accommodations; gorgeous vistas. **Cons:** not on the beach; numerous steps to climb; not easy to find; need a car to get around; no restaurant; tiny gym. [$] *Rooms from: $215* ✉ *156 Oyster Pond Rd., Oyster Pond* ☎ *599/543–6906, 800/441–7227 in the U.S.* 🌐 *www.princessheights.com* ⇨ *51 suites* 🍴 *No meals.*

★ Fodor's Choice 🏨 **Westin St. Maarten Dawn Beach Resort & Spa.**
$$ *Resort.* Straddling the border between the Dutch and
FAMILY French sides, the modern Westin sits on one of the island's best beaches. **Pros:** on Dawn Beach; plenty of activities; no smoking allowed. **Cons:** very big; a bit off the beaten track; time-share salespeople can be bothersome. [$] *Rooms from: $345* ✉ *144 Oyster Pond Rd., Oyster Pond* ☎ *599/543–6700, 800/228–3000 in the U.S.* 🌐 *www.westinstmaarten.com* ⇨ *317 rooms, 15 suites, 99 1-, 2-, and 3-bedroom condo units* 🍴 *No meals.*

PELICAN KEY

$ 🏨 **Atrium Beach Resort.** *Rental.* Lush tropical foliage in the
FAMILY glassed-in lobby—hence the name—makes a great first impression, welcoming guests to a property that makes a good base for island explorations. **Pros:** family-friendly environment; short walk to restaurants, free shuttle to Philipsburg. **Cons:** rooms lack private balconies; neighborhood is crowded; taxes and service charges add a whopping 25% to basic rates. [$] *Rooms from: $144* ✉ *6 Billy Folly Rd., Pelican Key* ☎ *721/784–6835* 🌐 *www.diamondresorts.com* ⇨ *87 rooms* 🍴 *No meals.*

★ Fodor's Choice 🏨 **Blue Pelican.** *Rental.* The 13 modern and chic
$$ apartment units hidden in this private enclave in Pelican Key were built by the owners of Hotel L'Esplanade and Le Petit Hotel on the French side and share the French management's vision, graciousness, obsessive attention to detail, and concern for the comfort and safety of their guests. **Pros:** nicest place to stay in the area; great pool; excellent management and security. **Cons:** residence, not a resort; not on the beach; definitely need a car to get around since there is no restaurant. [$] *Rooms from: $290* ✉ *Billy Folly Rd., Pelican Key* ☎ *0690/50–60–20* 🌐 *www.bluepelicansxm.com* ⇨ *13 apartments* 🍴 *No meals.*

$$ 🏨 **Diamond Resort International Flamingo Beach.** *Rental.* There
FAMILY are so many activities at this resort that you might not return to your room before bedtime. **Pros:** close to a variety of restaurants and nightlife; lots of activities. **Cons:** area gets crowded; small beach. [$] *Rooms from: $300* ✉ *6 Billy Folly Rd., Pelican Key* ☎ *721/544–3900, 800/438–2929 in the U.S.* 🌐 *www.diamondresorts.com* 🛏 *240 units* 🍴 *No meals.*

PHILIPSBURG

$ 🏨 **Holland House Beach Hotel.** *Hotel.* An ideal location for shoppers and sun worshippers, this historic hotel faces the Front Street pedestrian mall; to the rear are the boardwalk and a long stretch of Great Bay Beach. **Pros:** easy access to beach and shops; free Wi-Fi; young, engaging management. **Cons:** in a busy, downtown location; no pool; not very resort-y. [$] *Rooms from: $215* ✉ *43 Front St., Philipsburg* ☎ *721/542–2572* 🌐 *www.hhbh.com* 🛏 *48 rooms, 6 suites* 🍴 *Multiple meal plans.*

$ 🏨 **Sonesta Great Bay Beach Resort and Casino.** *Resort.* St.
FAMILY Maarten's only all-inclusive is well positioned even if it doesn't offer the height of luxury: away from the docks that are usually crawling with cruise ships, but only a 10-minute walk from downtown Philipsburg. **Pros:** all-inclusive unlimited food and bar; nice beach and pool; enough activities to keep you busy. **Cons:** hallways are white and bare, giving them a hospital-like feel; expensive Wi-Fi; although the beach is beautiful, pollution can be a problem; staff can be indifferent. [$] *Rooms from: $260* ✉ *19 Little Bay Rd., Philipsburg* ☎ *721/542–2446, 800/223–0757 in the U.S.* 🌐 *www.sonesta.com/greatbay* 🛏 *257 rooms* 🍴 *All-inclusive.*

SIMPSON BAY

★ **Fodor's**Choice 🏨 **The Horny Toad.** *B&B/Inn.* Because of its stu-
$ pendous view of Simpson Bay and the simple but comfortable rooms with creative décor, this lovely guesthouse is widely considered the best on this side of the island. **Pros:** tidy rooms; friendly vibe thanks to the fantastic owner; beautiful beach is usually deserted. **Cons:** rooms are very basic; need a car to get around; no kids under seven allowed; no pool. [$] *Rooms from: $218* ✉ *2 Vlaun Dr., Simpson Bay* ☎ *721/545–4323, 800/417–9361 in the U.S.* 🌐 *www.thtgh.com* 🛏 *8 rooms* 🍴 *No meals.*

$ 🏨 **La Vista.** *Rental.* Hibiscus and bougainvillea line brick walkways that connect the 32 wood-frame bungalows and beachfront suites of this intimate and friendly, family-owned time-share resort perched at the foot of Pelican Key. **Pros:** close to restaurants and bars. **Cons:** no-frills furnishings;

Condo Rentals

Condo rentals are another lodging option. They appeal to travelers who aren't interested in the one-size-fits-all activities offered by the resorts. Condos are much cheaper than villas, but you get many of the same amenities, including kitchens, and can save money by cooking your own meals. To rent a condo, contact the rental company or the individual owner.

The Cliff at Cupecoy Beach offers luxurious, high-rise condos rented out when the owners are not in residence. Depending on the owner's personal style, they can be downright fabulous. For extra privacy, separate elevators serve only two apartments on every floor. All units have large living and dining rooms plus fully equipped kitchens with stainless-steel appliances and granite countertops. All have sweeping vistas, but upper-level residences showcase Anguilla, Simpson Bay, and Basses Terres. The fitness center boasts a gym with sauna, whirlpool, and both indoor and outdoor pools. The megachic Dior Spa overlooks the huge indoor swimming pool. **Pros:** great views; good for families; close to Maho casinos and restaurants; tight security. **Cons:** it's apartment living, so if you're looking for resort-y or beachy, this is not your place; there is a concierge, but no other hotel services; no restaurant. ✉ *Rhine Rd., Cupecoy* ☎ *866/978–5839, 599/546–6633* ⊕ *www.cliffsxm.com.*

Jennifer's Vacation Villas. Condos near Simpson Bay Beach. ☎ *631/546–7345, 011/599–54–43107* ⊕ *www.jennifersvacationvillas.com.*

Sint Maarten Condos. Several condos on Pelican Key. ☎ *501/984–2483* ⊕ *www.stmaartencondos.com.*

need a car to get to more swimmable beaches. Ⓢ *Rooms from: $210* ✉ *53 Billy Folly Rd., Simpson Bay* ☎ *721/544–3005, 888/790–5264 in the U.S.* ⊕ *www.lavistaresort.com* ⤵ *50 suites, penthouses, and cottages* ⊙ *No meals.*

FRENCH SIDE

ANSE MARCEL

$$ ⊡ **Hotel Le Marquis.** *Hotel.* If you crave spectacular vistas and intimate surroundings and don't mind heights or steep walks, this is a fun property, with a funky St. Barth vibe. **Pros:** romantic honeymoon destination; doting staff; amazing views. **Cons:** not on the beach; on a steep hill. Ⓢ *Rooms* *from: $280* ✉ *Pigeon Pea Hill, Anse Marcel* ☎ *0590/29–42–30* 🌐 *www.hotel-marquis.com* 🛏 *17 rooms* 🍴 *Breakfast.*

$$$ FAMILY **Le Domaine Beach Resort and Spa by Christophe Leroy.** *Resort.* This classic property on 148 acres of lush gardens borders the exceptionally beautiful and secluded beach in Anse Marcel. **Pros:** all-inclusive option; lovely gardens; beachfront setting. **Cons:** some rooms have round bathtubs right in the middle of the room; you will need a car to get around; beach is shared with the busy Radisson Blu. [$] *Rooms from: $420* ✉ *Anse Marcel* ☎ *0590/52–35–35* 🌐 *www.hotel-le-domaine.com* 🛏 *124 rooms, 5 suites* ⏲ *Closed Sept. and Oct.* 🍴 *Multiple meal plans.*

★ $$$ FAMILY **Fodor's Choice** **Radisson Blu St. Martin Resort, Marina and Spa.** *Resort.* A $10-million renovation in 2011 has brought a new level of service, design, and comfort to this family-friendly resort with 18 prime acres on one of the island's prettiest beachy coves. **Pros:** attentive service; activities galore; great beach; excellent breakfast buffet. **Cons:** no oceanfront rooms, they either face the garden or the marina; need a car to get around; lots of families at school-vacation times; beach can be busy. [$] *Rooms from: $395* ✉ *BP 581, Anse Marcel* ☎ *0590/87–67–09, 800/333–3333 in the U.S.* 🌐 *www.radissonblu.com/resort-stmartin* 🛏 *189 rooms, 63 suites* 🍴 *Breakfast.*

BAIE LONGUE

★ $$$$ FAMILY **Fodor's Choice** **La Samanna.** *Resort.* A long stretch of pretty, white-sand beach borders this classic resort where service is warm and professional. **Pros:** chic new décor; great beach; convenient location; romantic; excellent spa. **Cons:** rather pricey for standard rooms; small pools. [$] *Rooms from: $845* ✉ *Baie Longue* ☎ *0590/87–64–00, 800/854–2252 in the U.S.* 🌐 *www.lasamanna.com* 🛏 *27 rooms, 54 suites* ⏲ *Closed Sept. and Oct.* 🍴 *Breakfast.*

BAIE NETTLÉ

$ FAMILY **Hotel Mercure St. Martin and Marina.** *Resort.* Families and couples who want to stay in a centrally located part of the island should try this modern option by a quiet beach bay. **Pros:** good location; pet and family-friendly; great spa; lots of activities, including for kids. **Cons:** beach isn't great for swimming; ground-floor rooms are noisy and have no view; no elevators. [$] *Rooms from: $232* ✉ *Baie Nettlé* ☎ *0590/87–54–54* 🌐 *www.mercure.com/gb/hotel-1100-hotel-mercure-saint-martin-marina/index.shtml* 🛏 *170 rooms* 🍴 *Breakfast.*

BAIE ORIENTALE

$$ 🏨 **Alamanda Resort.** *Resort.* One of the few resorts directly
FAMILY on the white-sand beach of Orient Bay, this hotel has a funky feel and spacious, colonial-style suites with terraces that overlook the pool, beach, or ocean. **Pros:** pleasant property; friendly staff; right on Orient Beach. **Cons:** some rooms are noisy; could still use some updating despite renovations. [$] *Rooms from: $375* ✉ *Baie Orientale* ☎ *0590/52–87–40, 800/622–7836* 🌐 *www.alamanda-resort.com* 🛏 *42 rooms* 🍴 *Breakfast.*

★ Fodor's Choice 🏨 **Caribbean Princess.** *Rental.* These 12 large,
$$$ well-equipped, and updated two- and three-bedroom con-
FAMILY dos have big kitchens and living rooms, lovely balconies over Orient Beach (a few steps away), and share a pretty pool. **Pros:** the comforts of home; nice interior design; direct beach access. **Cons:** not a full-service resort. [$] *Rooms from: $400* ✉ *C5 Parc de la Baie Orientale, Baie Orientale* ☎ *0590/52–94–94* 🌐 *www.caribbeanprincesscondos.com* 🛏 *12 condos* ⏲ *Closed Sept.* 🍴 *Breakfast.*

$$ 🏨 **Club Orient Resort.** *Resort.* For something rather different, consider letting it all hang out at this clothing-optional hotel on Baie Orientale. **Pros:** nice location; on-site convenience store. **Cons:** no TVs; rooms are the bare minimum. [$] *Rooms from: $300* ✉ *1 Baie Orientale, Baie Orientale* ☎ *0590/87–33–85, 877/456–6833 in the U.S.* 🌐 *www.cluborient.com* 🛏 *137 rooms* 🍴 *No meals.*

$$ 🏨 **Esmeralda Resort.** *Resort.* Almost all of these traditional
FAMILY Caribbean-style, kitchen-equipped villas, which can be configured to meet the needs of different groups, have their own private pool, and the fun of Orient Beach, where the hotel has its own private beach club, is a two-minute walk away. **Pros:** beachfront location; private pools; plenty of activities; frequent online promotions. **Cons:** need a car to get around; iffy Wi-Fi service. [$] *Rooms from: $375* ✉ *Baie Orientale* ☎ *0590/87–36–36, 800/622–7836* 🌐 *www.esmeralda-resort.com* 🛏 *65 rooms* ⏲ *Closed Sept. and Oct.* 🍴 *Breakfast.*

$$$$ 🏨 **Green Cay Village.** *Rental.* Surrounded by five acres of lush
FAMILY greenery high above Baie Orientale, these villas are perfect for families or groups of friends who are looking for privacy and the comforts of home. **Pros:** beautiful setting near Baie Orientale; perfect for families with teens or older kids. **Cons:** need a car to get around; beach is a five-minute walk; need to be vigilant about locking doors, as there have been reports of crime in the area. [$] *Rooms from: $660* ✉ *Parc*

de la Baie Orientale, Baie Orientale ☎ *0590/87–38–63* 🌐 *www.greencay.com* 🛏 *9 villas* 🍴 *Breakfast.*

$ FAMILY **Hotel La Plantation.** *Hotel.* Perched high above Orient Bay, this colonial-style hotel is a charmer. **Pros:** relaxing atmosphere; eye-popping views; lots of restaurants in the area. **Cons:** small pool; beach is a 10-minute walk away. $ *Rooms from: $240* ✉ *C5 Parc de La Baie Orientale, Baie Orientale* ☎ *0590/29–58–00* 🌐 *www.la-plantation.com* 🛏 *51 rooms* 🕒 *Closed Sept.–mid-Oct.* 🍴 *Breakfast.*

★ $ Fodor's Choice **Palm Court.** *Hotel.* The romantic beachfront units of this *hôtel de charme* are steps from the fun of Orient Beach yet private, quiet, and stylish. **Pros:** big rooms; fresh and new; nice garden. **Cons:** across from, but not on the beach. $ *Rooms from: $252* ✉ *Parc de la Baie Orientale, Baie Orientale* ☎ *0590/87–41–94* 🌐 *www.sxm-palm-court.com* 🛏 *24 rooms* 🕒 *Closed Sept.* 🍴 *Breakfast.*

FRENCH CUL DE SAC

★ $$ Fodor's Choice **Karibuni Lodge.** *B&B/Inn.* Lovely in every way, this super-chic yet reasonably priced enclave of spacious suites surrounded by gorgeous tropical gardens offer stunning views of tiny Pinel Island. **Pros:** stylish; eco-friendly; lushly comfortable; amazing views. **Cons:** removed from the action; definitely need a car; not a resort, and not on the beach. $ *Rooms from: $340* ✉ *29 Terrasses de Cul de Sac, French Cul de Sac* ☎ *690/64–38–58* 🌐 *www.lekaribuni.com* 🛏 *6 suites* 🍴 *Breakfast.*

GRAND CASE

$$ FAMILY **Bleu Emeraude.** *Rental.* The 11 spacious apartments in this tidy complex sit right on a sliver of Grand Case Beach. **Pros:** brand-new; walk to restaurants; attractive décor. **Cons:** it's not resort-y at all. $ *Rooms from: $360* ✉ *240 Bd. de Grand Case* ☎ *0590/87–27–71* 🌐 *www.bleuemeraude.com* 🛏 *4 studios, 6 1-bedroom apartments, 1 2-bedroom apartment* 🍴 *Breakfast.*

$$ FAMILY **Grand Case Beach Club.** *Resort.* This beachfront property on a cove at the east end of Grand Case has a friendly staff and spectacular sunset views. **Pros:** reasonably priced; comfortable rooms; walking distance to restaurants. **Cons:** small beach; dated décor and buildings; need a car to explore island. $ *Rooms from: $345* ✉ *21 Rue de Petit Plage, at north end of Bd. de Grand Case* ☎ *0590/87–51–87, 800/344–3016 in the U.S.* 🌐 *www.grandcasebeachclub.com* 🛏 *72 apartments* 🍴 *Breakfast.*

★ Fodor's Choice 🏨 **Hôtel L'Esplanade.** *Hotel.* Enthusiasts return
$$ again and again to the classy, loft-style suites in this immacu-
FAMILY ulate boutique hotel. **Pros:** attentive management; very clean; updated room décor; family-friendly feel. **Cons:** lots of stairs to climb; not on the beach. [$] *Rooms from: $295* ✉ *Grand Case* ☎ *0590/87–06–55, 866/596–8365 in the U.S.* 🌐 *www.lesplanade.com* 🛏 *24 units* 🍴 *No meals.*

★ Fodor's Choice 🏨 **Le Petit Hotel.** *Hotel.* Surrounded by some
$$ of the best restaurants in the Caribbean, this beachfront
FAMILY boutique hotel, sister hotel to Hôtel L'Esplanade, oozes charm and has the same caring, attentive management. **Pros:** walking distance to everything in Grand Case; friendly staff; clean, updated rooms. **Cons:** many stairs to climb; no pool. [$] *Rooms from: $315* ✉ *248 Bd. de Grand Case* ☎ *0590/29–09–65* 🌐 *www.lepetithotel.com* 🛏 *9 rooms, 1 suite* 🍴 *Breakfast.*

$ 🏨 **Love Hotel.** *B&B/Inn.* This cozy, seven-room guesthouse right on Grand Case Beach was renovated by the young owners themselves. **Pros:** young, fun vibe; in-town location. **Cons:** pretty basic rooms; ongoing construction; staff not always helpful; hotel can be noisy or hopping depending on your definition. [$] *Rooms from: $150* ✉ *140 Bd. de Grand Case* ☎ *00590/29–87–14* 🌐 *www.love-sxm.com* 🛏 *7 rooms* 🍴 *No meals.*

OYSTER POND

$ 🏨 **Captain Oliver's Resort.** *Hotel.* This cluster of pink bungalows is perched high on a hill above a lagoon with lots of lush landscaping and a fine view of the Caribbean and St. Barth. **Pros:** restaurant is reasonably priced; ferry trips leave from the hotel. **Cons:** not on the beach; not fancy or modern; must have a car to get around. [$] *Rooms from: $241* ✉ *Oyster Pond* ☎ *0590/87–40–26* 🌐 *www.captainolivers.com* 🛏 *50 suites* ⏲ *Closed Sept. and Oct.* 🍴 *Breakfast.*

NIGHTLIFE

St. Maarten has lots of evening and late-night action. To find out what's doing on the island, pick up *St. Maarten Nights* or *St. Maarten Events,* both of which are distributed free in the tourist office and hotels. The glossy *Discover St. Martin/St. Maarten* magazine, also free, has articles on island history and on the newest shops, discos, and restaurants. Or buy a copy of Thursday's *Daily Herald* newspaper, which lists all the week's entertainment.

The island's casinos—all 13 of them—are found only on the Dutch side. All have craps, blackjack, roulette, and slot machines. You must be 18 years or older to gamble. Dress is casual (but excludes bathing suits or skimpy beachwear). Most casinos are found in hotels, but there are also some independents.

DUTCH SIDE

COLE BAY

CASINOS

Princess Casino. One of the island's largest gaming halls, Princess Casino has a wide array of restaurants and entertainment options. ⊠ *Port de Plaisance, 155 Union Rd., Cole Bay* ☎ *721/544–4311* ⊕ *www.princessportdeplaisance.com.*

CUPECOY

CASINOS

Atlantis World Casino. With some of the best restaurants on the island, Atlantis World is a popular destination even for those who don't gamble. It has more than 400 slot machines and gaming tables offering roulette, baccarat, three-card poker, Texas Hold'em poker, and Omaha high poker, not to mention some of the best restaurants on the Dutch side of the island. ⊠ *106 Rhine Rd., Cupecoy* ☎ *721/545–4601* ⊕ *www.atlantisworld.com.*

MAHO

BARS AND CLUBS

Bliss. This open-air nightclub and lounge, which is good for dancing, rocks till late. Connect with them on social media for invitations to events. ⊠ *Caravanserai Resort, Maho* ☎ *721/544–3410* ⊕ *www.bliss-sxm.com.*

Cheri's Café. Across from Maho Beach Resort and Casino, Cheri's (you can't miss it—look for pink) is an open air club featuring Sweet Chocolate, a lively band that will get your toes tapping and your tush twisting. Snacks and hearty meals are available all day long on a cheerful verandah decorated with hundreds of inflatable beach toys. ⊠ *45 Rhine Rd., Maho* ☎ *721/545–3361* ⊕ *www.cheriscafe.com* ⊘ *Closed Tues.*

★ Fodor'sChoice **Sky Beach.** The Sky Beach Rooftop Beach and Lounge is perfect for visitors who don't want to leave the beach vibe after the sun goes down (there's also a tent in case of rain). The elegant rooftop pulses with techno and house music while guests lounge on beds in cabanas. There is sand volleyball for fun and great cocktails at the happening bar. Great views and stargazing come with the territory. In-the-know clubbers come here before Tantra starts to wake up after midnight. It's open every day from 4 pm until 1 am. ⊠ *Sonesta Maho Resort & Casino, 1 Rhine Rd., Maho* ☎ *721/520–1757* ⊕ *www.theskybeach.com.*

Soprano's. Starting each night at 8, the pianist at Soprano's takes requests for oldies, romantic favorites, or smooth jazz. Come for happy hour from 8 to 9 pm with a full menu that includes pizza. The bar is open until 3 am nightly. ⊠ *Sonesta Maho Beach Resort & Casino, 1 Rhine Rd., Maho* ☎ *721/545–2485* ⊕ *www.sopranospianobar.com.*

Sunset Bar and Grill. This popular spot offers a relaxed, anything-goes atmosphere. Enjoy live music Wednesday through Sunday as you watch planes from the airport next door fly directly over your head. Bring your camera for stunning photos, but expect a high noise level. ⊠ *Maho Beach, Beacon Hill #2, Maho* ☎ *721/545–2084* ⊕ *www. sunsetsxm.com.*

Tantra Nightclub & Sanctuary. This is definitely the hottest nightclub at the Sonesta Maho. Come late—things don't really get going until after 1 am. On Wednesday night ladies drink champagne for free, and drinks are $2 for everyone on Fridays. Celebrity DJs spin on Saturday. Feel free to dress up. There is bottle and table service by reservation. ⊠ *Sonesta Maho Beach Resort & Casino, 1 Rhine Rd., Maho Bay* ☎ *721/545–2861* ⊕ *www.tantrasxm.com.*

CASINOS

Casino Royale. This is the largest casino on the island, with some 1,300 square meters of gaming and a full theater with 750 seats for events and shows. There are 30 tables for gaming, including roulette (American and French), craps, blackjack, and poker (3-card and Caribbean). The 400 slot machines include a variety of classics and modern video slots. ⊠ *Maho Beach Resort & Casino, 1 Rhide Rd., Maho* ☎ *721/545–2590* ⊕ *www.playmaho.com.*

OYSTER POND

CASINOS

Westin Casino. This is somewhat more sedate than other island casinos. If you ever get tired of the slot machines and gaming tables, beautiful Dawn Beach is just outside the door. ⊠ *Westin Dawn Beach Resort and Spa, 144*

Oyster Pond Rd., Oyster Pond ☎ *721/543–6700* ⊕ *www. westinstmaarten.com.*

PHILIPSBURG

BARS AND CLUBS

Ocean Lounge. The quintessential people-watching venue, sip a guavaberry colada here and point your chair toward the boardwalk. ✉ *Holland House Hotel, 43 Front St., Philipsburg* ☎ *721/542–2572.*

CASINOS

Beach Plaza Casino. In the heart of the shopping area, Beach Plaza Casino has more than 180 slots and multigame machines with the latest in touch-screen technology. Because of its location, it is popular with cruise-ship passengers. ✉ *Front St., Philipsburg* ☎ *721/543–2031* ⊕ *www. atlantisworld.com.*

Coliseum Casino. The Coliseum is popular with fans of slots, blackjack, poker, or roulette. ✉ *Front St., Philipsburg* ☎ *721/543–2101* ⊕ *www.coliseumsxm.com.*

Diamond Casino. With 250 slot machines, plus the usual tables offering games like blackjack, roulette, and three-card poker, this casino is in the heart of Philipsburg. It opens at 9 am for slots on Tuesday and Wednesday. ✉ *1 Front St., Philipsburg* ☎ *721/543–2583* ⊕ *www.diamondcasinosxm.com.*

Golden Casino. The Sonesta Great Bay's casino is on the small side. But fans say the 84 slots machines and tables with Caribbean poker, blackjack, and roulette are more than enough. ✉ *Great Bay Beach Hotel, Little Bay Rd., Great Bay* ☎ *721/542–2446* ⊕ *www.sonesta.com/greatbay.*

Jump-Up Casino. On the main shopping street in Philipsburg and near the cruise-ship pier, the Jump-Up Casino attracts lots of day-trippers. ✉ *1 Emmaplein, Philipsburg* ☎ */21/542–0862.*

PELICAN KEY

CASINOS

Hollywood Casino. Centrally located to the Simpson Bay area, one of the island's entertainment hotspots is Pelican Key, where you'll find the Hollywood Casino. This attractive casino lets you play table games and slots, while enjoying the Hollywood Star Theme. ✉ *Pelican Resort, 37 Billy Folly Rd., Pelican Key* ☎ *721/544–4463.*

SIMPSON BAY

BARS AND CLUBS

Buccaneer Beach Bar. Located on Kim Sha Beach, this is the place to enjoy a BBC (Bailey's banana colada), a slice of pizza, a sunset, and a nightly fireball show. It's family-friendly and conveniently located. ✉ *Behind Atrium Beach Resort, 10 Billy Folly Rd., Simpson Bay* ☎ *721/522–9700* ⊕ *www.buccaneerbeachbar.com.*

Le Shore. This nighttime hot spot located in the middle of Simpson Bay will remind you of Miami or Vegas, with its special events and parties almost every night. It's billed as a private club, but if you call for a reservation or just dress nicely, you shouldn't have a problem getting in. ✉ *111 Welfare Rd., Simpson Bay* ☎ *721/586–4499* ⊕ *www. shoreclubsxm.com.*

Pineapple Pete. At Pete's you can groove to live music or visit the game room for a couple of rounds of pool. ✉ *Airport Rd., Simpson Bay* ☎ *721/544–6030* ⊕ *www. pineapplepete.com.*

Red Piano. This bar has a great pool room, terrific live music, and tasty cocktails every night till 3 am. On Mondays, check out the oldies hits of the '60s, '70s, and '80s. ✉ *Hollywood Casino, 35 Billy Folly Rd., Simpson Bay* ☎ *721/544–6008* ⊕ *www.theredpianosxm.com.*

CASINOS

Paradise Plaza Casino. Betting on sporting events is the big thing here, which explains the 20 televisions tuned to whatever game happens to be on at the time. There are also 250 slots and multigame machines. ✉ *69 Welfare Rd., Simpson Bay* ☎ *721/543–4721* ⊕ *www.paradisecasinosxm.com.*

FRENCH SIDE

BAIE DES PÈRES

BARS AND CLUBS

Kali's Beach Bar. This happening spot has feautred live music late into the night since the late 1980s. On the night of the full moon and on every Friday night, the beach bonfire and late-night party here is the place to be, but it's a great place to hang out all day long on chaises you can rent for the day. Be sure to ask Kali for some tastes of his homemade fruit-infused rum. ✉ *Baie des Pères* ☎ *690/49–06–81.*

GRAND CASE

BARS AND CLUBS

Calmos Café. Join the young local crowd at Caimos by just walking through the boutique and around the back to the sea, then pull up a beach chair or park yourself at a picnic table. It's open all day, but the fun really begins at the cocktail hour, when everyone enjoys tapas. The little covered deck at the end is perfect for romance. On Thursday and Sunday there is often live reggae on the beach. ⊠ *40 Bd. de Grand Case* ☎ *0590/29–01–85* ⊕ *www.lecalmoscafe.com.*

SHOPPING

It's true that the island sparkles with its myriad outdoor activities—diving, snorkeling, sailing, swimming, and sunning—but shopaholics are drawn to the sparkle in the jewelry stores. The huge array of stores is almost unrivaled in the Caribbean. In addition, duty-free shops can offer substantial savings—about 15% to 30% below U.S. and Canadian prices—on cameras, watches, liquor, cigars, and designer clothing, but not always, so make sure you know the U.S. price of anything you intend to buy to know if you're actually getting a deal. Stick with the big vendors that advertise in the tourist press, and you will be more likely to avoid today's ubiquitous fakes and replicas. On both sides of the island, be alert for idlers. They can snatch unwatched purses.

Prices are in dollars on the Dutch side, in euros on the French side. As for bargains, there are more to be had on the Dutch side; prices on the French side may sometimes be higher than those you'll find back home, and the fact that prices are in euros doesn't help affordability. Merchandise may not be from the newest collections, especially with regard to clothing, but there are items available on the French side that are not available on the Dutch side.

DUTCH SIDE

MAHO

You'll find a moderately good selection of stores in Maho Plaza, near the Sonesta resort in Maho. Many Americans prefer to shop here because they can pay in U.S. dollars and get better deals than on the French side. **Blue Mall,** a glitzy new shopping mall, opened in December 2013, but at this writing, the full list of shops is still shaping up.

Dutch Architecture along Philipsburg's pedestrian mall

CLOTHING

Hip Up. This outpost of the popular French retailer has a terrific selection of swimsuits, cute cover-ups, and beach accessories like rhinestone-studded flip-flops. Many of the swimsuits are sold as separates; you pick the top and the bottom in the size and style that suits you. There is another branch in Marigot. ✉ *Maho Pl., Maho* ☏ *721/545–4011* ⊕ *www.hipup.com.*

PHILIPSBURG

Philipsburg's **Front Street** has reinvented itself. Now it's mall-like, with a redbrick walk and streets, palm trees lining the sleek boutiques, jewelry stores, souvenir shops, outdoor restaurants, and the old reliables, such as McDonald's and Burger King. Here and there a school or a church appears to remind visitors there's more to the island than shopping. Back Street is where you'll find the **Philipsburg Market Place,** a daily open-air market where you can haggle for bargains on items such as handicrafts, souvenirs, and beachwear. **Old Street,** near the end of Front Street, has stores, boutiques, and open-air cafés offering French crêpes, rich chocolates, and island mementos.

CLOTHING

Façonnable. The refined men's line of cheery, well-fitting shirts is well represented, with a smattering of women's items in back. ✉ *16 Sint Rose Arcade, Front St., Philipsburg* ☏ *599/542–2444* ⊕ *www.faconnable.com.*

Liz Claiborne. This is a well-stocked shop from the well-known company. ⊠ *48A Front St., Philipsburg* ☎ *721/543–0380.*

Polo Ralph Lauren. Polo Ralph Lauren has men's and women's sportswear in preppy styles. ⊠ *48 Front St., Philipsburg* ☎ *721/543–0380.*

Tommy Hilfiger. This huge and attractive shop sells sportswear in the designer's trademark colors. ⊠ *28 Front St., Philipsburg* ☎ *721/542–6315.*

CRYSTAL AND CHINA
In addition to the stores listed here, both Little Europe and Little Switzerland carry china and crystal.

Lalique. Lalique has a fine collection of French crystal. ⊠ *13 Sint Rose Arcade, 26 Front St., Philipsburg* ☎ *721/542–0763.*

HANDICRAFTS
Guavaberry Emporium. Visitors to the Dutch side of the island come for free samples at the small factory where the Sint Maarten Guavaberry Company makes its famous liqueur. You'll find a multitude of versions, including one made with jalapeño peppers. Check out the hand-painted bottles. The store also sells the Gourmet BBQ & Hot Sauce Collection and souvenier hats ⊠ *8–10 Front St., Philipsburg* ☎ *721/542–2965* ⊕ *wwww.guavaberry.com.*

Shipwreck Shop. This company has outlets all over the island that stock a little of everything: colorful hammocks, handmade jewelry, and lots of the local Guavaberry liqueur, but the main store on Front Street in Philipsburg has the largest selection of wares. ⊠ *42 Front St., Philipsburg* ☎ *721/542–2962, 721/542–6710* ⊕ *www.shipwreckshops.com.*

JEWELRY AND GIFTS
Jewelry is big business on both the French and Dutch sides of the island, and many stores have outlets in both places. The so-called duty-free prices, however, may not give you much savings (if anything) over what you might pay at home, and sometimes prices are even higher. Compare prices in a variety of stores before you buy, and if you know you want to search for an expensive piece of jewelry or high-end watch, make sure you price your pieces at home and bargain hard to ensure you get a good deal.

Art of Time Jewelers. This store specializes in watches, Montblanc pens, and jewelry by David Yurman, Chopard, and

Mikimoto, among others. ✉ *26 Front St., Philipsburg* ☎ *721/542–2180* ⊕ *www.artoftimejewelers.com.*

Ballerina Jewelers. Here you can buy jewelry by Tacori and Pandora, and watches by Bell & Ross, Technomarine, Franck Muller, and other luxury brands. ✉ *56 Front St., Philipsburg* ☎ *721/542–4399* ⊕ *www.ballerina-jewelers.com.*

Cartier. The famous upscale jeweler has a lovely collection on sale here. ✉ *35 Front St., Philipsburg* ☎ *721/543–7700.*

Little Europe. Come here to buy fine jewelry, crystal, and china in the store's two branches in Philipsburg. ✉ *80 Front St., Philipsburg* ☎ *721/542–4371* ⊕ *www.littleeurope.com* ✉ *2 Front St., Philipsburg.*

Little Switzerland. The large Caribbean duty-free chain sells watches, fine crystal, china, perfume, and jewelry. ✉ *52 Front St., Philipsburg* ☎ *721/542–2523* ⊕ *www.littleswitzerland. com* ✉ *Westin Dawn Beach Resort & Spa, Dawn Beach* ☎ *721/543–6451* ⊕ *www.littleswitzerland.com.*

Oro Diamante. This store carries loose diamonds, jewelry, watches, perfume, and cosmetics. They specialize in natural colored diamonds, and also sell the popular stackable rings by Gabriel & Co. ✉ *62-B Front St., Philipsburg* ☎ *599/543–0342, 800/635–7950 in the U.S.* ⊕ *www.oro-diamante.com.*

PERFUME

Lipstick. Lipstick has an enormous selection of perfume and cosmetics. ✉ *31 Front St., Philipsburg* ☎ *721/542–6052.*

FRENCH SIDE

BAIE ORIENTALE

ART GALLERIES

Antoine Chapon. On the French side, the watercolor paintings of Antoine Chapon, reflecting the peaceful atmosphere of St. Martin and the sea surrounding it, can be seen at the artist's studio in Cul-de-Sac. Call for an appointment to view the work. ✉ *Terrasses de Cul-de-Sac, Baie Orientale* ☎ *0590/87–40–87* ⊕ *www.chaponartgallery.com.*

COLOMBIER

ART GALLERIES

Minguet Art Gallery. The Minguet Gallery, between Marigot and Grand Case, is managed by the daughter of the late artist Alexandre Minguet. The gallery carries original paintings, lithographs, posters, and postcards depicting

Marigot's waterfront market

island flora and landscapes by Minguet, as well as original works by Robert Dago and Loic BarBotin. ✉ *Rambaud Hill* ☎ *0590/87–76–06.*

GRAND CASE

ART GALLERIES

Tropismes Gallery. Contemporary Caribbean artists, including Paul Elliot Thuleau, who is a master of capturing the unique sunshine of the islands, and Nathalie Lepine, whose portraits show the influence of Modigliani, are showcased at Tropismes. This is a serious gallery with some very good artists. It's open 10 am until 1 pm, and then from 5 pm until 9 pm daily, so you can browse before dinner. ✉ *107 Bd. de Grand Case* ☎ *690/54–62–69* ⊕ *www.tropismesgallery.com.*

MARIGOT

On the French side, wrought-iron balconies, colorful awnings, and gingerbread trim decorate Marigot's smart shops, tiny boutiques, and bistros in the **Marina Port La Royale** complex and on the main streets, **rue de la Liberté** and **rue de la République.** Also in Marigot are the pricey **West Indies Mall** and the **Plaza Caraïbes,** which house designer shops, although some shops are closing in the economic downturn.

ART GALLERIES

Galerie Camaïeu. This gallery sells both originals and copies of works by Caribbean artists. ✉ *8 Rue de Kennedy, Marigot*

☏ *0590/87–25–78* ⊕ *www.camaieu-artgallery.com* ⊘ *Closed Sun., and Sat. May–Nov.*

CLOTHING
On the French side, the best luxury-brand shops are found either in the modern, air-conditioned West Indies Mall or the Plaza Caraïbes center across from Marina Port La Royale in Marigot. There is also a small center in Grand Case, called La Petite Favorite, with four shops and a café.

120% Lino. This store has nicely made classy shirts and pants made of pure linen in pastel tones. ✉ *21 Marina Port la Royale, Marigot* ☏ *0590/87–25–43* ⊕ *www.120percento. com/negozi/store-stmartin.*

Banana Moon. Find a terrific selection of bathing suits and other beachwear here on the Marina. There is a sister shop in Maho that sells discontinued styles at a discount. ✉ *Marina Port la Royale, Marigot* ☏ *0590/87–87–15* ⊕ *www. bananamoon.com.*

Lacoste. The preppy clothier has everything with the alligator logo for men, women, and children, and the offerings are generally the better-quality and more expensive made-in-France items, not the made-in-Peru items usually available in the United States. ✉ *West Indies Mall, Front de Mer, Marigot* ☏ *0590/52–84–84.*

Max Mara. Max Mara has beautifully made, tailored women's clothes with an elegant attitude. ✉ *6 Rue du Kennedy, Marigot* ☏ *0590/52–99–75.*

Vilebrequin St. Tropez. This shop on the marina has a vast selection of the brightly patterned status swimsuits for men and boys. ✉ *Marina Port la Royale, Marigot* ☏ *0590/29–13–09.*

JEWELRY AND GIFTS
Art of Time. This reputable shop carries Mikimoto, Pandora, and David Yurman, among many others, as well as high-end designer watches, including Chanel, Baum & Mercier, Technomarine, Bidat, and Chopard. ✉ *3 Rue du Général de Gaulle, Marigot* ☏ *0590/52–24–80* ⊕ *www. artoftimejewelers.com.*

Cartier. Cartier has a lovely collection of fine jewelry. ✉ *Rue de Général de Gaulle, Pl. Caraïbes, Marigot* ☏ *0590/ 52–40–02.*

Manek's. Here you'll find two floors selling electronics, luggage, perfume, jewelry, Cuban cigars, duty-free liquors, and tobacco products. ⊠ *Rue de la République, Marigot* ☎ *0590/87–54–91.*

LEATHER GOODS AND ACCESSORIES
Longchamp. This is the local outpost for the chic French leather-goods company, where you'll find an especially good selection of the Pliage line of foldable, durable, coated-zipper totes with leather handles. ⊠ *11 Rue de Général de Gaulle, Marigot* ☎ *0590/87–92–76* ⊕ *www.longchamp.com.*

PERFUME
Lipstick. Lipstick has an enormous selection of perfume and cosmetics. ⊠ *Rue du Kennedy, Pl. Caraïbes, Marigot* ☎ *0590/87–73–24.*

SPORTS AND ACTIVITIES

BIKING

Mountain biking is a great way to explore the island. Beginner and intermediate cyclists can ride the coastal trails from Cay Bay to Fort Amsterdam or Mullet Beach. More serious bikers can cruise the Bellevue Trail from Port de Plaisance to Marigot. Bring your bathing suit—along the way you can stop at Baie Rouge or Baie des Prunes for a dip. The bike trails to Fort Louis offer fabulous views. The most challenging ride is up Pic du Paradis. If you would feel better tackling this route with a guide, ask at one of the bike shops. Several locally known guides can help you make this trip.

DUTCH SIDE
FAMILY **TriSport.** Rent bikes here that come with helmets, water bottle, locks, and repair kits. Rates are $17 per half day, $24 overnight, and $110 per week. Guided bicycle tours are offered. TriSport also rents kayaks and stand-up paddle boards, and arranges hikes, outings, and even triathlons. ■**TIP→** If you are on the French side, there is a location in Marigot. ⊠ *14B Airport Rd., Simpson Bay* ☎ *721/545–4384* ⊕ *www. trisportsxm.com.*

The Quill, St. Eustatius' dormant volcano

FRENCH SIDE
Loterie Farm. Loterie Farm arranges mountain-biking tours around Pic du Paradis. ✉ *Rte. de Pic du Paradis 103, Rambaud* ☎ *721/87–86–16, 721/57–28–55* ⊕ *www.loteriefarm.com.*

BOATING AND SAILING

The island is surrounded by water, so why not get out and enjoy it? The water and winds are perfect for skimming the surf. It'll cost you around $1,200 to $1,500 per day to rent a 28- to 40-foot powerboat, considerably less for smaller boats or small sailboats. Drinks and sometimes lunch are usually included on crewed day charters.

DUTCH SIDE
Random Wind. This company offers full-day sailing and snorkeling trips on a traditional 54-foot clipper. Charter prices depend on the size of the group and whether lunch is served. The regularly scheduled Paradise Daysail costs $95 per person ($50 for kids) and includes food and drink. Departures are on the Dutch side, from Skipjack's at Simpson Bay, promptly at 8:30 am Tuesday through Friday. ■TIP➔ You can get the best rates by booking directly from the website, rather than through your hotel or cruise. ✉ *Ric's Place, Simpson Bay* ☎ *721/587–5742* ⊕ *www.randomwind.com.*

CLOSE UP

A Day in St. Eustatius

Unless you're a diver or a history buff, chances are you have never heard of St. Eustatius, or Statia, as it is often called. So many ships once crowded its harbor that it was tagged the Emporium of the Western World. That abruptly changed in 1776. With an 11-gun salute to the American *Andrew Doria,* Statia became the first country to recognize U.S. independence. Great Britain retaliated by economically devastating the island.

Fort Oranje, from where famous shots came, is a history buff favorite. In Oranjestad, it has protected the island beginning in 1636. Its courtyard houses the original Dutch Reformed Church (1776). Honen Dalim, one of the oldest synagogues

in the Caribbean (1738), is on Synagogepad (Synagogue Path).

The island's interior is gorgeous. For hikers, the Quill is the challenge. The long and windy trail to the top of the 1,968-foot crater is lined with wild orchids, frilly ferns, elephant ears, and various other kinds of flora. Beaches, on the other hand, hold little attraction. There's no real sandy spot on the Caribbean shore, and the beaches on the Atlantic side are too rough for swimming.

Statia is a pleasant change from the bustle of St. Maarten. No matter how much time you spend on the island, locals will wave or beep at you in recognition. You never feel like a stranger.

St. Maarten 12-Metre Challenge. Sailing experience is not necessary for the St. Maarten 12-Metre Challenge, one of the island's most popular activities. Participants compete on 68-foot racing yachts, including Dennis Connor's *Stars and Stripes* (the actual boat that won the America's Cup in 1987) and the *Canada II.* Anyone can help the crew grind winches, trim sails, and punch the stopwatch, or you can just sit back and watch everyone else work. The thrill of it is priceless, but book well in advance; this is the most popular shore excursion offered by cruise ships in the Caribbean. It's offered four times daily; the entire experience lasts about three hours. Only children over 12 are allowed. ⊠ *Bobby's Marina, Philipsburg* ☎ *721/542–0045* ⊕ *www.12metre.com.*

FRENCH SIDE

MP Yachting. You can rent boats here of all sizes, with or without a crew, for short trips and long, and it's conveniently located. ⊠ *Marina Port la Royale, Marigot* ☎ *690/53–37–40* ⊕ *www.mpyachting.com.*

Horseback riding in the surf, St. Maarten

Sun Evasion. This charter company has locations all over the world, including St. Martin. You can take a half- or full-day charter to Tintamarre, St. Barth, or Ilet Pinel on a mono- or multihull powerboat, available with or without a skipper. ■TIP→ Book online for a 10% discount. ✉ *Marina Port la Royale, Marigot* ☎ *690/35-03-18* ⊕ *www.sun-evasion.com.*

FISHING

You can angle for yellowtail snapper, grouper, marlin, tuna, and wahoo on deep-sea excursions. Costs range from $150 per person for a half day to $250 for a full day. Prices usually include bait and tackle, instruction for novices, and refreshments. Ask about licensing and insurance.

DUTCH SIDE

Lee's Deepsea Fishing. Organize your excursion through Lee's Deepsea Fishing and when you return, Lee's Roadside Grill will cook your tuna, wahoo, or whatever else you catch and keep. Rates start at $200 per person for a half-day. ✉ *84 Welfare Rd., Cole Bay* ☎ *721/544-4233* ⊕ *www.leesfish.com.*

Private Yacht Charter. For deep-sea fishing, snorkeling trips, and catamaran trips including snacks and drinks, check out Private Yacht Charter. ✉ *Oyster Pond Great House Marina, 14 Emerald Merit Rd., Oyster Pond* ☎ *0590/599-581-5305* ⊕ *www.privateyachtcharter-sxm.com.*

Rudy's Deep Sea Fishing. One of the more experienced sport-angling outfits, Rudy's has been around for years. A private charter trip for four people starts at $525 for a half-day excursion. ■**TIP➜** Check the website for great tips on fishing around St. Maarten. ⊠ *14 Airport Rd., Simpson Bay* ☎ *721/545–2177* ⊕ *www.rudysdeepseafishing.com.*

FRENCH SIDE

Big Sailfish Too. Your best bet for fishing excursions on the French side of the island operates out of the Radisson Blu Marina. ⊠ *Anse Marcel* ☎ *690/27–40–90.*

GOLF

DUTCH SIDE

Mullet Bay Golf Course. St. Maarten is not a golf destination. Nevertheless, there have been improvements to Mullet Bay Golf Course, on the Dutch side, which is now again an 18-hole course and the island's only choice. Although it seems to be improving, it's still not a major draw or a must-play. ⊠ *Airport Rd., north of airport, Mullet Bay* ☎ *721/545–3069.*

HORSEBACK RIDING

Island stables offer riding packages for everyone from novices to experts. A 90-minute ride along the beach costs $50 to $70 for group rides and $70 to $90 for private treks. Reservations are necessary. You can arrange rides directly or through most hotels.

DUTCH SIDE

Lucky Stables. These stables in Cay Bay offer two-hour rides three times a day and one-hour rides every hour on the hour all day long. For a romantic treat, book a sunset ride with champagne and a bonfire (complete with marshmallows) for $100 per person. All experience levels are welcome, but advanced riders can book private rides. ⊠ *64 Traybay Dr., Cay Bay* ☎ *721/544–5255* ⊕ *www.seasidenaturepark.com.*

KAYAKING

Kayaking is becoming very popular and is almost always offered at the many water-sports operations on both the Dutch and the French sides. Rental starts at about $15 per hour for a single and $19 for a double.

Sailing is a popular activity in St. Maarten/St. Martin.

DUTCH SIDE

TriSports. This company organizes kayaking and snorkeling excursions in addition to its biking operation. ⊠ *14B Airport Rd., Simpson Bay* ☎ *721/545–4384* ⊕ *www. trisportsxm.com.*

FRENCH SIDE

Kali's Beach Bar. On the French side, kayaks are available at Kali's Beach Bar. ⊠ *Friar's Bay* ☎ *690/49–06–81* ⊕ *www. kali-beach-bar.com.*

Wind Adventures. Near Le Galion Beach, Wind Adventures offers rentals and instruction in kayaking, kiteboarding, windsurfing, Hobie cats, and stand-up paddle surfing. ⊠ *Baie Orientale* ☎ *0590/29–41–57* ⊕ *www.windadventures.com.*

PARASAILING

FRENCH SIDE

Kontiki Watersports. Kontiki Watersports offers parasailing for $40 per half hour on Baie Orientale, giving you aerial views of Green Key, Tintamarre, Ilet Pinel, and St. Barth. You can also rent Jet Skis for $45 for a half hour. ⊠ *North beach entrance, Baie Orientale* ☎ *0590/87–43–27* ⊕ *www. kontiki-sxm.com.*

SCUBA DIVING

Diving in St. Maarten/St. Martin is mediocre at best, but those who want to dive will find a few positives. The water temperature here is rarely below 70°F (21°C) and visibility is often 60 to 100 feet. The island has more than 30 dive sites, from wrecks to rocky labyrinths. Right outside of Philipsburg, 55 feet under the water, is the HMS *Proselyte,* once explored by Jacques Cousteau. Although it sank in 1801, the boat's cannons and coral-encrusted anchors are still visible.

Off the north coast, in the protected and mostly current-free Grand Case Bay, is **Creole Rock.** The water here ranges in depth from 10 feet to 25 feet. Other sites off the north coast include **Ilet Pinel,** with its good shallow diving; **Green Key,** with its vibrant barrier reef; and **Tintamarre,** with its sheltered coves and geologic faults. On average, one-tank dives start at $55; two-tank dives are about $100. Certification courses start at about $400.

The Dutch side offers several full-service outfitters and SSI (Scuba Schools International) and/or PADI certification. There are no hyperbaric chambers on the island.

DUTCH SIDE

Dive Safaris. A shark-awareness dive occurs each Friday where participants can watch professional feeders give reef sharks a little nosh. The company also offers a full PADI training program and can tailor dive excursions and sophisticated instruction at any level. ✉ *16 Airport Blvd., Simpson Bay* ☎ *721/545–2401* ⊕ *www.divestmaarten.com.*

Ocean Explorers Dive Shop. St. Maarten's oldest dive shop offers different types of certification courses. Serious divers like the 6-person-maximum policy, but this means you should reserve in advance. ✉ *113 Welfare Rd., Simpson Bay* ☎ *721/544–5252* ⊕ *www.stmaartendiving.com.*

FRENCH SIDE

Octopus. Take advantage of PADI diving certification courses and all-inclusive dive packages, as well as private and group snorkel trips starting at $40, including all necessary equipment. The well-stocked dive shop also services regulators. ✉ *15 Bd. de Grand Case* ☎ *0590/29–11–27* ⊕ *www. octopusdiving.com.*

Ilet Pinel, St. Martin

SEA EXCURSIONS

DUTCH SIDE

FAMILY **Aqua Mania Adventures.** You can take day cruises to Prickly Pear Cay, off Anguilla, aboard the *Lambada*, or sunset and dinner cruises on the 65-foot sail catamaran *Tango* with Aqua Mania Adventures. The company also operates a floating playground called "Playstation 4 Kids" that kids love. ⊠ *Pelican Marina, Simpson Bay* ☎ 721/544–2640, 721/544–2631 ⊕ *www.stmaarten-activities.com.*

Bluebeard II. This 60-foot custom-built daysail catamaran is specially designed for maximum safety and comfort. *Bluebeard II* sails around Anguilla's south and northwest coasts to Prickly Pear Cay, where there are excellent coral reefs for snorkeling and powdery white sands for sunning. ⊠ *Simpson Bay* ☎ 721/587–5935 ⊕ *www.bluebeardcharters.com.*

Celine. For low-impact sunset and dinner cruises, try the catamaran *Celine.* ⊠ *Skip Jack's Restaurant, Simpson Bay* ☎ 721/526–1170, 721/552–1335 ⊕ *www.sailstmaarten.com.*

FAMILY **Golden Eagle.** The sleek 76-foot catamaran *Golden Eagle* takes day-sailors on eco-friendly excursions to outlying islets and reefs for snorkeling and partying. They can pick you up right from your hotel or condo. ⊠ *Bobby's Marina, Philipsburg* ☎ 721/542–3323 ⊕ *www.sailingsxm.com.*

SNORKELING

Some of the best snorkeling on the Dutch side can be found around the rocks below Fort Amsterdam off Little Bay Beach, in the west end of Maho Bay, off Pelican Key, and around the reefs off Oyster Pond Beach. On the French side, the area around Orient Bay—including Caye Verte, Ilet Pinel, and Tintamarre—is especially lovely and is officially classified and protected as a regional underwater nature reserve. Sea creatures also congregate around Creole Rock at the point of Grand Case Bay. The average cost of an afternoon snorkeling trip is about $45 to $55 per person.

DUTCH SIDE

FAMILY **Aqua Mania Adventures.** This company offers a variety of snorkeling trips. The newest activity, called Rock 'n Roll Safaris, lets participants not only snorkel, but navigate their own motorized rafts. ⊠ *Pelican Marina, Simpson Bay* ☎ *721/544–2640, 721/544–2631* ⊕ *www.stmaarten-activities.com.*

Eagle Tours. While Eagle Tours is geared more to cruise groups, anyone can sign on for the four-hour power rafting or sailing trips that include snorkeling, a beach break, and lunch. The sailing trips are done aboard a 76-foot catamaran. Some cruises stop in Grand Case or Marigot for a bit of shopping. ⊠ *Bobby's Marina, Philipsburg* ☎ *721/542–3323* ⊕ *www.sailingsxm.com.*

FRENCH SIDE

Kontiki Watersports. Arrange equipment rentals and snorkeling trips through Kontiki Watersports. ⊠ *North beach entrance, Parc de la Baie Orientale* ☎ *0590/87–46–89.*

SPAS

Spas have added a pampering dimension to several properties on both the French and Dutch sides of the island. Treatments and products vary depending on the establishment, but generally include several different massage modalities, body scrubs, facials, and mani-pedis; all the spas offer men's treatments, too. Be sure to phone to book in advance, however, as walk-ins are hardly ever accommodated. There are massage cabanas on some beaches, especially on the French side, and most of the beach clubs in Baie Orientale will have a blackboard where you can sign up or will give you the phone number for a massage therapist. Sometimes these beachside massages can be arranged on the spur of the moment. Hotels that don't have spas can usually arrange in-room treatments.

DUTCH SIDE

★ Fodor'sChoice **Christian Dior Spa.** With its oceanfront setting, the Christian Dior Spa is undeniably dramatic, and the treatments are certainly creative. The Intense Youthfulness Treatment combines a 30-minute back massage with a facial cleansing therapy and shiatsu head massage. A two-hour Harmonizing Body Massage combines several techniques such as reflexology and shiatsu. Guests have all-day use of the pool, steam room, and sauna. A full line of Dior products is available for purchase. The spa is open weekdays 9 to 6 and Saturday 9 to 4. ⊠ *The Cliff at Cupecoy Beach, Rhine Rd., Cupecoy* ☎ *721/546–6620* ⊕ *www.cliffsxm.com/the-christian-dior-spa.*

Good Life Spa. Good Life Spa offers aloe vera treatments (to combat sunburn) and a wide range of scrubs and wraps. There's also a large hydrotherapy pool with waterfalls and jets, and a fitness center. It's open weekdays from 9 to 8, weekends from 10 to 6. ⊠ *Sonesta Maho Beach Resort & Casino, 1 Rhine Rd., Maho* ☎ *721/545–2540, 721/545–2356* ⊕ *www.thegoodlifespa.com.*

Hibiscus Spa. Hibiscus Spa is an attractive facility offering the usual menu of facials, body treatment, and massages featuring Decleor products. The Hibiscus Expert Facial is formulated to benefit your skin type. It's open daily from 9 to 7. ⊠ *Westin Dawn Beach Resort & Spa, 144 Oyster Pond Rd., Oyster Pond* ☎ *599/543–6700* ⊕ *www.westinstmaarten.com/st-maarten-spa.*

FRENCH SIDE

★ Fodor'sChoice **La Samanna Spa.** You don't have to be a guest at the famous La Samanna Hotel to enjoy a treatment or a day package at this heavenly retreat considered to be one of the best spas on the island; just ring for an appointment and start to relax. In the lovely tropical garden setting, immaculate treatment rooms feature walled gardens with private outdoor showers. There are dozens of therapies for your body, face, hair, and spirit on the spa menu, and any can be customized to your desires or sensitivities. There are over a dozen different massage modalities offered, including Indian Ayurvedic, Thai, Japanese, and Chinese, and facials, scrubs, and soothing treatments for sunburn. The spa is open daily from 9 to

8. ⊠ *La Samanna, Baie Longue* ☎ *0590/87–65–69* ⊕ *www.lasamanna.orient-express.com.*

Le Spa. Le Spa offers a full menu of more than 40 services, including advanced skin-care therapies, integrative massages, exfoliation and body treatments, facials, and nail care performed by skilled Parisian-trained Carita therapists. Tropical ingredients are appropriate to the beach setting, so try the Lulur, Lotus, and Frangipani, a luxurious scrub that begins with a massage using rice, coconut powder, and flowers from Bali. ⊠ *Radisson St. Martin Resort, Marina & Spa, Anse Marcel* ☎ *0590/87–67–01* ⊕ *www.radissonblu.com/resort-stmartin/spa.*

WATERSKIING

Expect to pay $50 per half hour for waterskiing, $40 to $45 per half hour for jet-skiing.

FRENCH SIDE

FlyBoard St. Maarten. In St. Martin, you can try out the latest trend in water sports: FlyBoarding. Water jets connect to a jet-ski turbine and allow you to fly above the waves to a height of up to 10 feet. For $150 you get 15 minutes of ground instruction on how to operate the FlyBoard® and approximately 30 minutes of flight time with a certified instructor. ■TIP→ You must download and complete an online training program and sign a liability waiver beforehand. ⊠ *Front de Mer, Marigot* ☎ *690/76–22–32* ⊕ *www.flyboardstmaarten.com.*

Kontiki Watersports. On the French side, Kontiki Watersports offers rentals of windsurfing boards, Jet Skis, and Wave-Runners, as well as waterskiing, snorkling, and banana boating, and instruction for all of these sports. ⊠ *North beach entrance, Parc de la Baie Orientale* ☎ *0590/87–43–26* ⊕ *www.kontiki-sxm.com.*

WINDSURFING

The best windsurfing is on Galion Bay on the French side. From November to May, trade winds can average 15 knots.

FRENCH SIDE

Wind Adventures. Wind Adventures offers rentals and lessons in windsurfing, kiteboarding, stand-up paddleboarding, kayaking and more. One-hour lessons are about €40. The company also offers a fun vacation package that works out to a terrific deal: two hours of activities each day for five days for €199. ✉ *North beach entrance, Baie Orientale* ☎ *690/36–27–36* ⊕ *www.wind-adventures.com.*

Windy Reef. At its state-of-the-art facility, Windy Reef has offered surfing and windsurfing lessons and rentals since 1991. ✉ *Galion Beach, past Butterfly Farm* ☎ *690/34–21–85* ⊕ *www.windyreef.com.*

ST. BARTHÉLEMY

Updated
by Elise
Meyer

ST. BARTHÉLEMY BLENDS THE RESPECTIVE ESSENCES of the Caribbean, France, and *Architectural Digest* in perfect proportions. A sophisticated but unstudied approach to relaxation and respite prevails: you can spend the day on a beach, try on the latest French fashions, and watch the sunset while nibbling tapas over Gustavia Harbor, then choose from nearly 100 excellent restaurants for an elegant or easy evening meal. You can putter around the island, scuba dive, windsurf on a quiet cove, or just admire the lovely views.

A mere 8 square miles (21 square km), St. Barth is a hilly island, with many sheltered inlets providing visitors with many opportunities to try out picturesque, quiet beaches. The town of Gustavia wraps itself around a modern harbor lined with everything from size-matters megayachts to rustic fishing boats to sailboats of all descriptions. Red-roof villas dot the hillsides, and glass-front shops line the streets. Beach surf runs the gamut from kiddie-pool calm to serious-surfer dangerous, beaches from deserted to packed. The cuisine is tops in the Caribbean, and almost everything is tidy, stylish, and up-to-date. French *savoir vivre* prevails throughout the island.

Christopher Columbus discovered the island—called "Oua-nalao" by its native Caribs—in 1493; he named it for his brother Bartolomé. The first group of French colonists arrived in 1648, drawn by the ideal location on the West Indian Trade Route, but they were wiped out by the Caribs, who dominated the area. Another small group from Normandy and Brittany arrived in 1694. This time the settlers prospered—with the help of French buccaneers, who took advantage of the island's strategic location and protected harbor. In 1784 the French traded the island to King Gustav III of Sweden in exchange for port rights in Göteborg. The king dubbed the capital Gustavia, laid out and paved streets, built three forts, and turned the community into a prosperous free port. The island thrived as a shipping and commercial center until the 19th century, when earthquakes, fires, and hurricanes brought financial ruin. Many residents fled for newer lands of opportunity, and Oscar II of Sweden decided to return the island to France. After briefly considering selling it to America, the French took possession of St. Barthélemy again on August 10, 1877.

Today the island is a free port, and in 2007 it became a Collectivity, a French-administered overseas territory outside

LOGISTICS

Getting to St. Barth: There are no direct flights to St. Barth (SBH). You must fly to another island and then catch a smaller plane for the hop over, or you can take a ferry. Most Americans fly first to St. Maarten, and then take the 10-minute flight to St. Barth, but you can connect through St. Thomas or San Juan as well.

Hassle Factor: Medium–high.

On the Ground: Many hotels offer free airport transfers; before you arrive, they will contact you for your arrival information. Otherwise, there's a taxi stand at the airport; unmetered taxis cost about €10 to €25 to reach most hotels. If you are renting a car, you may pick it up from the airport; if you have a reservation (strongly recommended in high season), rental agents will meet you at the ferry if you arrive by boat.

Getting Around the Island: Most people coming to St. Barth rent a car. Taxis are expensive, but some visitors are happy to let an experienced driver negotiate the roads at night. Any restaurant will be happy to call a cab back to your hotel after dinner. Otherwise, there is no other transportation option on the island. It's also possible to rent a motorbike, but steep roads can make driving a stressful experience if you aren't experienced.

of continental France. Arid, hilly, and rocky, St. Barth was unsuited to sugar production and thus never developed an extensive slave base. Some of today's 3,000 current residents are descendants of the tough Norman and Breton settlers of three centuries ago, but you are more likely to encounter attractive French twenty- and thirtysomethings from Normandy and Provence who are friendly, English-speaking, and here for the sunny lifestyle.

The largest hotel on St. Barth has just over 70 rooms, which means you get a great deal of personal service and attention wherever you stay.

PLANNING

WHEN TO GO

High season in St. Barth is typical for the Caribbean, from mid-December through mid-April (or until after Easter). During busy holiday periods prices can shoot up to the highest levels, but in the summer (particularly June and July), there are some remarkable bargains on the island, though some restaurants still close over the summer months, and hotels tend to do their annual maintenance during this time as well.

ACCOMMODATIONS

Most hotels on St. Barth are small (the largest has fewer than 70 rooms) and stratospherically expensive, but there are some reasonable options. About half of the accommodations on St. Barth are in private villas. Prices drop dramatically after March, and summer is a great time for a visit. Check hotel websites for updates of discounts and special offers that seem to be becoming more common with the current economy.

HOTEL AND RESTAURANT PRICES

Prices in the restaurant reviews are the average cost of a main course at dinner or, if dinner is not served, at lunch; taxes and service charges are generally included. Prices in the hotel reviews are the lowest cost of a standard double room in high season, excluding taxes, service charges, and meal plans (except at all-inclusives). Prices for rentals are the lowest per-night cost for a one-bedroom unit in high season.

For expanded lodging reviews and current deals, visit Fodors.com.

WHAT IT COSTS IN EUROS			
$	$$	$$$	$$$$
Restaurants under €12	€12–€20	€21–€30	over €30
Hotels under €275	€276–€375	€376–€475	over €475

Restaurant prices are the average cost of a main course at dinner or, if dinner is not served, at lunch. Hotel prices are the lowest cost of a standard double room in high season.

EXPLORING

With a little practice, negotiating St. Barth's narrow, steep roads soon becomes fun. Recent infrastructure upgrades and the prevalence of small, responsive cars have improved things a lot. Free maps are everywhere, roads are smooth and well-marked, and signs will point the way. The tourist office has annotated maps with walking tours that highlight

Gustavia's waterfront promenade

sights of interest. Parking in Gustavia is still a challenge, especially during busy vacation times.

GUSTAVIA

You can easily explore all of Gustavia during a two-hour stroll. Some shops close from noon to 3 or 4—so plan lunch accordingly—but then stay open past 7 in the evening.

FAMILY **Le Musée Territorial de Saint Barthélemy.** On the far side of the harbor known as La Pointe is the charming Municipal Museum, where you can find watercolors, portraits, photographs, and historic documents detailing the island's history, as well as displays of the island's flowers, plants, and marine life. ⊠ *La Pointe, Gustavia* ☎ *0590/29–71–55* ⊡ *€2* ⊘ *Mon. and Tues. 8:30–1 and 2:30–5:30, Wed. 9–1, Thurs. and Fri. 8:30–1 and 2:30–5, Sat. 9–1. Call for summer closing hrs.*

Tourist Office. A good spot to park your car is rue de la République, alongside the catamarans, yachts, and sailboats. The tourist office on the pier can provide maps and a wealth of information. During busier holiday periods, the office may be open all day. ⊠ *Rue de la République, Gustavia* ☎ *0590/27–87–27* ⊕ *www.saintbarth-tourisme.*

St. Barthélemy

Restaurants

Bagatelle St. Barth, **3**
Bar'tô, **16**
Bonito, **2**
Do Brazil, **1**
Eddy's, **5**
La Langouste, **20**
La Plage, **19**
La Table de Jules, **15**
Le Carré d'Or, **9**
Le Case, **21**
Le Gaïac, **14**
Le Palace, **6**
Le Repaire, **10**
Le Ti St. Barth, **17**
Les Bananiers, **22**
L'Esprit, **13**
L'Isola, **8**
L'Isoletta, **7**
Maya's, **23**
Meat and Potatoes, **12**
Ocean, **4**
The Sand Bar, **18**
Santa Fé, **24**
Wall House, **11**

Hotels

Christopher, **8**
Eden Rock, **13**
Emeraude Plage, **11**
Hôtel Baie des Anges, **16**
Hotel Guanahani, **6**
Hôtel Le Toiny, **3**
Hôtel Le Village St Barth, **15**
Hotel Les Ondines Sur La Plage, **4**
Hotel St-Barth Isle de France, **18**
Hotel Taïwana, **17**
La Gloriette, **7**
Le P'tit Morne, **19**
Le Sereno, **5**
Le Tom Beach Hôtel, **12**
Les Îlets de la Plage, **14**
Les Mouettes, **10**
Normandie Hotel, **9**
Salines Garden Cottages, **2**
Sunset Hotel, **1**

KEY

- Beaches
- Dive Sites
- Ferry
- ❶ Restaurants
- ① Hotels
- ℹ️ Tourist info

ATLANTIC
OCEAN

Les Grenadiers

La Tortue

Pte. Milou   17 8

Anse de
Marigot

Anse Marechal

9 10

Anse de Grand
Cul de Sac

7

Anse de
Lorient

Marigot

4

16 6

5

Lorient

Anse de Petit
Cul de Sac

Vitet

Toiny

14 15 3

Mt. du
Grand Fond

Morne
Vitet

◆ Toiny Coast

2

Grand Fond

Anse à
Toiny

Pt. à Toiny

Grande Saline

Anse de
Grand Fond

12 13

Anse de
Grande Saline

Morne Rouge

Anse du
Gouverneur

Pt. Gouverneur

Gustavia

① R. de la République

🔟 R. Auguste Nyman

Municipal
Museum

11

Carré d'Or

9

8

7

R. de la Paix

R. du Port Oscar II

Fort
George

R. Duquesne

R. Charzy

R. Jeanne d'Arc

R. Schoelcher

R. Jean Bart

R. de la Colline

ℹ️

R. du Général de Gaulle R. Thiers

R. du Bord de Mer

6

5

R. Samuel Fahlberg

R. Roi Courbet R. Gambier

3

4

Post Office

R. I. de Bruyn

R. Victor Hugo

R. de l'Église

R. du Presbytère

R. des Normands

Fort Cart ◆

1

2

com ☙ *Mon. 8:30–12:30, Tues.–Fri. 8–noon and 2–5, Sat. 9–noon.*

COROSSOL

FAMILY Traces of the island's French provincial origins are evident in this two-street fishing village with a little rocky beach.

FAMILY **Inter Oceans Museum/Museum of Shells.** Ingenu Magras's Inter Oceans Museum has more than 9,000 seashells and an intriguing collection of sand samples from around the world. You can buy souvenir shells. ✉ *Corossol* ☎ *0590/27–62–97* 💶 *€3* ☙ *Tues.–Sun. 9–12:30 and 3–5.*

LORIENT

Site of the first French settlement, Lorient is one of the island's two parishes; a restored church, a school, and a post office mark the spot. Note the gaily decorated graves in the cemetery.

ELSEWHERE ON THE ISLAND

St-Jean. There is a monument at the crest of the hill that divides St-Jean from Gustavia. Called *The Arawak*, it symbolizes the soul of St. Barth. A warrior, one of the earliest inhabitants of the area (AD 800–1,800), holds a lance in his right hand and stands on a rock shaped like the island; in his left hand he holds a conch shell, which sounds the cry of nature; perched beside him are a pelican (which symbolizes the air and survival by fishing) and an iguana (which represents the earth). The half-mile-long crescent of sand at St-Jean is the island's most popular beach. A popular activity is watching and photographing the hair-raising airplane landings (though you should note that it is extremely dangerous to stand in the area at the beach end of the runway). You'll also find some of the best shopping on the island here, as well as several restaurants.

NEED A BREAK? **Maya's To Go.** If you find yourself in St-Jean and need a picnic or just want some food to take home to your villa for later, stop in at Maya's To Go, which can be found in the Galeries de Commerce shopping center across from the airport. A more casual offering from the owners of the Gustavia favorite, it is open daily from 7 to 7 (except Monday), has free Wi-Fi on the deck in front, and offers a full menu of prepared foods, baked goods, sandwiches, and salads for beach picnics or villa dinners. ⊠ *Galeries de Commerce, across from the airport, St-Jean* ☎ *0590/29–83–70* ⊕ *www.mayastogo.com* ⊙ *Closed Mon.*

Toiny Coast. Over the hills beyond Grand Cul de Sac is this much-photographed coastline. Stone fences crisscross the steep slopes of Morne Vitet, one of many small mountains on St. Barth, along a rocky shore that resembles the rugged coast of Normandy. Nicknamed the "washing machine" because of its turbulent surf, it is not recommended even to expert swimmers because of the strong undertow. ■TIP→ There is an tough but scenic hike around the point. Take the road past Le Toiny hotel to the top to find the start of the trail.

BEACHES

There is a beach in St. Barth to suit every taste. Whether you are looking for wild surf, a dreamy white-sand strand, or a spot at a chic beach club close to shopping and restaurants, you will find it within a 20-minute drive.

There are many *anses* (coves) and nearly 20 *plages* (beaches) scattered around the island, each with a distinctive personality; all are open to the public, even if the beach fronts the toniest of resorts. Because of the variety and number of beaches, even in high season you can find a nearly empty beach, despite St. Barth's tiny size. That's not to say that all the island's beaches are equally good or even equally suitable for swimming, but each beach has something unique to offer. Unless you are having lunch at a beachfront restaurant that has lounging areas set aside for its patrons, you should bring your own umbrella, beach mat, and water (all of which are easily obtainable all over the island if you haven't brought yours with you on vacation). Topless sunbathing is common, but nudism is supposedly forbidden—although both Grande Saline and Gouverneur are de facto nude beaches, albeit less today than in the past. Shade is scarce.

Anse à Colombier. The beach here is the least accessible, thus the most private, on the island; to reach it you must take either a rocky footpath from Petite Anse or brave the 30-minute climb down (and back up) a steep, cactus-bordered trail from the top of the mountain behind the beach. Appropriate footgear is a must, and you should know that once you get to the beach, the only shade is a rock cave. But this is a good place to snorkel. Boaters favor

this beach and cove for its calm anchorage. **Amenities:** none. **Best for:** snorkeling; swimming. ✉ *Colombier*.

Anse de Grand Cul de Sac. The shallow, reef-protected beach is nice for small children, fly-fishermen, kayakers, and windsurfers—and for the amusing pelicanlike frigate birds that dive-bomb the water, fishing for their lunch. There is a good dive shop. You needn't do your own fishing; you can have a wonderful lunch at one of the excellent restaurants, and use their lounge chairs for the afternoon. **Amenities:** food and drink; parking (no fee); toilets; water sports. **Best for:** swimming; walking.

> ## PICKING THE RIGHT BEACH
>
> For long stretches of talcum-soft pale sand choose Grande Saline, Gouverneur, or Flamands. For seclusion in nature, pick the tawny grains of Corossol. But the most remarkable beach on the island, Shell Beach, is right in Gustavia and hardly has sand at all! Millions of tiny pink shells wash ashore in drifts, thanks to an unusual confluence of ocean currents, sea-life beds, and hurricane action.

FAMILY **Fodor's**Choice **Anse de Grande Saline.** With its peaceful seclusion and sandy ocean bottom, this is just about everyone's favorite beach and is great for swimming, too. Without any major development (although there is some talk of developing a resort here), it's an ideal Caribbean strand, though there can be a bit of wind at times. In spite of the prohibition, young and old alike go nude. The beach is a 10-minute walk up a rocky dune trail, so be sure to wear sneakers or water shoes, and bring a blanket, umbrella, and beach towels. Although there are several good restaurants for lunch near the parking area, once you get here, the beach is just sand, sea, and sky. The big salt ponds here are no longer in use, and the place looks a little desolate when you approach, but don't despair. **Amenities:** parking (no fee). **Best for:** nudists; swimming; walking.

FAMILY **Anse de Lorient.** This beach is popular with St. Barth's families and surfers, who like its rolling waves and central location. Be aware of the level of the tide, which can come in very quickly. Hikers and avid surfers like the walk over the hill to Point Milou in the late afternoon sun when the waves roll in. **Amenities:** parking (no fee). **Best for:** snorkeling; surfing; swimming.

Anse des Flamands. This is the most beautiful of the hotel beaches—a roomy strip of silken sand. Come here for lunch and then spend the afternoon sunning, enjoying long beach walks, and swimming in the turquoise water. From the beach, you can take a brisk hike along a paved sidewalk to the top of the now-extinct volcano believed to have given birth to St. Barth. **Amenities:** food and drink; toilets. **Best for:** snorkeling; swimming; walking.

FAMILY **Anse du Gouverneur.** Because it's so secluded, this beach is a popular place for nude sunbathing. It is truly beautiful, with blissful swimming and views of St. Kitts, Saba, and St. Eustatius. Venture here at the end of the day and watch the sun set behind the hills. The road here from Gustavia also offers spectacular vistas. Legend has it that pirates' treasure is buried in the vicinity. There are no restaurants, toilets, or other services here, so plan accordingly. **Amenities:** parking (no fee). **Best for:** nudists; sunset; swimming; walking.

FAMILY **Baie de St-Jean.** Like a mini Côte d'Azur—beachside bistros, terrific shopping, bungalow hotels, bronzed bodies, windsurfing, and day-trippers who tend to arrive on BIG yachts—the reef-protected strip is divided by Eden Rock promontory. Except when the hotels are filled to capacity you can rent chaises and umbrellas at La Plage restaurant or at Eden Rock, where you can lounge for hours over lunch. **Amenities:** food and drink; toilets. **Best for:** partiers, walking.

WHERE TO EAT

Dining on St. Barth compares favorably to almost anywhere in the world. Varied and exquisite cuisine, a French flair in the décor, sensational wine, and attentive service make for a wonderful epicurean experience in almost any of the more than 80 restaurants. On most menus, freshly caught local seafood mingles on the plate with top-quality provisions that arrive regularly from Paris. Interesting selections on the Cartes de Vins are no surprise, but don't miss the sophisticated cocktails whipped up by island bartenders. They are worlds away from cliché Caribbean rum punches with paper umbrellas. The signature drink of St. Barth is called "'ti punch," a rum concoction similar to a Brazilian caipirinha. It's also fun to sit at a bar and ask the attractive bartenders for their own signature cocktail.

Most restaurants offer a chalkboard full of daily specials that are usually a good bet. But even the pickiest eaters will find something on every menu. Some level of compliance can be paid to dietary restrictions within reason, and especially if explained in French; just be aware that French people generally let the chef work his or her magic. Expect your meal to be costly; however, you can dine superbly and somewhat economically if you limit pricey cocktails, watch wine selections, share appetizers or desserts, and pick up snacks and picnic meals from one of the well-stocked markets. Or you could follow the locals to small crêperies, cafés, sandwich shops, and pizzerias in the main shopping areas. Lunch is usually less costly than dinner. *Ti Creux* means "snack" or "small bite."

Lavish publications feature restaurant menus and contacts. Ask at your hotel or look on the racks at the airport for current issues. Reservations are strongly recommended and, in high season, essential. Lots of restaurants now accept reservations through their website or by email. Check social media. Except during the Christmas–New Year's season it's not usually necessary to book far in advance. A day's—or even a few hours'—notice is usually sufficient. At the end of the meal, as in France, you must request the bill. Until you do, you can feel free to linger at the table and enjoy the complimentary vanilla rum that's likely to appear.

Check restaurant bills carefully. A *service compris* (service charge) is always added by law, but you should leave the server 5% to 10% extra in cash. You'll usually come out ahead if you charge restaurant meals on a credit card in euros instead of paying with American currency, as your credit card might offer a better exchange rate than the restaurant (though since some credit cards nowadays have conversion surcharges around 3%, the benefit of using plastic is rapidly disappearing). Many restaurants serve locally caught *langouste* (lobster); priced by weight, it's usually the most expensive item on a menu and, depending on its size and the restaurant, will range in price from $40 to $60. *In menu prices below, it has been left out of the range.*

What to Wear: A bathing suit and gauzy top or shift is acceptable at beachside lunch spots, but not really in Gustavia. Jackets are never required and are rarely worn by men, but most people do dress fashionably for dinner. Casual chic is the idea; women wear whatever is hip, current, and sexy. You can't go wrong in a tank dress or anything clingy and ruffly with white jeans and high sandals. The sky is the limit for high fashion at nightclubs and lounges in high season, when you might (correctly) think everyone in sight is a model. Leave some space in your suitcase; you can buy the perfect outfit here on the island. Nice shorts (not beachy ones) at the dinner table may label a man *américain,* but many locals have adopted the habit, and nobody cares much. Wear them with a pastel shirt to really fit in (never tucked in). Pack a light sweater or shawl for the occasional breezy night.

ANSE DE TOINY

$$$ ✕ **La Table de Jules.** *Bistro.* Reinvented for 2013, the former K'fe Massai is now a charming and attractive "Bistrot Gourmand." The restaurant's décor and music pays homage to French jazz singers like Edith Piaf, Charles Aznavour, and Jacques Brel, and the cuisine is the perfect match. French bistro classics like soup de poisson, house-made foie gras, and herb-wrapped beef tenderloin join tasty fish and grilled dishes, and the Tarte Tatin is the best on the island. [$] *Average main: €23* ✉ *, Anse de Toiny* ☎ *0590/29–76–78.*

★ **Fodor's Choice** ✕ **Le Gaïac.** *Modern French.* Hôtel Le Toiny's

$$$$ dramatic, tasteful, cliffside dining porch showcases gastronomic art. Less stuffy than you might remember from seasons past, the food is notable for its innovation and extraordinary presentation, and the warm but consummately professional service sets a high standard. The menu changes frequently but rare ingredients and unique preparations always delight: beet ravioli filled with raspberries; tender roasted Iberian pork grilled and confit; lamb medallions accompanied by tender zucchini toasts. A greenhouse on-site produces organic produce for the restaurant. Tuesday is Fish Market Night when you choose your own fish to be grilled; there's a €43 buffet brunch on Sunday from 11 to 2. [$] *Average main: €36* ✉ *Hôtel Le Toiny, Anse de Toiny* ☎ *0590/29–77–47* 🌐 *www.letoiny.com* ✍ *Reservations essential* ⊗ *Closed Sept.–mid-Oct.*

FLAMANDS

$$$ ✕ **La Langouste.** *French Fusion.* This tiny but friendly beachside restaurant in the pool courtyard of Hôtel Baie des Anges lives up to its name by serving fresh-grilled local lobster, and lobster thermidor, at prices that are somewhat gentler than at most other island venues. Try starters like

creole stuffed crab, scallop carpaccio, a warm goat cheese salad, or one of the five soups including classic Caribbean fish soup and lobster bisque. The well-prepared fish or pasta dishes are great main options, and there are choices for meat fans as well. Classic French desserts like Floating Island with vanilla sauce, crepes suzette, and mango tart are worth the calories. [$] *Average main: €27* ✉ *Hôtel Baie des Anges, Anse des Flamands* ☎ *0590/27–63–61* 🌐 *www.hotelbaiedesanges.fr* ✍ *Reservations essential* 🕓 *Closed Aug. 26–Oct. 15.*

★ $$$ **Fodor's Choice** ✕ **Le Case a L'Isle.** *Modern French.* You can't top the view or the fine service at this waterfront restaurant at the renowned Hotel Isle de France. Light and tasty fare with a hint of Asia is served at lunch and dinner; at lunch you can have your toes in the sand and a perfect club sandwich. There is something for everyone on the dinner menu, from sparkling fresh local tuna tartare with guacamole sauce to lobster risotto scented with coconut and lime, and the rack of lamb is beyond compare. A fashion show featuring the lovely beachwear from the on-site boutique occurs during lunch daily and during dinner Tuesday. ■ **TIP→** At night, there is no more romantic a spot on St. Barth. [$] *Average main: €27* ✉ *Hotel Isle de France, Flamands Beach, Flamands* ☎ *0529/27–61–81* 🌐 *www.isle-de-france.com* ✍ *Reservations essential.*

GRAND CUL DE SAC

$$$$ FAMILY ✕ **Bar'tô.** *Italian.* Locavores will like the pretty restaurant in the gardens of the Hotel Guanahani, which showcases the refined cuisine of executive chef Philippe Masseglia. Influenced by Provence and Italy, dishes are presented beautifully, and use some organic and local products. Try the burrata with lightly smoked tomato, which is garnished with anchovy, olives, and basil seeds, or splurge on the black truffle risotto. There are €90 and €120 tasting menus if the whole table is adventurous and likes to eat on the early side. Don't miss the caramelized pear cloaked in almond brittle and chocolate. There is a €20 children's menu too, and veggie and gluten-free items are marked on the menu. ■ **TIP→** Long pants are required at dinner. [$] *Average main: €42* ✉ *Hotel Guanahani, Grand Cul de Sac* ☎ *0590/27–66–60* ✍ *Reservations essential* 🕓 *Closed Mon. and Tues.*

$$$ ✕ **La Gloriette.** *Caribbean.* For a beachside lunch with your toes in the sand, La Gloriette is a dream. Picnic tables under the cocoloba trees are shady, and everyone is having a great time. Longtime visitors will remember the original

creole restaurant here, and will be happy to know that the *accras* (salt-cod fritters with spicy sauce) are as good as ever. There are huge, fresh salads and many daily specials on the blackboard. Superfresh grilled fish is a great choice, and the sushi-style tatakis are light and delicious. At dinner there are good pizzas for dining in or taking back to your villa. Don't miss the artisanal, island-flavor rums offered after your meal, and available at the tiny shop. Ⓢ *Average main: €23* ✉ *Plage de Grand Cul de Sac, Grand Cul de Sac* ☎ *690/29–85–71* ⊘ *Closed Wed.*

GRANDE SALINE

★ Fodor'sChoice ✕ **L'Esprit.** *Modern French.* Jean-Claude Dufour, a renowned chef on the island (formerly of Eden Rock) brings tasty and innovative dishes to a romantic terrace close to Saline Beach. The menu has lots of variety, from light French dishes with a Provençale twist to interesting salads (like house-smoked mahimahi on fennel slaw), pastas, burgers, and steak. Tasty vegetarian options keep non–meat eaters happy, too. Don't miss the chocolate tart for dessert, but the memory of the sweet service will last longer. Ⓢ *Average main: €36* ✉ *Anse de Grande Saline, Grande Saline* ☎ *0590/52–46–10* ⊘ *No lunch Wed. and Sun.*
$$$$
FAMILY

$$$ ✕ **Meat and Potatoes.** *Steakhouse.* If you think that St. Barth is sometimes too "girly," you will love this restaurant at the end of the road to Saline Beach. The white interior is lined with banquettes heaped with red, black, and gray pillows; there are almost a dozen different cuts of steak, from tenderloins to T-bones, at least a dozen starchy sides, and some vegetables for good measure (all à la carte). There is also fresh fish for the red-meat averse, and a vegetarian menu. Don't miss the Provençal *pommes ratte,* wedges of potatoes cooked in duck fat, fresh rosemary, and sea salt. The wine list is full of complimentary bottles, heavy on Bordeaux's best. Ⓢ *Average main: €30* ✉ *Grande Saline* ☎ *0590/51–15–98.*

$$$$ ✕ **Santa Fé.** *French.* Perched at the top of the Lurin hills on the way to Gouverneur Beach, this relaxed and scenic restaurant serves panoramic views with both lunch and dinner to visitors and locals alike. The chef comes from Provence, and trained at some of the region's best restaurants before moving to the Caribbean. Salads and light lunch offerings are perfect on the way to the beach, but come back for dinner—especially if you are a fan of authentic French cuisine—for delicious veal osso bucco, coq au vin, and
FAMILY

crisp tomato tarts with pesto. $ *Average main: €34* ⊠ *Rte. de Lurin, Grande Saline* ☎ *0590/27–61–04* ⊗ *Closed Sept.– mid-Oct. No dinner Wed.*

GUSTAVIA

$$$$ ✕ **Bagatelle St. Barth.** *Bistro.* New in 2012, the sophisticated St-Tropez-inspired interior, right on the harbor, is a scene-y place to watch big boats and enjoy a menu of classic French bistro favorites such as truffled roast chicken, pastis-flamed shrimp, and steak tartare. There are platters of charcuterie and fromage for sharing, and a great wine list. Fans of the popular sister establishments in New York's Meatpacking District and Los Angeles will recognize the friendly service and lively atmosphere, and the great music provided by resident DJs—come late, the party really gets going after 11. Book a table on the terrace. $ *Average main: €34* ⊠ *Rue Samuel Fahlberg, Gustavia* ☎ *0590/27–51–51* ⊕ *www.bistrotbagatelle.com* ⚭ *Reservations essential.*

★ **Fodor's**Choice ✕ **Bonito.** *Latin American.* Decorated like a chic
$$$$ beach house, Bonito features big, white, canvas couches for lounging in the center, tables around the sides, an open kitchen, and three bar areas—all located on a hill above Gustavia Harbor. The young Venezuelan owners go to great lengths to see that guests are having as much fun as they are. The specialty is ceviche with eight different varieties, in combos that are prettily arrayed on poured-glass platters for culinary experimentation. Try octopus and shrimp, or wahoo garnished with sweet potatoes and popcorn. Traditionalists might like the fricassee of escargots, or foie gras served with mango, soy, and preserved lemon. Carnivores will love the rack of lamb. French pastry classics are on the dessert menu. ■TIP→ A sister location, with the same terrific food, but a quieter ambience is open in the chic beachside Le Sereno resort. $ *Average main: €35* ⊠ *Rue Lubin Brin, Gustavia* ☎ *0590/27–96–96* ⊕ *www.ilovebonito.com* ⚭ *Reservations essential* ⊗ *Closed Mon. in low season. No lunch.*

$$$ ✕ **Dō Brazil.** *Eclectic.* Right on Gustavia's Shell Beach, this restaurant is open every day for lunch and dinner and offers live music for sundown cocktail hour on Thursday, Friday, and Saturday evenings, as well as top DJs spinning the latest club mixes for evening events, which are listed in the local papers. You'll find tasty light fare like chilled soups, fruit-garnished salads with tuna, shrimp, and chicken, plus sandwiches, burgers, pastas, and grilled fresh fish for lunch. Everyone loves the Dō Brazil hot pot: mahimahi, shrimp, and sea scallops in a sauce of lemongrass and coconut milk.

The extensive cocktail menu tempts, but at €12 each, your bar bill can quickly exceed the price of dinner. There is a €10 children's menu. $ *Average main: €26* ✉ *Shell Beach, Gustavia* ☎ *0590/29–06–66* 🌐 *www.dobrazil.com.*

$$$ 🍴 **Eddy's.** *Asian.* By local standards, dinner in the pretty, open-air, tropical garden here is reasonably priced. The cooking is French-creole-Asian. Fish specialties, especially the tuna sushi sampler, are fresh and delicious, and there are always plenty of notable daily specials. Just remember some mosquito repellent for your ankles. $ *Average main: €24* ✉ *12 Rue Samuel Fahlberg, Gustavia* ☎ *0590/27–54–17* ✍ *Reservations not accepted* ⏲ *Closed Sun., and Sept. and Oct. No lunch.*

$$$ 🍴 **Le Carré d'Or.** *Eclectic.* Franck Mathevet, the esteemed Burgundy-born chef formerly of Wall House, opened this attractive and lively outdoor restaurant in 2012, right in the center of Le Carré d'Or, Gustavia's glam shopping enclave. Team terrific cocktails with tasty and modern small plates, fresh seafood from the Raw Bar, or sandwiches like lobster rolls and pastrami-cured salmon on bagels. Sliders, both beef and mahimahi, are a favorite on the lunch menu, while fun sharable appetizers and simple grills make a perfect combo at night. The restaurant is open for breakfast, lunch, snacks, dinner, and Sunday brunch—and it's a great spot for a special event, too. $ *Average main: €21* ✉ *Rue Auguste Nyman, Gustavia* ☎ *0590/52–46–11* 🌐 *www.lecarresbh.com.*

$$$$ 🍴 **Le Palace.** *Caribbean.* Tucked into a tropical garden, this popular in-town restaurant, also known as Pipiri Palace, is famous for its barbecue ribs, beef filet, and rack of lamb; it is consistently one of our absolute favorites. Fish-market specialties like red snapper cooked in a banana leaf or grilled tuna are good here, as are grilled duck with mushroom sauce and a skewered surf-and-turf with a green curry sauce. The blackboard lists daily specials that are usually a great choice, like St. Marcellin cheese roasted in a crock of honey. $ *Average main: €31* ✉ *Rue Général-de-Gaulle, Gustavia* ☎ *0590/27–53–20* ✍ *Reservations essential* ⏲ *Closed Sun., and mid-June–July.*

$$ 🍴 **Le Repaire.** *Brasserie.* This friendly classic French bras-
FAMILY serie overlooks Gustavia's harbor, and is a popular spot from its early morning opening to its late-night closing. The flexible hours are great if you arrive on the island midafternoon and need a substantial snack before dinner. Grab a cappuccino, pull a captain's chair up to the streetside rail, and watch the pretty people go by. The

menu ranges from cheeseburgers, which are served only at lunch along with the island's best fries, to simply grilled fish and meat, pastas, and risottos. The mixed salads always please. Wonderful ice cream sundaes round out the menu. [$] *Average main: €19* ✉ *Rue de la République, Gustavia* ☎ *0590/27–72–48* ⊗ *Closed Sun. in June.*

$$$ 🍴 **Les Bananiers.** *French.* Ask the locals where to eat, and they will surely recommend this casual spot in Colombier adjacent to a wonderful bakery. The food is classic French, the service is warm, the prices are gentle, and you can eat in or take out. Choose from dishes like grilled duck breast, classic escargots in garlic butter, pizza, or fresh fish. The classic fish soup is a favorite. [$] *Average main: €23* ✉ *Rte. de Columbier, Colombier* ☎ *0590/27–93–48.*

★ **Fodor's Choice** 🍴 **L'Isola.** *Italian.* St. Barth's chic sister to the
$$$ Santa Monica (California) favorite, Via Veneto, packs in happy guests for classic Italian dishes, dozens of house-made pasta dishes, prime meats, and the huge, well-chosen wine list. Restaurateur Fabrizio Bianconi wants it all to feel like a big Italian party, and with all the celebrating you can hear at dinner in this pretty and romantic room, it sure sounds like he succeeded. Favorite dishes include a hearty veal chop in a sage-butter sauce, and heavenly risotto with either wild mushrooms or wild boar. [$] *Average main: €27* ✉ *33 Rue du Roi Oscar II, Gustavia* ☎ *0590/51–00–05* 🌐 *www.lisolastbarth.com* ✍ *Reservations essential* ⊗ *Closed Sept. and Oct.*

$ 🍴 **L'Isoletta.** *Pizza.* New in 2012, this casual Roman-style pizzeria run by the popular L'Isola restaurant is a chic lounge-style gastropub serving delicious thin-crust pizzas by the slice or by the meter. Lasagnas and sandwiches are also available to eat in or take out. Stop in anytime as they are open from lunch straight through until 11 pm. Don't miss the dessert pizzas. [$] *Average main: €10* ✉ *Rue du Roi Oscar II, Gustavia* ☎ *0590/52–02–02* 🌐 *www.lisolettastbarth.com* ✍ *Reservations not accepted.*

$$$$ 🍴 **Maya's.** *French.* New Englander Randy Gurley and his wife Maya (the French-born chef) provide returning guests with a warm welcome and a very pleasant albeit expensive dinner on their cheerful dock decorated with big, round tables and crayon-color canvas chairs, all overlooking Gustavia Harbor. A market inspired menu of good, simply prepared and garnished dishes—like roasted quail and Indian-spiced fish—changes daily, assuring the ongoing popularity of a restaurant that seems to be on everyone's

list of favorites. [$] *Average main: €39* ✉ *Public, Gustavia* ☎ *0590/27–75–73* 🌐 *www.mayas-stbarth.com* ✍ *Reservations essential* ⏲ *Closed Sun.*

$$$ ✕ **Ocean.** *Seafood.* New in 2013, this romantic and delicious seafood restaurant is family-run and features fresh-caught local fish and attentive, friendly service. Plates are distinctive, creative, refined, and beautifully presented—think a whole sea bass baked in a salt-pastry shell. There are also beautiful steaks on offer for non–fish lovers, and spectacular, classic French desserts to round out your meal. The daily prix fixe lunch menu, which includes a main course and dessert, ranges from €11 to €19; the choices are listed on their Facebook page. ■ **TIP→** Long-time visitors will fondly remember this as the charming old-St.=Barth-style space that once housed Le Sapotillier. [$] *Average main: €26* ✉ *13 Rue Samuel Falberg, Gustavia* ☎ *0590/52–45–31* ✍ *Reservations essential.*

$$$$ ✕ **Wall House.** *Eclectic.* There's a new chef at the helm of this steakhouse-style restaurant on the far side of Gustavia Harbor. Favorite dishes, such as the light-as-air gnocchi with pesto and the roasted duck marinated in honey, remain while others have been revised or replaced. Steaks are USDA Prime Angus beef, offered in sizes from "queen" to "emperor." There are vegetarian options too. Local businesspeople crowd the restaurant for the bargain €11 prix-fixe lunch menu (posted daily on their Facebook page), with classic dishes like duck-leg confit, but there are big salads too. For €18 the menu includes the main dish or salad of the day, coffee and petits fours, and a glass of wine or beer. An old-fashioned dessert trolley showcases yummy classic sweets. [$] *Average main: €33* ✉ *La Pointe, Gustavia* ☎ *0590/27–71–83* 🌐 *www.wallhouserestaurant.com* ✍ *Reservations essential* ⏲ *No lunch Sun.*

POINTE MILOU

★ **$$$$** Fodor's Choice ✕ **Le Ti St. Barth Caribbean Tavern.** *Eclectic.* Chef-owner Carole Gruson captures the funky, sexy spirit of the island in her wildly popular hilltop hot spot. We always come here to dance to great music with the attractive crowd lingering at the bar, lounge at one of the pillow-strewn banquettes, or chat on the torchlit terrace. By the time your appetizers arrive, you'll be best friends with the next table. Top-quality fish and meats are cooked on the traditional charcoal barbecue; big spenders will love the Angus beef filet Rossini with truffles, but there are lighter options like wok shrimp with Chinese noodles, and seared tuna with caviar. Provocatively named desserts, such as Nymph Thighs (airy lemon cake with vanilla custard), Daddy's Balls (passion-fruit sorbet and ice cream), and Sweet Thai Massage (kiwi, pineapple, mango, and lychee salad) end the meal on a fun note. Around this time someone is sure to be dancing on top of the tables. There's an extensive wine list. The famously raucous full-moon parties, cabarets, and Monday's "Plastic Boots" Ladies' Night are all legendary. [$] *Average main: €53* ✉ *Pointe Milou* ☎ *0590/27–97–71* 🌐 *www.letistbarth.com* ✍ *Reservations essential* ⏲ *Closed Sun. and Mon.*

3

ST-JEAN

$$$$ ✕ **La Plage.** *French.* Beachfront dining in quintessential St. Barth style is spot-on at this eatery in the Tom Beach Hotel. Passion-fruit martinis are a must, as is the fresh-caught grilled spiny lobsters and roasted beet "carpaccio." There are beach lounges for daytime, and music all day long. It's a prime spot for people-watching and all the action on Plage de St-Jean. Check local papers for special events like the Full Moon White Party or Saturday Bikini Brunch. [$] *Average main: €36* ✉ *Tom Beach Hotel, Plage de St-Jean* ☎ *0590/27–53–13* 🌐 *www.tombeach.com.*

★ **$$$$** **Fodor's Choice** ✕ **The Sand Bar.** *Eclectic.* At this Eden Rock Hotel eatery, lunch on the terrace with the beautiful blue water sparkling beyond is incomparable. Star chef Jean-Georges Vongerichten's cuisine is tailored to the setting and the ambience—you'll find all the things you would expect to be tempted to eat at the beach. Delicious light salads, soups, and carpaccio are menu highlights, but there are also heartier salads with fish and chicken, and simple grilled fish and meat entrees. The wood-oven pizzas are delicious—try the fontina and truffle option. Beautiful and delicious desserts include the chocolate and lemon tart dessert. And, there's brunch on Sunday. You can be sure of world-class people-watching opportunities at the The Sand Bar—you never know who'll be checking out a menu next to you. [$] *Average main: €32* ✉ *Eden Rock Hotel, Baie de St-Jean* ☎ *0590/29–79–99* 🌐 *www.edenrockhotel.com* ✍ *Reservations essential.*

WHERE TO STAY

There's no denying that hotel rooms and villas on St. Barth carry high prices. You're paying primarily for the privilege of staying on the island, and even at $800 a night the bedrooms tend to be small. Still, if you're flexible—in terms of timing and in your choice of lodgings—you can enjoy a holiday in St. Barth and still afford to send the kids to college.

The most expensive season falls during the holidays (mid-December to early January), when hotels are booked far in advance, may require a 10- or 14-day stay, and can be double the high-season rates. A 5% government tourism tax on room prices (excluding breakfast) is in effect; be sure to ask if it is included in your room rate or added on.

When it comes to booking a hotel on St. Barth, the reservation manager can be your best ally. Rooms within a property can vary greatly. It's well worth the price of a phone call or the time investment of an email correspondence to make a personal connection, which can mean a lot when it comes to arranging a room that meets your needs or preferences. Details of accessibility, views, recent redecorating, meal options, and special package rates are topics open for discussion. Quoted hotel rates are per room, not per person, and include service charges and, often, airport transfers. Bargain rates found on Internet booking sites can sometimes yield unpleasant surprises in terms of the actual room you get. Consider contacting the hotel about a reservation and mentioning the rate you found. Often they will match it, and you'll end up with a better room.

VILLAS AND CONDOMINIUMS

On St. Barth the term *villa* is used to describe anything from a small cottage to a luxurious, modern estate. Today almost half of St. Barth's accommodations are in villas, and we recommend considering this option, especially if you're traveling with friends or family. Ever more advantageous to Americans, villa rates are usually quoted in dollars, thus bypassing unfavorable euro fluctuations. Most villas have a small private swimming pool and maid service daily except Sunday. They are well furnished with linens, kitchen utensils, and such electronic playthings as CD and DVD players, satellite TV, and broadband Internet. Weekly in-season rates range from $1,400 to "OMG." Most villa-rental companies are based in the United States and have extensive websites that allow you to see pictures

St. Barth's Spas

Visitors to St. Barth can enjoy more than the comforts of home by taking advantage of any of the myriad spa and beauty treatments that are available on the island. The major hotels, the Isle de France, the Guanahani, and Le Christopher, have beautiful, comprehensive, on-site spas. Others, including the Hôtel le Village St-Jean, Le Sereno, and Le Toiny, have added spa cottages, where treatments and services can be arranged on-site. Depending on availability, all visitors to the island can book services at all of these. In addition, scores of independent therapists will come to your hotel room or villa and provide any therapeutic discipline you can think of, including yoga, Thai massage, shiatsu, reflexology, and even manicures, pedicures, and hairdressing. You can get up-to-date recommendations at the tourist office in Gustavia.

or panoramic videos of the place you're renting; their local offices oversee maintenance and housekeeping and provide concierge services to clients. Just be aware that there are few beachfront villas, so if you have your heart set on "toes in the sand" and a cute waiter delivering your Kir Royale, stick with the hotels or villas operated by hotel properties.

VILLA RENTAL CONTACTS

Marla. This local St. Barth villa-rental company represents more than 100 villas, many of which are not listed with other companies. ⊠ *Rue du Roi Oscar II, Gustavia* ☎ *0590/27–62–02* ⊕ *www.marlavillas.com.*

St. Barth Properties, Inc. Owned by American Peg Walsh—a regular on St. Barth since 1986, St. Barth Properties, Inc. represents more than 120 properties and can guide you to the perfect place to stay. Weekly peak-season rates range, depending on the property's size, location, and amenities. The excellent website offers virtual tours of most of the villas and even details of availability. An office in Gustavia can take care of any problems you may have and offers some concierge-type services. ⊠ *Gustavia* ☎ *508/528–7727, 800/421–3396* ⊕ *www.stbarth.com.*

Wimco. Based in Rhode Island, Wimco oversees bookings for more than 230 properties on St. Barth. Rents range from $2,000 to $10,000 for two- and three-bedroom villas; larger villas rent for $7,000 per week and up. Properties can be previewed and reserved on Wimco's website (which occasionally lists last-minute specials). There are even interactive floor plans, so you can see exactly what you will be getting, or you can obtain a catalog by mail. The company will arrange babysitters, massages, chefs, and other in-villa services for clients, as well as private air charters. ☎ *800/932–3222* 🌐 *www.wimco.com.*

ANSE DE TOINY

★ Fodor's Choice **Hôtel Le Toiny.** *Hotel.* The privacy, serenity, and
$$$$ personalized service please the international-mogul set. It's remote, but you never have to leave if you don't want to. **Pros:** extremely private; luxurious rooms; flawless service; environmental awareness. **Cons:** not on the beach; isolated (at least half an hour's drive from town). $ *Rooms from: €1350* ✉ *Anse de Toiny* ☎ *0590/27–88–88* 🌐 *www.letoiny.com* 🛏 *14 1-bedroom villas, 1 3-bedroom villa* ⏲ *Closed Sept.–late Oct.* 🍴 *Breakfast.*

COLOMBIER

$ **Le P'tit Morne.** *B&B/Inn.* Each of the modestly furnished but clean and freshly decorated, painted mountainside studios has a private balcony with panoramic views of the coastline. **Pros:** reasonable rates; great area for hiking. **Cons:** rooms are basic; remote location. $ *Rooms from: €204* ✉ *Colombier* ☎ *0590/52–95–50* 🌐 *www.timorne.com/fr* 🛏 *14 rooms* 🍴 *Breakfast.*

FLAMANDS

$$$ **Hôtel Baie des Anges.** *Hotel.* Everyone is treated like fam-
FAMILY ily at this casual retreat with 10 clean, spacious units, two of which are brand-new, two-bedroom oceanfront suites. **Pros:** on St. Barth's longest beach; family-friendly; excellent value. **Cons:** the area is a bit remote from the town areas, necessitating a car. $ *Rooms from: €385* ✉ *Anse des Flamands* ☎ *0590/27–63–61* 🌐 *www.hotel-baie-des-anges.com* 🛏 *10 rooms* ⏲ *Closed Sept.* 🍴 *No meals.*

★ Fodor's Choice **Hotel St-Barth Isle de France.** *Resort.* An obses-
$$$$ sively attentive management team ensures that this intimate, casual, refined resort remains among the very best accommodations in St. Barth—if not the entire Caribbean. **Pros:** prime beach location; terrific management; great spa; excellent restaurant. **Cons:** you will definitely want a car to get around; unfortunately, the day will come when

you will have to leave this paradise. $ *Rooms from: €725* ✉ *B.P. 612 Baie des Flamands, Flamands* ☎ *0590/27–61–81* 🌐 *www.isle-de-france.com* 🛏 *32 rooms, 2 villas* ⏲ *Closed Sept.–mid-Oct.* 🍴 *Breakfast.*

★ $$$$ FAMILY Fodor's Choice **Hotel Taïwana.** *Resort.* This classic island retreat reopened in 2012 under new management to the delight of the young, international guests who appreciate the spiffy updates to the spacious rooms and suites clustered around a charming atrium garden. **Pros:** newly renovated; busy social scene; great beach access. **Cons:** maybe too scene-y for some; every room is different, so choose carefully. $ *Rooms from: €538* ✉ *Baie des Flamands, Anse des Flamands* ☎ *0590/29–80–08* 🌐 *www.hoteltaiwana.com* 🛏 *7 rooms, 15 suites* 🍴 *Breakfast.*

GRAND CUL DE SAC

★ $$$$ FAMILY Fodor's Choice **Hotel Guanahani and Spa.** *Resort.* The largest full-service resort on the island has lovely rooms and suites (14 of which have private pools) and impeccable personalized service, not to mention one of the island's only children's programs (though it's more of a nursery). **Pros:** fantastic spa; beachside sports; family-friendly; great service. **Cons:** lots of walking all around the property; steep walk to beach. $ *Rooms from: €646* ✉ *Grand Cul de Sac* ☎ *0590/52–90–00* 🌐 *www.leguanahani.com* 🛏 *36 suites, 31 rooms* ⏲ *Closed Sept.* 🍴 *Breakfast.*

$$$ FAMILY **Hotel Les Ondines Sur La Plage.** *Rental.* Right on the beach of Grand Cul de Sac, this reasonably priced, intimate gem comprises modern, comfortable apartments with room to really spread out. **Pros:** spacious beachfront apartments; close to restaurants and water sports; pool; airport transfers. **Cons:** not a resort; beach is narrow in front of the property; will need a car to get around. $ *Rooms from: €425* ✉ *Grand Cul de Sac* ☎ *0590/27–69–64* 🌐 *www.stbarth-lesondineshotel.com* 🛏 *6 rooms* 🍴 *Breakfast.*

★ $$$$ Fodor's Choice **Le Sereno.** *Resort.* Those seeking a restorative, sensous escape will discover true nirvana at the quietly elegant, aptly named Le Sereno, set on a beachy cove of turquoise sea, between the island's highest mountain and the foamy waves. **Pros:** romantic rooms; beach location; superchic comfort; friendly atmosphere. **Cons:** no a/c in bathrooms; some construction planned for this part of the island over the next few years. $ *Rooms from: €730* ✉ *B.P. 19 Grand Cul de Sac* ☎ *0590/29–83–00* 🌐 *www.lesereno.com* 🛏 *37 suites and villas* 🍴 *Multiple meal plans.*

GRANDE SALINE

$ 🏨 **Salines Garden Cottages.** *Rental.* Budget-conscious beach lovers who don't require a lot of coddling need look no further than these petite garden cottages, a short stroll from what is arguably St. Barth's best beach. **Pros:** only property walkable to Anse de Grande Saline; quiet; reasonable rates. **Cons:** far from town; not very private; strict cancellation policy. [$] *Rooms from: €160* ✉ *Grand Saline* ☎ *0590/51–04–44* 🌐 *www.salinesgarden.com* 🛏 *5 cottages* 🕒 *Closed mid-Aug.–mid-Oct.* 🍴 *Breakfast.*

GUSTAVIA

$ 🏨 **Sunset Hotel.** *Hotel.* Ten simple, utilitarian rooms (one can accommodate three people) right in Gustavia sit across from the harbor and offer an economical and handy, if not luxurious option for those who want to stay in town. **Pros:** reasonable rates; in town. **Cons:** no elevator; not resort-like in any way. [$] *Rooms from: €110* ✉ *Rue de la République, Gustavia* ☎ *0590/27–77–21* 🌐 *www.saint-barths.com/sunset-hotel* 🛏 *10 rooms* 🍴 *No meals.*

LORIENT

$ 🏨 **Les Mouettes.** *Rental.* This guesthouse offers clean, simply FAMILY furnished, and economical bungalows that open directly onto the beach. **Pros:** right on the beach; family-friendly. **Cons:** rooms are basic; right near the road; strict prepayment and cancellation policies; no pool; no TV. [$] *Rooms from: €150* ✉ *Anse de Lorient* ☎ *0590/27–77–91* 🌐 *www.lesmouetteshotel.com* 🛏 *7 bungalows* 💳 *No credit cards* 🍴 *No meals.*

$ 🏨 **Normandie Hotel.** *B&B/Inn.* The immaculate rooms here are small but stylish, and there's nothing on the island at this price range that compares. **Pros:** friendly management; pleasant atmosphere; good value. **Cons:** tiny rooms; small bathrooms. [$] *Rooms from: €135* ✉ *Lorient* ☎ *0590/27–61–66* 🌐 *www.normandiehotelstbarts.com* 🛏 *8 rooms (7 doubles, 1 single)* 🍴 *Breakfast.*

POINTE MILOU

$$$$ 🏨 **Christopher.** *Resort.* This longtime favorite of European FAMILY families delivers a high standard of courteous professionalism and personalized service. **Pros:** comfortable elegance; family-friendly; reasonable price. **Cons:** resort is directly on the water but not on a beach; three-night minimum stay.

§ *Rooms from: €480* ⊠ *Pointe Milou* ☎ *0590/27–63–63*
⊕ *www.hotelchristopher.com* ⇆ *42 rooms* ⊙ *Closed Sept.–mid-Oct.* ❍ *Breakfast.*

ST-JEAN

★ **Fodor's** Choice ⊞ **Eden Rock.** *Resort.* Even on an island known
$$$$ for gourmet cuisine and luxury hotels, this iconic property
FAMILY stands out—thanks to its two Jean-Georges Vongerichten
eateries, spacious rooms, stunning bay views, and cosseting
service. **Pros:** two Vongerichten-overseen restaurants; chic
clientele; beach setting; stylish facilities; walk to shopping
and restaurants. **Cons:** some suites are noisy because of
proximity to street. § *Rooms from: €715* ⊠ *Baie de St-Jean* ☎ *0590/29–79–99, 877/563–7015 in U.S.* ⊕ *www.edenrockhotel.com* ⇆ *32 rooms, 2 villas* ⊙ *Closed Aug. 29–Oct. 17* ❍ *Breakfast.*

★ **Fodor's** Choice ⊞ **Emeraude Plage.** *Hotel.* Right on the Plage de
$$$ St-Jean, this petite resort consists of small but immaculate
FAMILY bungalows and villas with modern, fully equipped outdoor
kitchens on small private patios. **Pros:** beachfront and in-town location; good value; cool kitchens on each porch.
Cons: smallish rooms. § *Rooms from: €405* ⊠ *Baie de St-Jean* ☎ *0590/27–64–78* ⊕ *www.emeraudeplage.com* ⇆ *28 bungalows* ⊙ *Closed Sept.–mid-Oct.* ❍ *No meals.*

★ **Fodor's** Choice ⊞ **Hôtel le Village St. Barth.** *Hotel.* You get the
$$ advantages of a villa and the services of a hotel at Hôtel
FAMILY Le Village, where for two generations the Charneau fam-ily has offered friendly service and reasonable rates, mak-ing guests feel like a part of the family. **Pros:** great value;
convenient location; wonderful management; friendly cli-entele. **Cons:** a walk up a steep hill to the hotel; can be
noisy, depending on how close your room is to the street
below. § *Rooms from: €280* ⊠ *Colline de St-Jean* ☎ *0590/27–61–39, 800/651–8366* ⊕ *www.villagestjeanhotel.com* ⇆ *5 rooms, 20 cottages, 1 3-bedroom villa, 2 2-bedroom villas* ❍ *Breakfast.*

$$ ⊞ **Le Tom Beach Hôtel.** *Hotel.* This chic but casual boutique
hotel right on busy St-Jean beach is fun for social types,
and the nonstop house party often spills out onto the ter-races and lasts into the wee hours. **Pros:** party central at
beach, restaurant, and pool; in-town location. **Cons:** trendy
social scene is not for everybody, especially light sleepers.
§ *Rooms from: €320* ⊠ *Plage de St-Jean* ☎ *0590/52–81–20*
⊕ *www.tombeach.com* ⇆ *12 rooms* ❍ *Breakfast.*

$$$ 🏠 **Les Îlets de la Plage.** *Rental.* FAMILY On the far side of the airport, tucked away at the far corner of Baie de St-Jean, these well-priced, comfortably furnished, island-style one-, two-, and three-bedroom bungalows (four right on the beach, seven up a small hill) have small kitchens, pleasant open-air sitting areas, and comfortable bathrooms. **Pros:** beach location; apartment conveniences; front porches. **Cons:** TVs by request only and offer limited French programming; a/c only in bedrooms; right next to the airport. [$] *Rooms from: €460* ✉ *Plage de St-Jean* ☎ *0590/27–88–57* 🌐 *www.lesilets.com* 🛏 *11 bungalows* 🕒 *Closed Sept.–Nov. 1* 🍴 *No meals.*

WORD OF MOUTH

"We've seen up and down nightlife in Gustavia and St-Jean in March and April, better experiences in June, late September/October, and November. Depends who and what fancy boats are in dock and whether the jet set are partying publicly or privately. Some nights the bars can be a snooze, other times packed and Bohemian."

—Mathieu

NIGHTLIFE

Most of the nightlife in St. Barth is centered on Gustavia, though there are a few places to go outside of town. "In" clubs change from season to season, so you might ask around for the hot spot of the moment, but none really get going until about midnight. Theme parties are the current trend. Check the daily *St. Barth News* or *Le Journal de Saint-Barth* for details. A late reservation (10 pm or later) at one of the club-restaurants will eventually become a front-row seat at a party. *Saint-Barth Collector Guest Book* contains current information about sports, spas, nightlife, and the arts.

GUSTAVIA

Bar de l'Oubli. This is where young locals gather for drinks. Bring cash, they don't accept plastic. ✉ *Rue du Roi Oscar II, Gustavia* ☎ *0590/27–70–06.*

Le Repaire. This restaurant lures a crowd for cocktail hour and its pool table. ✉ *Rue de la République, Gustavia* ☎ *0590/27–72–48.*

Le Sélect. This is St. Barth's original hangout, commemorated by Jimmy Buffett's song "Cheeseburger in Paradise." The boisterous garden is where the barefoot boating set gathers for a cold Carib beer, at prices somewhat lower than usual. ⊠ *Rue du Centenaire, Gustavia* ☎ *0590/27–86–87.*

Le Yacht Club. Although ads call it a private club, dress right and you can probably get in to this hot spot anyway. Nothing much happens 'til midnight, when the terrific DJs get things going. Check the local papers for details of special parties. Above the Yacht Club you'll find one of the island's newest hotspots, The First Floor, where there are tapas, drinks, and music. Check the club's Facebook page or local papers for details of current events. ⊠ *Rue Jeanne d'Arc, Gustavia* ☎ *0690/49–23–33* ⊕ *www.caroleplaces.com.*

ST-JEAN

Le Nikki Beach. This place rocks on weekends during lunch—especially Sunday afternoons—when the scantily clad young and beautiful lounge on the white canvas banquettes. ⊠ *St-Jean* ☎ *0590/27–64–64* ⊕ *www.nikkibeach.com.*

SHOPPING

★ **Fodor's Choice** St. Barth is a duty-free port, and with its sophisticated crowd of visitors, shopping in the island's 200-plus boutiques is a definite delight, especially for beachwear, accessories, jewelry, and casual wear. It would be no overstatement to say that shopping for fashionable clothing, jewels, and designer accessories is better in St. Barth than anywhere else in the Caribbean. New shops open all the time, so there's always something to discover. Some stores close for lunch from noon to 3, but they are open until 7 in the evening. A popular afternoon pastime is strolling about the two major shopping areas in Gustavia and St-Jean.

In Gustavia, boutiques line the three major shopping streets. Quai de la République, which is right on the harbor, rivals New York's Madison Avenue or Paris's avenue Montaigne for high-end designer retail, including shops for **Louis Vuitton, Bulgari, Cartier, Chopard, Eres,** and **Hermès.** These shops often carry items that are not available in the United States. The elegant Carré d'Or plaza is great fun to explore. Shops are also clustered in **La Savane Commercial Center** (across from the airport), **La Villa Créole** (in St-Jean), and **Espace Neptune** (on the road to Lorient). It's worth working your way from one end to the other at these shopping complexes—just to see or, perhaps, be seen. Boutiques in all three areas carry the latest in French and Italian sportswear and some haute couture. Bargains may be tough to come by, but you might be able to snag that *Birkin* that has a long waiting list stateside, and in any case, you'll have a lot of fun hunting around.

If you are looking for locally made art and handicrafts, call the tourist office, which can provide information, and arrange visits to the studios of some of the island artists, including Christian Bretoneiche, Robert Danet, Nathalie Daniel, Patricia Guyot, Rose Lemen, Aline de Lurin, and Marion Vinot. A few good gallery/craft boutiques are also scattered around Gustavia, Villa Créole, and the larger hotels.

ANSE DE TOINY

HANDICRAFTS

Chez Pompi. Chez Pompi is little more than a cottage whose first room is a gallery for the naive paintings of Pompi (also known as Louis Ledée). ⊠ *Rte. de Toiny, Petit Cul de Sac* ☎ *0590/29–76–90.*

GRAND CUL DE SAC

LIQUOR AND TOBACCO

La Cave de Saint-Barths. For more than 30 years, this cellar has maintained its excellent collection of French vintages and small-production rums in temperature-controlled cellars. ⊠ *Marigot* ☎ *0590/27–63–21.*

GUSTAVIA

ART GALLERIES

Le P'tit Collectionneur. Encouraged by his family and friends, André Berry opened his private museum in early 2007 to showcase his lifelong passion for collecting fascinating objects such as 18th-century English pipes and the first phonograph to come to the island. He will happily show you his treasures. ⊠ *La Pointe, Gustavia* ☎ €2 ⊗ *Mon.–Sat. 10–noon and 4–6.*

BOOKS

Clic Bookstore and Gallery. This bookstore is an island outpost of the SoHo NYC and Hamptons concept gallery–bookstore devoted to books on photography and monthly exhibits of fine modern photography. It's the brainchild of

Calypso founder Christine Celle. ⊠ *Rue de la République, Gustavia* ☎ *0590/29–70–17* ⊕ *www.clicgallery.com.*

La Case Aux Livres. This is a full-service bookstore and newsstand with hundreds of English titles for adults and kids. Booklovers can follow their blog to learn about author appearances. ⊠ *Quai de la République, 9 Rue de la République, Gustavia* ☎ *0590/27–15–88* ⊕ *lacaseauxlivres.over-blog.com.*

CLOTHING

Bamboo St. Barth. Beach fashions like cotton tunics, cocktails-on-the-yacht dresses, and sexy Australian swimsuits by Nicole Olivier and Seafolly, can be paired with sassy sandals and costume jewelry. ⊠ *Pélican Beach, St-Jean* ☎ *0590/52–08–82.*

Black Swan. This shop has an unparalleled selection of bathing suits for men, women, and children. The wide range of styles and sizes is appreciated. They also have souvenir-appropriate island logo-wear and whatever beach equipment you might require. ⊠ *Le Carré d'Or, Gustavia* ☎ *0590/52–48–30.*

Boutique Lacoste. This store has a huge selection of the once-again-chic alligator-logo wear, as well as a shop next door with a complete selection of the Petit Bateau line of T-shirts popular with teens. ⊠ *Rue du Bord de Mer, Gustavia* ☎ *0590/27–66–90.*

Calypso. This well-known retailer carries sophisticated, sexy resort wear and accessories by Balenciaga, Chloe, and D Squared, among others. ⊠ *Le Carré d'Or, Gustavia* ☎ *0590/27–69–74* ⊕ *www.saint-barths.com/calypso.*

Hermès. The Hermès store in St. Barth is an independently owned franchise, and prices are slightly below those in the States. ⊠ *Rue de la République, Gustavia* ☎ *0590/27–66–15.*

Human Steps. Two boutiques, one for women and one for men, have a well-edited selection of chic shoes and leather accessories from names like YSL, Prada, Balenciaga, Miu Miu, and Jimmy Choo. ⊠ *39 Rue de la République, Gustavia* ☎ *0590/27–93–79* ⊕ *www.human-steps.fr.*

Kokon. This boutique offers a nicely edited mix of designs for on-island or off, including the bo'em, Lotty B. Mustique, and Day Birger lines, and cute shoes to go with them by Heidi Klum for Birkenstock. ⊠ *Rue Samuel Fahlberg, Gustavia* ☎ *0590/29–74–48.*

Shops on rue de la France, Gustavia

La Chemise Tropezienne. Beautiful tailored cotton shirts in fun prints and stripes for men and women, and colorful Bermuda shorts to coordinate, are popular in St-Tropez and St. Barth. ⊠ *Le Carré d'Or, Gustavia* ☎ *0590/27–54–33* ⊕ *www.be-shorts.com.*

Linde Gallery. Linde sells vintage sunglasses, accessories, vintage ready-to-wear from the 1970s and '80s, as well as books, CDs, and DVDs. ⊠ *Les Hauts de Carré d'Or, Gustavia* ☎ *0590/29–73–86* ⊕ *www.lindegallery.com.*

Linen. This shop offers tailored linen shirts for men in a rainbow of soft colors, and their soft slip-on driving mocs in classic styles are a St. Barth must. ⊠ *Rue Lafayette, Gustavia* ☎ *0590/27–54–26.*

Lolita Jaca. Don't miss this store for trendy, tailored sportswear. ⊠ *Le Carré d'Or, Gustavia* ☎ *0590/27–59–98* ⊕ *www. lolitajaca.com.*

Longchamp. Fans of the popular travel bags, handbags, and leather goods will find a good selection at about 20% off stateside prices. ⊠ *Rue du Général de Gaulle, Gustavia* ☎ *0590/51–96–50.*

Mademoiselle Hortense. Shop for cute tops and dresses for the young and young at heart in pretty Liberty prints, which are made right on the island. You'll also find great crafty bracelets and necklaces to accent your new styles. ⊠ *Rue de la République, Gustavia* ☎ *0590/27–13–29.*

Marina St. Barth. A great spot for the typical sexy resort-wear worn by the young and the beautiful on the island. If you forgot your floaty beachwear, you can stop here. Lines include Ondade, Façonnable, and Caffé. ⊠ *Rue du Roi Oscar II, Gustavia* ☎ *0590/29–37–30* ⊕ *www.marina-stbarth.com.*

Pati de Saint Barth. This is the largest of the three shops that stock the chic, locally made T-shirts, totes, and beach wraps that have practically become the logo of St. Barth. The newest styles have hand-done graffiti-style lettering. The shop also has some handicrafts and other giftable items. ⊠ *Rue du Bord de Mer, Gustavia* ☎ *0590/29–78–04* ⊕ *www.madeinstbarth.com.*

Poupette St. Barth. All the brilliant color-crinkle silk, chiffon batik, and embroidered peasant skirts and tops are designed by the owner. There also are great belts and beaded bracelets. A new outpost is at Hotel Taïwana. ⊠ *Rue de la République, Gustavia* ☎ *0590/27–55–78* ⊕ *www. poupettestbarth.com.*

Saint-Barth Stock Exchange. On the far side of Gustavia Harbor is the island's consignment and discount shop. It's a blast to explore. ⊠ *La Pointe-Gustavia, Gustavia* ☎ *0590/27–68–12.*

Stéphane & Bernard. This store stocks a large, well-edited selection of superstar French fashion designers, including Rykiel, Missoni, Valentino, Versaci, Ungaro, Christian Lacroix, and Eres beachwear. ⊠ *Rue de la République, Gustavia* ☎ *0590/27–65–69* ⊕ *www.stephaneandbernard.com.*

St. Tropez KIWI. Look to this popular boutique in St-Jean for resort wear for every member of the family. ⊠ *Villa Creole, St-Jean* ☎ *0590/27–57–08.*

Vanita Rosa. This store showcases beautiful lace and linen sundresses and peasant tops, with accessories galore, as well as some very cool designer vintage. ⊠ *Rue du Roi Oscar II, Gustavia* ☎ *0590/52–43–25* ⊕ *www.vanitarosa.com.*

Victoire. Classic, well-made sportswear in luxurious fabrics and great colors, with a French twist on preppy, will please shoppers eager for finds that will play as well in Nantucket or Greenwich as they do on St. Barth. There is even a small sidewalk cafe with Wi-Fi if you need a pick-me-up or a simple lunch. ⊠ *Rue du Général de Gaulle, Gustavia* ☎ *0590/29–84–60* ⊕ *www.victoire-paris.com.*

FOODSTUFFS

A.M.C. This supermarket is a bit older than Marché U in St-Jean but able to supply nearly anything you might need for housekeeping in a villa or for a picnic. ⊠ *Quai de la République, Gustavia.*

La Rotisserie. For exotic groceries, dinner at your villa, or picnic fixings, stop by St. Barth's gourmet *traiteur* (take-out shop) for salads, prepared meats, groceries from Fauchon, and Iranian caviar. ⊠ *Rue du Roi Oscar II, Gustavia* ☎ *0590/27–63–13.*

HANDICRAFTS

Fabienne Miot. Look for unusual and artistic jewelry featuring rare stones and natural pearls at this shop. ⊠ *Rue de la République, Gustavia* ☎ *0590/27–73–13* ⊕ *www.saint-barths.com/fabiennemiot.*

French Indies Design. This beautiful shop on the far side of Gustavia Harbor is the brainchild of Karine Bruneel, a St. Barth-based architect and interior designer. There are lovely items to accent your home (or yacht) including furniture, textiles, glassware, and unusual decorative baskets, candles, and pottery. ⊠ *Maison Suédoise, Gustavia* ☎ *0590/29–66–38* ⊕ *www.frenchindiesdesign.fr.*

Kalinas Perles. Beautiful freshwater pearls are knotted onto the classic St. Barth–style leather thongs by artist Jeremy Albaledejo, who also showcases other artisans' works in a gallery-like setting. ⊠ *23 Rue du Général de Gaulle, Gustavia* ☎ *690/65–93–00.*

JEWELRY

Bijoux de la Mer. This store carries beautiful and artistic jewelry made of South Sea pearls in wonderful hues strung in clusters on leather to wrap around the neck or arms. ⊠ *Rue de la République, Gustavia* ☎ *0590/52–37–68* ⊕ *www.bijouxdelamerstbarth.com.*

Carat. Carat has Chaumet and a large selection of Breitling watches, plus rarities by Richard Mille and Breguet. ⊠ *Rue de la République, Gustavia* ☎ *0590/27–67–22* ⊕ *www.caratsaintbarth.com.*

Cartier. For fine jewelry, visit this branch of the famous jeweler. ⊠ *Quai de la République, Gustavia.*

Diamond Genesis. A good selection of watches, including Patek Phillippe and Chanel, can be found at this store. Pendants and charms in the shape of the island are a popular purchase. ⊠ *Rue du Général de Gaulle, Gustavia* ☎ *0590/27–66–94* ⊕ *www.diamondgenesis.com.*

Donna del Sol. Designer Donna del Sol carries beautiful handmade gold chains, Tahitian pearl pieces, and baubles in multicolor diamonds of her own designs. Have something special in mind? She'll work with clients to design and produce custom items. ⊠ *Quai de la République, Gustavia* ☎ *0590/27–90–53* ⊕ *www.donnadelsol.com.*

Sindbad. This tiny shop, an island favorite since 1977, curates funky, unique couture fashion jewelry by Gaz Bijou of St-Tropez, crystal collars for your pampered pooch, and other reasonably priced, up-to-the-minute styles. Current favorites are the south-sea pearls strung on leather thongs or colorful silky cords. ⊠ *Le Carré d'Or, Gustavia* ☎ *0590/27–52–29* ⊕ *www.sindbad-st-barth.com.*

Time St. Barth. Specializing in exclusive watches by Girard Perregaux, Bell & Ross, Jacquet Droz, Omega, Gérard Genta, Swatch, Technomarine, Hublot, Sector, Redline, Panagonda, and Welder. ⊠ *Rue de la République, Gustavia,* ☎ *0590/27–99–10.*

LIQUOR AND TOBACCO

M'Bolo. Be sure to sample the varieties of infused rums, including lemongrass, ginger, and the island favorite, vanilla. Bring some home some in beautiful hand-blown bottles. Chefs will like the selection of Laguiole knives, and the local spices too. ⊠ *Rue du Général de Gaulle, Gustavia* ☎ *0590/27–90–54.*

LORIENT

COSMETICS

St. Barth Spa. Don't miss the superb skin-care products made on site from local tropical plants by this St. Barth company. Call in advance to request personal visits from the beauticians or therapists at your villa or yacht. ⊠ *Rte. de Saline, Lorient* ☎ *0590/27–82–63* ⊕ *www.lignestbarth.com.*

FOODSTUFFS

JoJo Supermarché. JoJo is the well-stocked counterpart to
Gustavia's large supermarket and gets daily deliveries of
bread and fresh produce. JoJoBurger, next door is the
local surfers' favorite spot for a (very good) quick burger.
⊠ *Lorient* ☎ *0590/27–63–53.*

ST-JEAN

CLOTHING

Black Swan. Black Swan has an unparalleled selection of
bathing suits. The wide range of styles and sizes is appreciated. ⊠ *La Villa Créole, St-Jean* ☎ *0590/52–48–30* ⊕ *www.
blackswanstbarth.com.*

Iléna. This boutique has incredible beachwear and lingerie
by Chantal Thomas, Sarda, and others, including Swarovski
crystal–encrusted bikinis for the young and gorgeous. ⊠ *La
Villa Creole, St-Jean* ☎ *0590/29–84–05.*

Lili Belle. Check out Lili Belle for a nice selection of
wearable and current styles. ⊠ *Pélican Plage, St-Jean*
☎ *0590/87–46–14.*

Morgan. This shop has a line of popular casual wear in the
trendy vein. ⊠ *La Villa Créole, St-Jean* ☎ *0590/27–71–00.*

St. Tropez KIWI. Look to this popular boutique with two
branches (one in Gustavia and one in St-Jean) for resort
wear. ⊠ *3 rue de la Villa Créole, St-Jean* ☎ *0590/27–57–08.*

SUD SUD.ETC.Plage. This store stocks everything for the
beach: inflatables, mats, bags, and beachy shell jewelry, as
well as bikinis and gauzy cover-ups. ⊠ *Galeries du Commerce, St-Jean* ☎ *0590/27–90–56.*

FOODSTUFFS

La Rotisserie. For exotic groceries or picnic fixings, stop by
St. Barth's gourmet traiteur for salads, sandwiches, pre-
pared meats, groceries from Fauchon, and Iranian caviar.
⊠ *Centre Vaval, St-Jean* ☎ *0590/29–75–69.*

Marche U. This modern, fully stocked supermarket across
from the airport has a wide selection of French cheeses,
pâtés, cured meats, produce, fresh bread, wine, and
liquor. There is also a good selection of prepared foods
and organic grocery items. ⊠ *Face à l'aéroport, St-Jean*
☎ *0590/27–68–16.*

Maya's to Go. This is the place to go for prepared picnics, meals, salads, rotisserie chickens, and more from the kitchen of the popular restaurant in Gustavia. ⊠ *Galeries du Commerce, St-Jean* ☎ *0590/29–83–70* ⊕ *www.mayastogo. com* ⊙ *Closed Mon.*

HANDICRAFTS

Cabane St. Barth. Stocked with stenciled cotton, gauzy beach tops, and caftans (for all ages), this shop is open nonstop every day. ⊠ *Pelican Plage, St-Jean* ☎ *0590/51–21–02.*

Couleurs Provence. This store stocks beautiful, handcrafted, French-made items like jacquard table linens in brilliant colors; decorative tableware, including trays in which dried flowers and herbs are suspended; and the island home fragrance line by L'Occitane. ⊠ *Rte. de Saline, St-Jean* ☎ *0590/52–48–51.*

SPORTS AND ACTIVITIES

BOATING AND SAILING

St. Barth is a popular yachting and sailing center, thanks to its location midway between Antigua and St. Thomas. Gustavia's harbor, 13 to 16 feet deep, has mooring and docking facilities for 40 yachts. There are also good anchorages available at Public, Corossol, and Colombier. You can charter sailing and motorboats in Gustavia Harbor for as little as a half day, staffed or bare-boat. Stop at the tourist office in Gustavia, or ask at your hotel for an up-to-the minute list of recommended charter companies.

Carib Waterplay. On St. Jean beach for 30 years, Carib Waterplay let's you try windsurfing, kayaking, and stand-up paddling. They also have new waterbikes for rent and there are kids' windsurfing lessons, too. ⊠ *St-Jean* ☎ *0590/61–80–81* ⊕ *www.caribwaterplay.net.*

Jicky Marine Service. This company offers full-day outings, either on a variety of motorboats, Zodiacs, or 42- or 46-foot catamarans, to the uninhabited Île Fourchue for swimming, snorkeling, cocktails, and lunch. The cost starts at about $100 per person; an unskippered motor rental runs about $260 a day. ⊠ *26 rue Jeanne D'Arc, Gustavia* ☎ *0590/27–70–34* ⊕ *www.jickymarine.com.*

FAMILY **Yellow Submarine.** Go "six feet under" (the surface of the sea) for a one-hour, close-up view of St. Barth's coral reefs

Snorkeling at Anse à Colombier

through large glass portholes. It costs €40 for adults, €25 for children under 11. Trips depart daily, from the Ferry Dock in Gustavia with departures at 11 am and 2 pm, with Night Excursions Wednesday and Friday at 5:45 but more often depending on demand, so call first. ⊠ *Ferry Dock, Gustavia* ☎ *0590/52–40–51* ⊕ *www.yellow-submarine.fr*.

DIVING AND SNORKELING

Several dive shops arrange scuba excursions to local sites. Depending on weather conditions, you may dive at **Pain de Sucre, Coco Island,** or toward nearby **Saba.** There's also an underwater shipwreck to explore, plus sharks, rays, sea tortoises, coral, and the usual varieties of colorful fish. The waters on the island's leeward side are the calmest. For the uncertified who still want to see what the island's waters hold, there's an accessible shallow reef right off the beach at Anse de Cayes that you can explore if you have your own mask and fins, and a hike down the hill to the beach at Corossol brings you to a very popular snorkeling spot for locals.

FAMILY **Plongée Caraïbe.** This company is recommended for its up-to-the-minute equipment and dive boat. Their Scuba discovery program is very well regarded. They also run two-hour group snorkeling trips on the *Blue Cat Catamaran*; a half day is €40. ☎ *0590/27–55–94* ⊕ *www.plongee-caraibes.com*.

Réserve Marine de St-Barth. Most of the waters surrounding St. Barth are protected in the island's Réserve Marine de St-Barth, which also provides information at its office in Gustavia. The diving here isn't nearly as rich as in the more dive-centered destinations like Saba and St. Eustatius, but the options aren't bad either, and none of the smaller islands offer the ambience of St. Barth. ⊠ *Gustavia* ☎ *0590/27–88–18* ⊕ *www.reservenaturellestbarth.com.*

Splash. In Gustavia, Splash offers PADI and CMAS (Confederation Mondiale des Activites Subaquatiques—World Underwater Federation) courses in diver training at all levels. All the instructors speak French, Russian, and English. Although their boat normally leaves daily at 9 am, 11:30 am, 2 pm, and in the evening for a night dive, they will adjust their times to suit your preferences. They feature "seabob" scuba scooters. ⊠ *Gustavia* ☎ *0590/56–90–24* ⊕ *www.divestbarth.com.*

FISHING

Most fishing is done in the waters north of Lorient, Flamands, and Corossol. Popular catches are tuna, marlin, wahoo, and barracuda. There's an annual St. Barth Open Fishing Tournament, organized by Océan Must, in mid-July.

Jicky Marine Service. This private marina in the heart of Gustavia organizes catamaran day charters, champagne sunset sails, luxury motorboat day cruise, interisland transfer, bareboat sailboat rentals, diving, Jet Skiing, and more. ⊠ *Gustavia* ☎ *0590/27–70–34* ⊕ *www.jickymarine.com.*

Océan Must Marina. This outfitter arranges deep-sea fishing expeditions as well as bare boat and staffed boat charters. ⊠ *La Pointe, Gustavia* ☎ *0590/27–62–25* ⊕ *www. oceanmust.com.*

GUIDED TOURS

You can arrange island tours by minibus or car at hotel desks or through any of the island's taxi operators in Gustavia or at the airport. The tourist office runs a variety of tours with varying itineraries that run about €46 for a half day for up to eight people. You can also download up-to-the-minute walking and driving tour itineraries from the Tourist Board's website.

JC Taxi. Since 1986, native-born Jean-Claude has been providing safe and comfortable transportation for island visitors and residents alike in a 10-passenger minivan. Island tours and night driving are available. ✉ *Gustavia* ☎ *0690/49–02–97.*

Mat Nautic. This company can arrange for you to tour the island by water on a Jet Ski or WaveRunner. ✉ *Quai du Yacht Club, Rue Jeanne d'Arc, Gustavia* ☎ *0690/49–54–72.*

ANGUILLA

Updated
by Elise
Meyer

PEACE, PAMPERING, GREAT FOOD, and a wonderful local music scene are among the star attractions on Anguilla (pronounced ang-*gwill*-a). Beach lovers may become giddy when they first spot the island from the air; its blindingly white sand and lustrous blue-and-aquamarine waters are intoxicating. And if you like sophisticated cuisine served in casually elegant open-air settings, this may be your culinary Shangri-la.

The island's name, a reflection of its shape, is most likely a derivative of *anguille*, which is French for "eel." (French explorer Pierre Laudonnaire is credited with having given the island this name when he sailed past it in 1556.) In 1631 the Dutch built a fort here, but so far no one has been able to locate its site. English settlers from St. Kitts colonized the island in 1650, with plans to cultivate tobacco and, later, cotton and then sugar. But the thin soil and scarce water doomed these enterprises. Except for a brief period of independence, when it broke from its association with St. Kitts and Nevis in the 1960s, Anguilla has remained a British colony ever since.

From the early 1800s various island federations were formed and disbanded, with Anguilla all the while simmering over its subordinate status and forced union with St. Kitts. Anguillians twice petitioned for direct rule from Britain and twice were ignored. In 1967, when St. Kitts, Nevis, and Anguilla became an associated state, the mouse roared; citizens kicked out St. Kitts's policemen, held a self-rule referendum, and for two years conducted their own affairs. To what *Time* magazine called "a cascade of laughter around the world," a British "peacekeeping force" of 100 paratroopers from the Elite Red Devil unit parachuted onto the island, squelching Anguilla's designs for autonomy but helping a team of royal engineers stationed there to improve the port and build roads and schools. Today Anguilla elects a House of Assembly and its own leader to handle internal affairs, and a British governor is responsible for public service, the police, the judiciary, and external affairs.

The territory of Anguilla includes a few islets (or cays, pronounced "keys"), such as Scrub Island, Dog Island, Prickly Pear Cay, Sandy Island, and Sombrero Island. The 16,000 or so residents are predominantly of African descent, but there are also many of Irish background, whose ancestors came over from St. Kitts in the 1600s. Historically, because

LOGISTICS

Getting to Anguilla: There are no nonstop flights to Anguilla (AXA) from the United States, so you will almost always have to fly through San Juan, St. Maarten, or some other Caribbean island. You'll ordinarily be making the hop on a smaller plane. You can also take a variety of boats and ferries from the airport in St. Maarten, or Marigot on the French side.

Hassle Factor: Medium.

On the Ground: Some hotels provide transfers from the airport or ferry pier, especially the more expensive ones. For everyone else, if you don't rent a car, the taxi ride from the airport to your hotel will be less than $25 even to the West End (and considerably less if you're going to Sandy Ground).

Getting Around the Island: It's possible to base yourself in Sandy Ground, Rendezvous Bay, Meads Bay, or Shoal Bay without a car, but restaurants and resorts are quite spread out, so for the sake of convenience you may wish to rent a car for a few days or for your entire stay. If you do, prepare to drive on the left. Taxis are fairly expensive on Anguilla, another reason to consider renting a car.

the limestone land was unfit for agriculture, attempts at enslavement never lasted long. Consequently, Anguilla doesn't bear the scars of slavery found on so many other Caribbean islands. Instead, Anguillians became experts at making a living from the sea and are known for their boat-building and fishing skills. Tourism is the stable economy's growth industry, but the government carefully regulates expansion to protect the island's natural resources and beauty. New hotels are small, select, casino-free, and generally expensive; Anguilla emphasizes its high-quality service, serene surroundings, and friendly people.

PLANNING

WHEN TO GO
As in much of the Caribbean, high season runs mid-December through mid-April, and some resorts in Anguilla still close September through mid-December, though many remain open year-round. A few resorts require long minimum stays until after New Year's Day.

ACCOMMODATIONS

Anguilla is known for its luxurious resorts and villas, but there are also some places that mere mortals can afford (and a few that are downright bargains).

HOTEL AND RESTAURANT PRICES

Prices in the restaurant reviews are the average cost of a main course at dinner or, if dinner is not served, at lunch; taxes and service charges are generally included. Prices in the hotel reviews are the lowest cost of a standard double room in high season, excluding taxes, service charges, and meal plans (except at all-inclusives). Prices for rentals are the lowest per-night cost for a one-bedroom unit in high season.

For expanded lodging reviews and current deals, visit Fodors.com.

WHAT IT COSTS IN U.S. DOLLARS			
$	**$$**	**$$$**	**$$$$**
Restaurants under $12	$12–$20	$21–$30	over $30
Hotels under $275	$276–$375	$376–$475	over $475

Restaurant prices are the average cost of a main course at dinner or, if dinner is not served, at lunch. Hotel prices are the lowest cost of a standard double room in high season.

EXPLORING

TOP ATTRACTIONS

Exploring on Anguilla is mostly about checking out the spectacular beaches and resorts. The island has only a few roads. Locals are happy to provide directions, but using the readily available tourist map is the best idea. Visit the Anguilla Tourist Board, centrally located on Coronation Avenue in The Valley.

The Anguilla Heritage Trail is a free, self-guided tour of 10 important historical sights that can be explored independently in any order. Wallblake House, in The Valley, is the main information center for the trail, or you can just look for the large boulders with descriptive plaques.

Bethel Methodist Church. Not far from Sandy Ground, this charming little church is an excellent example of skillful

Cacti growing on one of Anguilla's scrub-covered coral flats

island stonework. It also has some colorful stained-glass windows. ⊠ *South Hill.*

Heritage Museum Collection. Don't miss this remarkable opportunity to learn about Anguilla. Old photographs and local records and artifacts trace the island's history over four millennia, from the days of the Arawaks. The tiny museum (complete with gift shop) is painstakingly curated by Colville Petty. High points include the historical documents of the Anguilla Revolution and the albums of photographs chronicling island life, from devastating hurricanes to a visit from Queen Elizabeth in 1964. You can see examples of ancient pottery shards and stone tools along with fascinating photographs of the island in the early 20th century—many depicting the heaping and exporting of salt and the christening of schooners—and a complete set of beautiful postage stamps issued by Anguilla since 1967. ⊠ *East End at Pond Ground* ☎ *264/235–7440* ✉ *$5* ⊘ *Mon.–Sat. 10–5.*

Island Harbour. Anguillians have been fishing for centuries in the brightly painted, simple, handcrafted fishing boats that line the shore of the harbor. It's hard to believe, but skillful pilots take these little boats out to sea as far as 50 or 60 miles (80 or 100 km). Late afternoon is the best time to see the day's catch. ■TIP→ Hail the free boat to Gorgeous Scilly Cay, a classic little restaurant offering sublime lobster and Eudoxie Wal-

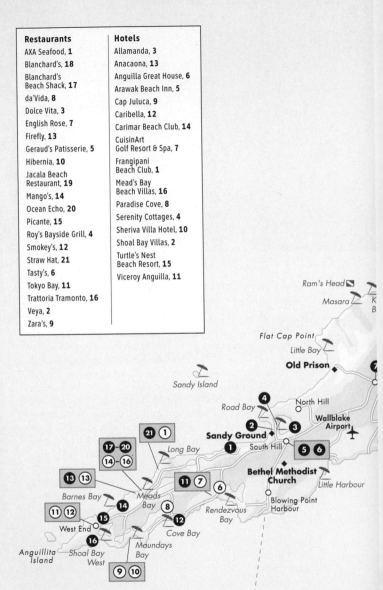

Restaurants

AXA Seafood, **1**
Blanchard's, **18**
Blanchard's
Beach Shack, **17**
da'Vida, **8**
Dolce Vita, **3**
English Rose, **7**
Firefly, **13**
Geraud's Patisserie, **5**
Hibernia, **10**
Jacala Beach
Restaurant, **19**
Mango's, **14**
Ocean Echo, **20**
Picante, **15**
Roy's Bayside Grill, **4**
Smokey's, **12**
Straw Hat, **21**
Tasty's, **6**
Tokyo Bay, **11**
Trattoria Tramonto, **16**
Veya, **2**
Zara's, **9**

Hotels

Allamanda, **3**
Anacaona, **13**
Anguilla Great House, **6**
Arawak Beach Inn, **5**
Cap Juluca, **9**
Caribella, **12**
Carimar Beach Club, **14**
CuisinArt
Golf Resort & Spa, **7**
Frangipani
Beach Club, **1**
Mead's Bay
Beach Villas, **16**
Paradise Cove, **8**
Serenity Cottages, **4**
Sheriva Villa Hotel, **10**
Shoal Bay Villas, **2**
Turtle's Nest
Beach Resort, **15**
Viceroy Anguilla, **11**

Ram's Head
Masara
K
B
Flat Cap Point
Little Bay
Old Prison
Sandy Island
North Hill
Road Bay
**Wallblake
Airport**
Sandy Ground
South Hill
Long Bay
**Bethel Methodist
Church**
Little Harbour
Barnes Bay
Meads
Bay
Blowing Point
Harbour
Rendezvous
Bay
West End
Cove Bay
Maundays
Bay
*Anguillita
Island*
Shoal Bay
West

TO ST. MAARTEN/
ST. MARTIN

Anguilla

ATLANTIC
OCEAN

Little Scrub Island

Scrub Island

Upper Flats

Stoney Bay Marine Park

Grouper Bowl

Island Harbour

Island Harbour

Scilly Cay

Captain's Bay

2

Shoal Bay

Crocus Bay

9 **3** **4** **5**

Island Harbour

10

Heritage Museum Collection

8

Savannah Bay

Katouche Bay

Mimi Bay

Sea Feathers Bay

7

The Valley

The Quarter

Sandy Hill Bay

◆ **Old Factory**

◆ **Warden's Place**

◆ **Wallblake House**

Long Salt Pond

Forest Bay

our

KEY	
⚲	*Beaches*
◰	*Dive Sites*
❶	*Restaurants*
①	*Hotels*
⛴	*Ferry lines*

0		2 mi
0		2 km

TOP ATTRACTIONS

Beautiful Beaches: Miles of brilliant beach ensure you have a high-quality spot in which to lounge.

Great Restaurants: The dining scene offers both fine dining and delicious casual food.

Fun, Low-Key Nightlife: A funky late-night local music scene features reggae and string bands.

Upscale Accommodations: Excellent luxury resorts coddle you in comfort.

Hidden Bargains: You'll find a few relative bargains if you look hard enough.

lace's knockout rum punches on Wednesday and Sunday. ⊠ *Island Harbor Rd.* ⊕ *www.scillycayanguilla.com.*

Old Factory. For many years the cotton grown on Anguilla and exported to England was processed in this beautiful historic building. Later it was a General Store, and now it's the home of Sotheby's Real Estate. There is a small art gallery on the lower level in an old stone cellar. ⊠ *Government Corner, The Valley* ☎ *264/497–2759* ⊕ *www.oldfactory-anguilla.ai* ☏ *Free* ⊗ *Weekdays 10–noon and 1–4.*

Old Prison. The ruins of this historic jail on Anguilla's highest point—213 feet above sea level—have outstanding views. ⊠ *Valley Rd. at Crocus Hill.*

Sandy Ground. Almost everyone who comes to Anguilla stops by this central beach, home to several popular open-air bars and restaurants, as well as boat-rental operations. This is where you catch the ferry for tiny Sandy Island, 2 miles (3 km) offshore.

Wallblake House. The only surviving plantation house in Anguilla, Wallblake House was built in 1787 by Will Blake (Wallblake is probably a corruption of his name). The place is associated with many a tale involving murder, high living, and the French invasion in 1796. On the grounds are an ancient vaulted stone cistern and an outbuilding called the Bakery (which wasn't used for making bread at all but for baking turkeys and hams). Tours of the thoroughly and thoughtfully restored house and grounds are usually offered three days a week, and you can only visit on a guided tour. It's also the information center for the Anguilla Heritage Tour. ⊠ *Wallblake Rd., The Valley* ☎ *264/497–6613*

⊕ *www.wallblake.ai* ✉ *Free* ☉ *Tours Mon., Wed., and Fri. at 10 and 2.*

Warden's Place. This former sugar-plantation greathouse was built in the 1790s and is a fine example of island architecture. It now houses KoalKeel restaurant and a sumptuous bakery upstairs. But for many years it served as the residence of the island's chief administrator, who also doubled as the only medical practitioner. Across the street you can see the oldest dwelling on the island, originally built as slave housing. It's a stop on the Heritage Trail. ■TIP→ Go in the morning from 8 to 10 for breakfast, then tour the historic building. ✉ *Coronation Ave., The Old Valley* ☎ *264/497–2930* ⊕ *www.koalkeel.com.*

BEACHES

Anguilla's beaches are among the best and most beautiful in the Caribbean. You can find long, deserted stretches suitable for sunset walks, or beaches lined with lively bars and restaurants—all surrounded by crystal clear warm waters in several shades of turquoise. The sea is calmest at 2½-mile-long Rendezvous Bay, where gentle breezes tempt sailors. But Shoal Bay (East) is the quintessential Caribbean beach. The white sand is so soft and abundant that it pools around your ankles. Cove Bay and Maundays Bay, both on the southeast coast, must also rank among the island's best beaches. Maundays is the location of the island's famous resort, Cap Juluca, Meads Bay's arc is dominated by the tony Viceroy Resort, and smaller Cove Bay is just a walk away. In contrast to the French islands, Anguilla doesn't permit topless sunbathing.

NORTHEAST COAST

Captain's Bay. On the north coast just before the eastern tip of the island, this quarter-mile stretch of perfect white sand is bounded on the left by a rocky shoreline where Atlantic waves crash. If you make the tough, four-wheel-drive-only trip along the dirt road that leads to the northeastern end of the island toward Junk's Hole, you'll be rewarded with peaceful isolation. The surf here slaps the sands with a vengeance, and the undertow is strong—so wading is the safest water sport. **Amenities:** none. **Best for:** solitude.

Island Harbour. These mostly calm waters are surrounded by a slender beach. For centuries Anguillians have ventured from these sands in colorful handmade fishing boats. It's not much of a beach for swimming or lounging, but there are

Shoal Bay, considered by many to be the most beautiful beach on Anguilla

several restaurants (Hibernia, Arawak Café, and Smitty's), and this is the departure point for the three-minute boat ride to Scilly Cay, where a thatch-roof beach bar serves seafood. Just hail the restaurant's free boat and plan to spend most of the day (the all-inclusive lunch starts at $40 and is worth the price—Wednesday and Sunday only). **Amenities:** food and drink. **Best for:** partiers.

NORTHWEST COAST

Little Bay. Little Bay is on the north coast between Crocus Bay and Shoal Bay, not far from the Valley. Sheer cliffs lined with agave and creeping vines rise behind a small gray-sand beach, usually accessible only by water (it's a favored spot for snorkeling and night dives). The easiest way to get here is a five-minute boat ride from Crocus Bay (about $10 round-trip). The young and agile can clamber down the cliffs by rope to explore the caves and surrounding reef; this is the only way to access the beach from the road and is not recommended to the inexperienced climber. Do not leave personal items in cars parked here, because theft can be a problem. **Amenities:** none. **Best for:** snorkeling.

Road Bay (*Sandy Ground*). The big pier here is where the cargo ships dock, but so do some pretty sweet yachts, sailboats, and fishing boats. The brown-sugar sand is home to terrific restaurants that hop from dusk till dawn, including Veya, Roy's Bayside Grille, Ripples, Barrel Stay, the Pumphouse, and Elvis', the quintessential beach bar. There are

all kinds of boat charters available here. The snorkeling isn't very good, but the sunset vistas are glorious, especially with a rum punch in your hand. **Amenities:** food and drink. **Best for:** sunset.

Sandy Island. A popular day trip for Anguilla visitors, tiny Sandy Island shelters a pretty lagoon nestled in coral reefs about 2 miles (3 km) from Road Bay, with a restaurant that serves lunch and great islandy cocktails. November through August, you can take the "Happiness" sea shuttle from Sandy Ground ($10). ■TIP→ The reef is great for snorkeling. **Amenities:** food and drink. **Best for:** partiers; snorkeling; swimming. ⊕ *www.mysandyisland.com.*

FAMILY **Fodor's**Choice **Shoal Bay.** Anchored by sea grape and coconut
★ trees, the 2-mile (3-km) powdered-sugar strand at Shoal Bay (not to be confused with Shoal Bay West at the other end of the island) is one of the world's prettiest beaches. You can park free at any of the restaurants, including Elodia's, Uncle Ernie's, or Gwen's Reggae Grill, most of which either rent or provide chairs and umbrellas for patrons for about $20 per person per day. There is plenty of room to stretch out in relative privacy, or you can barhop or take a ride on Junior's Glass Bottom Boat. The relatively broad beach has shallow water that is usually gentle, making this a great family beach; a coral reef not far from the shore is a wonderful snorkeling spot. Sunsets over the water are

spectacular. **Amenities:** food and drink. **Best for:** sunset; swimming; walking.

SOUTHEAST COAST

Sandy Hill. You can park anywhere along the dirt road to Sea Feathers Bay to visit this popular fishing center. What's good for the fishermen is also good for snorkelers. But the beach here is not much of a lounging spot; the sand is too narrow and rocky for that. However, it's a great place to buy lobsters and fish fresh out of the water in the afternoon. **Amenities:** food and drink. **Best for:** walking.

SOUTHWEST COAST

★ Fodor'sChoice **Cove Bay.** Follow the signs to Smokey's at the end of Cove Road, and you will find water that is brilliantly blue and sand that's as soft as sifted flour. It's just as spectacular as its neighbors Rendezvous Bay and Maundays Bay. You can walk here from Cap Juluca for a change of pace, or you can arrange a horseback ride along the beach. Weekend barbecues with terrific local bands at Smokey's are an Anguillian must. **Amenities:** food and drink. **Best for:** partiers; swimming; walking.

★ Fodor'sChoice **Maundays Bay.** The dazzling, mile-long platinum-white beach is especially great for swimming and long beach walks. It's no wonder that Cap Juluca, one of Anguilla's premier resorts, chose this as its location. Public parking is straight ahead at the end of the road near Cap Juluca's Pimms restaurant. You can have lunch or dinner at Cap Juluca (just be prepared for the cost). Depending on the season you can book a massage in one of the beachside tents. **Amenities:** food and drink; parking; toilets. **Best for:** partiers; swimming; walking.

Rendezvous Bay. Follow the signs to Anguilla Great House for public parking at this broad swath of pearl-white sand that is some 1½ miles (2½ km) long. The beach is lapped by calm, bluer-than-blue water and a postcard-worthy view of St. Martin. The expansive crescent is home to three resorts; stop in for a drink or a meal at one, or rent a chair and umbrella at one of the kiosks. Don't miss the daylong party at the treehouse Dune Preserve, where Bankie Banx, Anguilla's most famous musician, presides. **Amenities:** food and drink; parking; toilets. **Best for:** partiers; swimming; walking.

Shoal Bay West. This glittering bay bordered by mangroves and sea grapes is a lovely place to spend the day. The mile-long beach is home to Covecastles villas. The tranquility is sublime, with coral reefs for snorkeling not too far from shore. Punctuate your day with a meal at beachside Trattoria Tramonto. Reach the beach by taking the main road to the West End and bearing left at the fork, then continuing to the end. Note that similarly named Shoal Bay is a separate beach on a different part of the island. **Amenities:** food and drink; parking; toilets. **Best for:** solitude; swimming; walking.

WHERE TO EAT

Despite its small size, Anguilla has around 70 restaurants: stylish temples of haute cuisine; classic, barefoot beachfront grills; roadside barbecue stands; food carts; and casual cafés. Many have breeze-swept terraces for dining under the stars. Call ahead—in winter to make a reservation, and in late summer and fall to confirm whether the place you've chosen is even open at that time. Anguillian restaurant meals are leisurely events, and service is often at a relaxed pace, so settle in and enjoy. Most restaurant owners are actively and conspicuously present, especially at dinner. It's a special treat to take the time to get to know them a bit when they stop by your table to make sure you are enjoying your meal.

What to Wear: During the day, casual clothes are widely accepted: shorts will be fine, but don't wear bathing suits and cover-ups unless you're at a beach bar. In the evening, shorts are okay at the extremely casual eateries. Elsewhere, women wear sundresses or nice casual slacks; men will be fine in short-sleeve shirts and casual pants. Some hotel restaurants are slightly more formal, but that just means long pants for men.

$$$$ 🍴 **AXA Seafood.** *Italian.* New on the Anguilla dining scene in 2013 is this lively seafood restaurant. Longtime visitors will remember Luna Rosa, formerly in this location, and Axa Seafood brings Abi and Sylvestro back together. There is a lively bar, frequent live music, and a menu full of tasty fresh seafood (and meat) choices including a crowd-pleasing paella, a signature lobster mac-and-cheese, and several daily specials according to the day's "catch." The desserts are a standout, especially the espresso-mascarpone mousse garnished with white chocolate. [$] *Average main: $38* ✉ *South Hill* ☎ *264/497–7979* 🌐 *www.axaseafoodhouse.com.*

★ $$$$ Fodor's Choice ✕ **Blanchard's.** *Eclectic.* This absolutely delightful restaurant is one of the best in the Caribbean. Proprietors Bob and Melinda Blanchard moved to Anguilla from Vermont in 1994 to fulfill their culinary dreams. A festive atmosphere pervades the handsome, airy white room, which is accented with floor-to-ceiling teal-blue shutters to let in the breezes, and colorful artwork by the Blanchards' son Jesse on the walls. A masterful combination of creative cuisine, an upscale atmosphere, attentive service, and an excellent wine cellar (including a selection of aged spirits) pleases the star-studded crowd. The nuanced contemporary menu is ever changing but always good; house classics like corn chowder, lobster and shrimp cakes, and a Caribbean sampler are crowd-pleasers, and vegetarians will find ample choices. For dessert, you'll remember concoctions like the key lime "pie-in-a-glass" or the justly famous "cracked coconut" long after your suntan has faded. [$] *Average main: $49* ✉ *Meads Bay* ☎ *264/497–6100* 🌐 *www.blanchardsrestaurant.com* ✍ *Reservations essential* ⏲ *Closed Sun., Mon., May–mid-Dec., and Sept. 1–Oct. 17.*

$$ FAMILY ✕ **Blanchard's Beach Shack.** *American.* You'll find the perfect antidote to high restaurant prices at this spinoff, right on the sands of Meads Bay Beach. Opened in late 2011 right next to Blanchard's, this chartreuse-and-turquoise cottage serves yummy lunches and dinners of lobster rolls, all-natural burgers, tacos, and terrific salads and sandwiches—you can dine at nearby picnic tables or rent a beach chair. Frozen drinks like mango coladas and icy mojitos please grown-ups, while kids dig into the fresh-made frozen yogurt concoctions. Organic produce and happy smiles are always on offer. Lots of choices for kids and vegetarians, too. ■ **TIP→** Diners are welcome to hang around on the beach. [$] *Average main: $12* ✉ *Meads Bay* ☎ *264/498–6100* 🌐 *www.blanchardsrestaurant.com* ⏲ *Closed Sun., and Sept. 1–Oct. 17.*

$$$$ FAMILY ✕ **da'Vida.** *Caribbean.* Sometimes you really can have it all. Right on exquisite Crocus Bay, this beautifully designed resort, restaurant, and club is a place where you could spend the whole day dining, drinking, and lounging under umbrellas on the comfortable chairs. Snorkeling equipment and kayaks are available for rent, and there's a boutique as well as a beachside spa. You can picnic at the Beach Grill (burgers, hot dogs, wraps, salads) or head inside the main building for dumplings, soups, pastas, and pizzas. Lunch starts at 11, and you can get tapas and sunset drinks from about 3. At dinner, the stylish wood inte-

rior (built by craftsmen from St. Vincent) is accented by candlelight. On the menu are such dishes as tasty seared snapper with gingered kale, coconut-crusted scallops, and Angus steaks. Go for the music on Friday and Saturday nights. The owners, siblings David and Vida Lloyd, who also operate Lloyd's Guest House, grew up right here, and they have taken pains to get it all just right. ■ TIP→ Call for information about their nightly shuttle service. $ *Average main: $33* ✉ *Crocus Bay* ☎ *264/498–5433* 🌐 *www.davidaanguilla.com* ⊗ *Closed Mon.*

$$$$ 🍴 **Dolce Vita Italian Beach Restaurant & Bar.** *Italian.* Serious Italian cuisine and warm and attentive service are provided here, in a romantic beachside pavillion in Sandy Ground for lunch and dinner. Freshly made pasta stars in classic lasagna, fettuccini bolognese, pappardelle with duck sauce, and a meatless eggplant parmigiana. A carniverous quartet can pre-order suckling pig, or a sample first-quality chops and steaks. Pizza is offered only at lunch. Italian wine fans will discover new favorites from the cellar. What's for dessert? How about Nutella cheesecake? $ *Average main: $34* ✉ *Sandy Ground* ☎ *264/497–8668* 🌐 *www.dolcevitasandyground.com* ✍ *Reservations essential* ⊗ *Closed Sun., and Sept. 1–Oct. 15. No lunch Sat.*

4

$$ 🍴 **English Rose Bar and Restaurant.** *Caribbean.* Lunchtime finds this neighborhood hangout packed with locals: cops flirting with sassy waitresses, entrepreneurs brokering deals with politicos, schoolgirls in lime-green outfits doing their homework. The décor is nothing to speak of, but this is a great place to eavesdrop or people-watch while enjoying island-tinged specialties like beer-battered shrimp, jerk-chicken Caesar salad, snapper creole, and buffalo wings. There is karaoke on Friday. $ *Average main: $12* ✉ *Carter Rey Blvd., The Valley* ☎ *264/497–5353* ⊗ *Closed Sun.*

$$$ 🍴 **Firefly Restaurant.** *Caribbean.* Set on a breezy poolside
FAMILY patio, Firefly—the restaurant at Anacaona Boutique Hotel—serves huge portions of tasty Caribbean fare by a longtime Anguillian chef. The pumpkin-coconut soup is a winner, as are the local snapper, mahimahi, and crayfish. Breakfast and lunch are also served. Lunch and drinks delivered to the beach is also a possibility here. ■ TIP→ For agreat value and terrific fun, book a table at the Thursday night buffet, with a lively performance by the folkloric theater company, Mayoumba, or the Tuesday night Chinese feast. Friday night is Latin night: great food and music for practicing your salsa and your merengue with a professional dancer. $ *Average main: $28* ✉ *Meads Bay* ☎ *264/497–6827* 🌐 *anacaonahotel.com.*

$$ ✕ **Geraud's Patisserie.** *French.* A stunning array of absolutely delicious French pastries and breads—and universal favorites like cookies, brownies, and muffins—are produced by Le Cordon Bleu dynamo Geraud Lavest in this well-located shop. Come in the early morning for cappuccino and croissants, or healthy fresh juices and smoothies, and pick up fixings for a wonderful and thrifty lunch later (or choose from among the list of tempting daily lunch specials). The little shop carries a small selection of interesting condiments, teas, and gourmet goodies. During the high season (December through May), a terrific Sunday brunch is available. Geraud also does a large amount of off-site catering, from intimate villa and yacht dinners to weddings. His sophisticated wedding cakes are an island wonder. Follow on facebook for daily specials. $ *Average main: $13* ✉ *South Hill Pl.* ☎ *264/497–5559* ⊕ *www.anguillacakesandcatering. com* ⊗ *Closed Mon. No dinner. Weekends 5:30 am–noon.*

★ **Fodor's Choice** ✕ **Hibernia Restaurant and Art Gallery.** *Eclectic.*
$$$$ Some of the island's most creative dishes are served in this wood-beam cottage restaurant overlooking the water at the far eastern end of Anguilla. Unorthodox yet delectable culinary pairings—inspired by chef-owners Raoul Rodriguez and Mary Pat's annual travels to Asia—bring new tastes and energy to the tables. The restaurant uses local organic products whenever possible. Long-line fish is served with a gratin of local pumpkin, shiitake mushrooms, and an essence of bitter oranges grown beside the front gate. Every visit here is an opportunity to share the owners' passion for life, expressed through the vibrant combination of setting, art, food, unique tableware, beautiful gardens, and thoughtful hospitality. In 2012 the restaurant acquired the stellar wine collection from the Malliouhana Hotel. There is a shuttle service available for dinner, call for details. ■TIP→ Mary Pat stocks the tiny art gallery here with amazing, and reasonable, finds from her travels around the globe. $ *Average main: $36* ✉ *Harbor Ridge Dr., Island Harbour* ☎ *264/497–4290* ⊕ *www.hiberniarestaurant.com* ⊗ *Closed mid-July–Nov. Call for seasonal hrs.*

★ **Fodor's Choice** ✕ **Jacala Beach Restaurant.** *French.* Right on beau-
$$$ tiful Meads Bay, this restaurant opened to raves in 2010. Alain the chef and Jacques the maître d' (from Malliouhana) have joined forces, and the happy result is carefully prepared and nicely presented French food served with care in a lovely open-air restaurant, accompanied by good wines and a lot of personal attention. A delicious starter terrine of feta and grilled vegetables is infused with pesto.

For an entrée, you must try hand-chopped steak tartare, or seared and marinated sushi-grade tuna on a bed of delightful mashed plantain. Lighter lunchtime options include a tart cucumber-yogurt soup garnished with piquant tomato sorbet. After lunch you can digest on the beach in one of the "Fatboy" loungers. In any case, save room for the chocolate pot de crème. $ *Average main: $30* ✉ *Meads Bay* ☎ *264/498–5888* ⚮ *Reservations essential* ◷ *Closed Mon. and Tues., and Aug. and Sept.*

$$$$ ✕ **Mango's.** *Seafood.* Sparkling-fresh fish specialties have
FAMILY starring roles on the menu here. Light and healthy choices include spicy grilled whole snapper, and Cruzan Rum barbecued chicken. Save room for dessert—the warm apple tart and the coconut cheesecake are worth the splurge. Come at lunch for sandwiches and burgers. There's an extensive wine list, and the Cuban cigar humidor is a luxurious touch. $ *Average main: $36* ✉ *Barnes Bay* ☎ *264/497–6479* ⊕ *www.mangosseasidegrill.com* ⚮ *Reservations essential* ◷ *Closed Tues., and Aug.–Oct.*

$$$$ ✕ **Ocean Echo.** *Caribbean.* Newly opened in 2012, this
FAMILY relaxed and friendly restaurant is great for salads, burgers, grills, pasta and fresh fish. Heartier appetites will enjoy the ribs and steaks. It's nonstop every day from lunch until late. Sunday, Friday, and Wednesday there is live music as well as the enticing possibility of a bit of dancing with an islandy cocktail in hand. $ *Average main: $31* ✉ *Mead's Bay, West End* ☎ *264/498–5454* ⊕ *www.oceanechoanguilla.com.*

$$$ ✕ **Picante.** *Mexican.* This casual, wildly popular bright-red
FAMILY roadside Caribbean taquería, opened by a young California couple, serves huge, tasty burritos with a choice of fillings, fresh warm tortilla chips with first-rate guacamole, huge (and fresh) taco salads, seafood enchiladas, and tequila-lime chicken grilled under a brick. Passion-fruit margaritas are a must, and the creamy Mexican chocolate pudding makes a great choice for dessert. Seating is at picnic tables; the friendly proprietors cheerfully supply pillows on request. Reservations are recommended. $ *Average main: $21* ✉ *West End Rd., West End* ☎ *264/498–1616* ⊕ *www.picante-restaurant-anguilla.com* ◷ *Closed Tues. Dec.–May, and Mon. and Tues. May–Aug. No lunch.*

$$$ ✕ **Roy's Bayside Grille.** *Caribbean.* Some of the best grilled
FAMILY lobster on the island is served here, along with burgers, great fish-and-chips, and good homestyle cooking. On Friday from 5 to 7 there's a happy hour with a special menu. On Sunday you can get roast beef and Yorkshire pudding, and there's free Wi-Fi. The $35 prix fixe here is a good

deal with lots of choices, and Ray's is very accomodating toward kids and people with food allergies. $ *Average main: $27* ✉ *Road Bay, Sandy Ground* ☎ *264/497–2470* 🌐 *www.roysbaysidegrill.com.*

$$$ FAMILY 🍴 **Smokey's.** *Caribbean.* This quintessential Anguillian beach barbecue, part of the Gumbs family mini-empire of authentic and delicious eateries, is on pretty Cove Bay. On the beach, lounges with umbrellas welcome guests. Hot wings, honey-coated smoked ribs, curry goat, smoked chicken salad, and grilled lobsters are paired with local staple side dishes such as spiced-mayonnaise coleslaw, hand-cut sweet-potato strings, and crunchy onion rings. If your idea of the perfect summer lunch is a roadside lobster roll, be sure to try the version here, served on a home-baked roll with a hearty kick of hot sauce. The dinner menu includes lobster fritters, grilled tuna with lemon-caper butter, and rum chicken. On Saturday afternoon, a popular local band enlivens the casual, laid-back atmosphere, and on Sunday the restaurant is party central for locals and visitors alike. $ *Average main: $25* ✉ *Cove Rd., Cove Bay* ☎ *264/497–6582* 🌐 *www.smokeysatthecove.com.*

★ $$$$ FAMILY **Fodor's Choice** 🍴 **Straw Hat.** *Eclectic.* Charming owners, a gorgeous oceanfront location, sophisticated and original food, and friendly service are the main reasons this stylish restaurant has been in business since the late 1990s. Whether for breakfast, lunch, or dinner, you will find appealing, tasty, and fresh choices to mix up or share for the perfect meal. Try Anguilla's only "real" bagel, tuna flatbread, jerk-braised pork belly, lobster spring rolls, or curried goat. "Fish of the day" truly means fish caught that day. Vegetarians and kids will find many options. A small garden out in the back is the source for the superfresh greens. The big flat-screens with satellite TV in the bar make it a fine place to catch the game or make some new friends. $ *Average main: $39* ✉ *Frangipani Beach Club, Meads Bay* ☎ *264/497–8300* 🌐 *www.strawhat.com* ✍ *Reservations essential* ⊗ *Closed Sept. and Oct.*

$$$ 🍴 **Tasty's.** *Caribbean.* Once your eyes adjust to the quirky kiwi, lilac, and coral color scheme, you'll find that breakfast, lunch, or dinner at Tasty's is, well, very tasty. It's open all day long, so if you come off a midafternoon plane starving, head directly here—it's near the airport and the ferry terminal. Chef-owner Dale Carty trained at Malliouhana, and his careful, confident preparation bears the mark of French culinary training, but the menu is classic Caribbean with a creole edge. It's worth leaving

Straw Hat's outdoor patio on Forest Bay

the beach at lunch for the lobster salad here. A velvety pumpkin soup garnished with roasted coconut shards is superb, as are the seared jerk tuna and the garlic-infused marinated conch salad. Don't be stuffy—try the goat stew. Yummy desserts end meals on a high note. This is one of the few restaurants that don't allow smoking, so take your Cubans elsewhere for an after-dinner puff. The popular Sunday brunch buffet features island specialties like saltfish cakes. There is live music on Saturday night. $ *Average main: $23* ⊠ *Main Rd., South Hill Village, South Hill* ☏ *264/497–2737* ⊕ *www.tastysrestaurant.com* ⌖ *Reservations essential* ⊗ *Closed Thurs.*

$$$$ ✕ **Tokyo Bay.** *Sushi.* This chic sushi and teppanyaki res-
FAMILY taurant, dramatically lit and perched at the top of CuisinArt's spa building, opened to raves in 2012. Chances are that this is where you will find many local chefs and other restaurant people on their night out. The sake bar features terrific cocktails with names like Eager Ninja and Saketini, and Japanese chefs slice up ocean-fresh fish for sushi both traditional and otherwise. Hot pots, rice dishes, wagyu beef, and yakitori skewers round out the menu. "Chocolate Sushi" is an amusing finale to dinner. $ *Average main: $42* ⊠ *CuisinArt Resort and Spa, Rendevous Bay* ☏ *264/498–2000* ⊕ *www.cuisinartresort.com* ⊗ *Closed Tues. No lunch.*

$$$ ✕ **Trattoria Tramonto and Oasis Beach Bar.** *Italian.* The island's
FAMILY only beachfront Italian restaurant features a dual (or duel-

ing) serenade of Andrea Bocelli on the sound system and gently lapping waves a few feet away. Chef Valter Belli artfully adapts recipes from his home in Emilia-Romagna. Try the delicate lobster ravioli in truffle-cream sauce. For dessert, don't miss the tiramisu. Though you might wander in here for lunch after a swim, when casual dress is OK, you'll still be treated to the same impressive menu. You can also choose from a luscious selection of champagne fruit drinks, a small and fairly priced Italian wine list, and homemade grappa. Hang out on chairs on the spectacular beach before or after your meal. $ *Average main: $28* ✉ *Shoal Bay West* ☎ *264/497–8819* ⊕ *www. trattoriatramonto.com* ⌂ *Reservations essential* ⊙ *Closed Mon., and Aug.–Oct.*

★ **Fodor's**Choice ✕ **Veya.** *Eclectic.* On the suavely minimalist
$$$$ four-sided verandah, the stylishly appointed tables glow with flickering candlelight (in matte-white, sea urchin–shape votive holders made of porcelain). A lively lounge where chic patrons mingle and sip mojitos to the purr of soft jazz anchors the room. Inventive, sophisticated, and downright delicious, Carrie Bogar's "Cuisine of the Sun" features ingenious preparations of first-rate provisions. Ample portions are sharable works of art—sample Moroccan-spice shrimp "cigars" with roast tomato–apricot chutney or Vietnamese-spice calamari. Jerk-spice tuna is served with a rum-coffee glaze on a juicy slab of grilled pineapple with curls of plantain crisps, and crayfish in beurre blanc is divine. ■TIP➔ Consider a splurge on the $85 five-course tasting menu. Dessert is a must—the sublime warm chocolate cake with chili-roasted banana ice cream and caramelized bananas steals the show. Great music in the lounge invites after-dinner lingering. $ *Average main: $38* ✉ *Sandy Ground* ☎ *264/498–8392* ⊕ *www.veya-axa.com* ⌂ *Reservations essential* ⊙ *Closed Sun., June–Aug., and weekends June–Oct. Restaurant closed Sept. 1–Oct. 16.*

$$$ ✕ **Zara's.** *Eclectic.* Chef Shamash Brooks presides at this under-the-radar but cozy restaurant with beam ceilings, terra-cotta floors, and colorful artwork. His kitchen turns out tasty fare that combines Caribbean and Italian flavors with panache (Rasta Pasta is a specialty). Standouts include a velvety pumpkin soup with coconut milk, crunchy calamari, lemon pasta scented with garlic, herbed rack of lamb served with a roasted applesauce, and spicy fish fillet steamed in banana leaf. Follow the signs to Allamanda. $ *Average main: $25* ✉ *Allamanda Beach Club, Upper Shoal Bay* ☎ *264/497–3229* ⊙ *No lunch.*

WHERE TO STAY

Tourism on Anguilla is a fairly recent phenomenon—most development didn't begin until the early 1980s. The lack of native topography and, indeed, vegetation, and the blindingly white expanses of beach have inspired building designs of some interest; architecture buffs might have fun trying to name some of the most surprising examples. Inspiration largely comes from the Mediterranean: the Greek Islands, Morocco, and Spain, with some Miami-style art deco thrown into the mixture.

Anguilla accommodations basically fall into two categories: grand resorts and luxury resort-villas, or low-key, simple, locally owned inns and small beachfront complexes. The former can be surprisingly expensive, the latter surprisingly reasonable. In the middle are some condo-type options, with full kitchens and multiple bedrooms, which are great for families or for longer stays. Private villa rentals are becoming more common and are increasing in number and quality every season as development on the island accelerates.

A good phone chat or email exchange with the management of any property is a good idea, as units within the same complex can vary greatly in layout, accessibility, distance to the beach, and view. When calling to reserve a room, ask about special discount packages, especially in spring and summer. Most hotels include continental breakfast in the price, and many have meal-plan options. But keep in mind that Anguilla is home to dozens of excellent restaurants, before you lock yourself into an expensive meal plan that you may not be able to change. All hotels charge a 10% tax, a $1 per room per day tourism marketing levy, and—in most cases—an additional 10% service charge. A few properties include these charges in the published rates, so check carefully when you are evaluating prices.

PRIVATE VILLAS AND CONDOS

The tourist office publishes an annual *Anguilla Travel Planner* with informative listings of available vacation apartment rentals.

Anguilla Connection. You can contact the Anguilla Connection for condo and villa listings. ☎ *264/498–0123* ⊕ *www. luxuryvillas.com.*

Anguilla Luxury Collection. This operator also manages the Anguilla Affordable Collection, another group of less-expensive villas. ☎ *264/497–6049* 🌐 *www.anguillaluxurycollection.com.*

Ani Villas. Two stunning cliffside villas for up to 24 guests offer breathtaking views and total luxury to families or groups looking for total pampering. Included in the rental rate comes private boat transfers from St. Martin/St. Maarten, rental car, a full service team: concierge, butler, chef, housekeepers, breakfasts, dinner chef service, and all beverages. Tennis pros, spa services, trainers and guides are all available on demand. There is room for 100 guests for a party or a wedding; and a dramatic and romantic promontory for the ceremony. A tennis court, bikes, fitness room, pool, cliffside hot-tubs, and playrooms mean that except for beachgoing, you never have to leave. Check for promotions that include unlimited golf at the CuisinArt Golf Course. ☎ *264/497–7888* 🌐 *www.anivillas.com.*

4

myCaribbean. Gayle Gurvey and her staff manage and rent more than 100 local villas, and have been in business since 2000; it's he largest local company for private villa rentals. The "last minute" deals on the website offer good deals for the impulsive. ☎ *321/392–0828* 🌐 *www.mycaribbean.com.*

RECOMMENDED HOTELS AND RESORTS

$ 🏨 **Allamanda Beach Club.** *Rental.* Youthful, active couples FAMILY from around the globe happily fill this casual, three-story, white-stucco building hidden in a palm grove just off the beach, opting for location and price over luxury. **Pros:** front row for all Shoal Bay's action; young crowd; good restaurant. **Cons:** location requires a car; rooms are pleasant, but not at all fancy. [$] *Rooms from: $175* ✉ *The Valley* ☎ *264/497–5217, 305/396–4472* 🌐 *www.allamanda.ai* 🛏 *20 units* ⏲ *Closed Sept.* 🍴 *No meals.*

$ 🏨 **Anacaona Boutique Hotel.** *Resort.* Imbued with the culture FAMILY and traditions of the island, this resort makes low-key yet chic hideaway (its name is pronounced "an-nah-cah-*oh*-na"). **Pros:** friendly clientele; sensitive to local culture; modern and good value; nice high-tech amenities. **Cons:** bit of a walk to beach; smallish rooms. [$] *Rooms from: $265* ✉ *Meads Bay* ☎ *264/497–6827, 877/647–4736* 🌐 *www.anacaonahotel.com* 🛏 *27 rooms and suites* 🍴 *Multiple meal plans.*

$$ 🏨 **Anguilla Great House Beach Resort.** *Resort.* These tradi-FAMILY tional West Indian–style bungalows are strung along one of Anguilla's longest beaches. **Pros:** real, old-school Caribbean;

right on the gorgeous beach; young crowd; good prices. **Cons:** rooms are very simple; Internet access is spotty. *$ Rooms from: $310 ✉ Rendezvous Bay ☎ 264/497–6061, 800/583–9247 🌐 www.anguillagreathouse.com 🛏 31 rooms 🍴 Multiple meal plans.*

$ 🏨 **Arawak Beach Inn.** *B&B/Inn.* These hexagonal two-story villas are a good choice for a funky, budget-friendly, low-key guesthouse experience. **Pros:** funky, casual crowd; friendly owners; very competitive rates. **Cons:** not on the beach; a/c included only in premium rooms; isolated location makes a car a must. *$ Rooms from: $265 ✉ The Valley, Island Harbour ☎ 264/497–4888, 877/427–2925 for reservations 🌐 www.arawakbeach.com 🛏 17 rooms 🍴 Multiple meal plans.*

$$$$ 🏨 **Cap Juluca.** *Resort.* Strung along 179 acres of breathtaking Maundays Bay, the romantic, domed, Moorish-style villas have been an Anguilla favorite for 25 years, thanks to caring staff, great sports facilities, and plenty of room for privacy and comfort. **Pros:** lots of space to stretch out on miles of talcum-soft sand; warm service; romantic atmosphere. **Cons:** ongoing renovations; comparatively high rates; some of the units are currently closed. *$ Rooms from: $995 ✉ Maundays Bay ☎ 264/497–6779, 888/858–5822 in U.S. 🌐 www.capjuluca.com 🛏 69 rooms, 7 patio suites, 6 pool villas 🍴 Some meals.*

$$$ 🏨 **Caribella.** *Rental.* These spacious Mediterranean-style villas on the broad sands of Barnes Bay are a good deal at the much-discounted weekly rate. **Pros:** huge amount of space for the cost; beautiful views from huge balconies. **Cons:** basic décor. *$ Rooms from: $450 ✉ Barnes Bay ☎ 264/497–6045 🌐 www.lambertventures.com 🛏 6 units 🍴 No meals.*

$$$ FAMILY 🏨 **Carimar Beach Club.** *Rental.* This horseshoe of bougainvillea-draped Mediterranean-style buildings on beautiful Meads Bay has the look of a Sun Belt condo. **Pros:** tennis courts; easy walk to restaurants and spa; great beach location; laundry facilities. **Cons:** no pool or restaurant. *$ Rooms from: $435 ✉ Meads Bay ☎ 264/497–6881, 866/270–3764 🌐 www.carimar.com 🛏 24 apartments ⏲ Closed Sept.–mid-Oct. 🍴 Multiple meal plans.*

★ $$$$ FAMILY **Fodor's Choice** 🏨 **CuisinArt Golf Resort and Spa.** *Resort.* Anguilla's only family-friendly full-service resort has it all: miles of stunning beach, world-class golf, a gorgeous spa and health club, top dining, and sports galore. **Pros:** family-friendly; great spa and sports; gorgeous beach and gardens. **Cons:** food service can be slow; pool area is noisy; beach lounges need replacement. $ *Rooms from: $800* ✉ *Rendezvous Bay* ☎ *264/498–2000, 800/943–3210* 🌐 *www.cuisinartresort.com* 🛏 *100 rooms, 2 penthouses, 6 villas* ⏲ *Closed Sept. and Oct.* 🍴 *Multiple meal plans.*

$$$ FAMILY 🏨 **Frangipani Beach Club.** *Resort.* This flamingo-pink Mediterranean-style property perches on the beautiful champagne sands of Meads Bay. **Pros:** great beach; good location for restaurants and resort-hopping; first-rate on-site restaurant; helpful staff. **Cons:** some rooms lack a view, so be sure to ask, if you care. $ *Rooms from: $400* ✉ *Meads Bay* ☎ *264/497–6442, 877/593–8988* 🌐 *www.frangipaniresort.com* 🛏 *19 rooms* ⏲ *Closed Sept. and Oct.* 🍴 *Breakfast.*

$$$$ FAMILY 🏨 **Meads Bay Beach Villas.** *Rental.* These gorgeous one-, two-, and three-bedroom villas set right on Meads Bay have a cult following, so it's sometimes hard to book them. **Pros:** big private apartments; beautiful beach location; private plunge pools; free phone calls to the U.S. **Cons:** more condo than hotel in terms of service. $ *Rooms from: $550* ✉ *Meads Bay Rd.* ☎ *264/497–0271* 🌐 *www.meadsbaybeachvillas.com* 🛏 *4 villas* 🍴 *No meals.*

$$ FAMILY 🏨 **Paradise Cove.** *Rental.* Located 500 yards away from Cove Beach, this simple complex of huge, reasonably priced studios, one-, and two-bedroom apartments has two whirlpools, a large pool, and tranquil tropical gardens where you can pluck fresh guavas for breakfast. **Pros:** reasonable rates; great pool; lovely gardens. **Cons:** a bit far from the beach; bland décor. $ *Rooms from: $320* ✉ *The Cove* ☎ *264/497–6959, 264/497–6603* 🌐 *www.paradise.ai* 🛏 *12 studio suites, 17 1- and 2-bedroom apartments* 🍴 *No meals.*

$$ FAMILY 🏨 **Serenity Cottages.** *Rental.* Despite the name, these aren't cottages but rather large, fully equipped, and relatively affordable one- and two-bedroom apartments (and studios created from them) in a small complex set in a lush garden at the farthest end of glorious Shoal Bay Beach. **Pros:** big apartments; quiet end of beach; snorkeling right outside the door; very reasonable rates for weeklong packages. **Cons:** no pool; more condo than hotel in terms of staff; location at the end of Shoal Bay pretty much requires a car and some extra time to drive to the West End. $ *Rooms from: $325* ✉ *Shoal Bay East* ☎ *264/497–3328* 🌐 *www.serenity.ai* 🛏 *2 1-bedroom suites, 8 2-bedroom apartments* ⏲ *Closed Sept.* 🍴 *No meals.*

$$$$ FAMILY 🏨 **Sheriva Villa Hotel.** *Rental.* This intimate, luxury-villa hotel is made up of three cavernous villas with a total of 20 guest rooms and seven private swimming pools, which overlook a broad swath of turquoise sea. **Pros:** incredible

staff; all the comforts of home and more; good value for large family groups. **Cons:** not on the beach; you risk being spoiled for life by the staff's attentions; expensive. *$ Rooms from: $1500 ✉ Maundays Bay Rd., West End ☎ 264/498–9898 🌐 www.sheriva.com 🛏 20 rooms 🍴 Multiple meal plans.*

$$$ FAMILY 🏨 **Shoal Bay Villas.** *Rental.* This old-style property well located right on Shoal Bay's incredible 2-mile beach. **Pros:** friendly; casual; full kitchens; beachfront. **Cons:** not fancy; you'll want a car to get around; there's construction going on in the area, so check on progress before booking. *$ Rooms from: $410 ✉ Shoal Bay ☎ 264/497–2051 🌐 www.sbvillas.ai 🛏 12 units 🍴 No meals.*

$$ FAMILY 🏨 **Turtle's Nest Beach Resort.** *Rental.* This collection of studios and one- to three-bedroom oceanfront condos is right on Meads Bay beach, with some of the island's best restaurants a sandy stroll away. **Pros:** beachfront location; huge apartments; well-kept grounds and pool. **Cons:** no elevator, so avoid booking a fourth-floor unit if you don't want to climb a lot of stairs (despite the great views). *$ Rooms from: $340 ✉ Meads Bay ☎ 264/462–6378 🌐 www.turtlesnestbeachresort.com 🛏 29 units 🍴 No meals.*

★ $$$$ FAMILY **Fodor's Choice** 🏨 **Viceroy Anguilla.** *Resort.* On a promontory over 3,200 feet of the gorgeous pearly sand on Meads Bay, Kelly Wearstler's haute-hip showpiece wows international sophisticates. **Pros:** state-of-the-art luxury; cutting-edge contemporary design; spacious rooms. **Cons:** international rather than Caribbean in feel; very large resort; kind of a see-and-be-seen scene; really expensive. *$ Rooms from: $795 ✉ Barnes Bay, West End ☎ 264/497–7000, 866/270–7798 in U.S. 🌐 www.viceroyhotelsandresorts.com 🛏 163 suites, 3 villas ⊙ Closed Sept. 🍴 Breakfast.*

NIGHTLIFE

In late February or early March, on the first full moon before Easter, reggae star and impresario Bankie Banx stages Moonsplash, a three-day music festival that showcases local and imported talent. The boat races on Anguilla Day in May is the most important island sporting event of the year. At the end of July is the Anguilla Summer Festival, with boat races by day and Carnival parades, calypso competitions and parties at night. Some years there is a Jazz Festival, check the Tourist Board website for information.

Most hotels and many restaurants offer live entertainment in high season and on weekends: it might include pianists, jazz combos, or traditional steel and calypso bands. Friday and Saturday, Sandy Ground is the hot spot; Wednesday and Sunday the action shifts to Shoal Bay East.

The nightlife scene here runs late into the night—the action doesn't really start until after 11 pm. If you do not rent a car, be aware that taxis are not readily available at night. If you plan to take a taxi back to your hotel or villa at the end of the night, be sure to make arrangements in advance with the driver who brings you or with your hotel concierge.

Dune Preserve. The funky Dune Preserve is the driftwood-fabricated home of Bankie Banx, Anguilla's famous reggae star. He performs here weekends and during the full moon. There's a dance floor and a beach bar, and sometimes you can find a sunset beach barbecue in progress. In high season there's a $15 cover charge. ✉ *Rendezvous Bay* ☎ *264/497–6219* ⊕ *www.bankiebanx.net.*

★ **Fodor'sChoice Elvis' Beach Bar.** This is the perfect locale (it's actually a boat) to hear great music and sip the best rum punch on earth. The bar is open every day but Tuesday, and there's live music Wednesday through Sunday nights during the high season—as well as food until 1 am. Check to see if there's a full-moon LunaSea party. You won't be disappointed. ✉ *Sandy Ground* ☎ *264/772–0637.*

Johnno's Beach Stop. Things are lively at Johnno's, where there is live music and alfresco dancing every night and on Sunday afternoon, when just about everybody drops by (on Sunday night, there's live jazz). This is *the* classic Caribbean beach bar, attracting a funky, eclectic mix, from locals to movie stars. It's open Tuesday through Sunday from 11 to 9. ✉ *Sandy Ground* ☎ *264/497–2728* ☉ *Closed Mon.*

★ **Fodor'sChoice Pumphouse.** At the Pumphouse, in the old rock-salt factory, you can find live music most nights—plus surprisingly good food from snacks like wings and calvados-flamed Camembert to burgers and steaks. Check out the minimuseum of artifacts and equipment from 19th-century salt factories. There's entertainment every night: Tuesday is Lady's night, and trivia is Sunday. ✉ *Sandy Ground* ☎ *264/497–5154* ⊕ *www.pumphouse-anguilla.com.*

SHOPPING

Anguilla is by no means a shopping destination. In fact, if your suitcase is lost, you will be hard-pressed to secure even the basics on-island. If you're a hard-core shopping enthusiast, a day trip to nearby St. Martin will satisfy. Well-heeled visitors sometimes organize boat or plane charters through their hotel concierge for daylong shopping excursions to St. Barth, and Anguilla Air Services started a reasonably priced daily round trip to St. Barth in 2012. The island's tourist publication, *What We Do in Anguilla,* has shopping tips and is available free at the airport and in shops. For upscale designer sportswear, check out the small boutiques in hotels (some are branches of larger stores in Marigot on St. Martin). Outstanding local artists sell their work in galleries, which often arrange studio tours (you can also check with the Anguilla Tourist Office).

Cheddie's Carving Studio. Cheddie's showcases Cheddie Richardson's fanciful wood carvings and coral and stone sculptures. ⊠ *Driftwood Haven, The Cove* ☎ *264/497–6027* ⊕ *www.news.ai/web/cheddie* ⊘ *Closed Sun.*

Devonish Art Gallery. This gallery purveys the wood, stone, and clay creations of Courtney Devonish, an internationally known potter and sculptor, plus creations by his wife, Carolle, a bead artist. Also available are works by other Caribbean artists and regional antique maps. ⊠ *West End Rd., George Hill* ☎ *264/497–2949* ⊕ *www.devonishart.com.*

The Galleria at World Art and Antiques. The peripatetic proprietor of World Arts, Christy Douglas, displays a veritable United Nations of antiquities: exquisite Indonesian ikat hangings to Thai teak furnishings, Aboriginal didgeridoos to Dogon tribal masks, Yuan Dynasty jade pottery to Uzbeki rugs. There is also handcrafted jewelry and handbags, and Anguilla souvenirs also. ⊠ *West End Rd., West End* ☎ *264/497–5950, 264/497–2767* ⊕ *www.worldartandantiques.com.*

Hibernia Restaurant and Gallery. Hibernia has striking pieces culled from the owners' travels, from contemporary Eastern European artworks to traditional Indo-Chinese crafts. ⊠ *Island Harbour* ☎ *264/497–4290* ⊕ *www.hiberniarestaurant.com.*

Savannah Gallery. Here you'll find works by local Anguillian artists as well as other Caribbean and Central American art, including oil paintings by Marge Morani. You'll also find works by artists of the renowned Haitian St. Soleil school, as well as Guatemalan textiles, Mexican pottery, and brightly painted metalwork. ⊠ *Coronation St., Lower Valley* ☎ *264/497–2263* ⊕ *www.savannahgallery.com.*

CLOTHING

Boutique Blu. This store at CuisinArt carries custom designs by the renowned jewelers Alberto e Lina, as well as Helen Kaminski accessories and more brand-name merchandise. ⊠ *CuisinArt Resort and Spa, Rendezvous Bay* ☎ *264/498–2000.*

Irie Life. This popular boutique sells vividly hued beach- and resort wear and flip-flops, as well as attractive handcrafts, jewelry, and collectibles from all over the Caribbean. ⊠ *South Hill* ☎ *264/497–6526* ⊕ *www.irielife.com.*

ZaZaa. Sue Ricketts, the first lady of Anguilla marketing, owns ZaZaa boutiques in South Hill on the Main Road, and near the entrance of Anacaona Resort, on Meads Bay. Buy Anguillian crafts as well as wonderful ethnic jewelry and beachwear from around the globe, such as sexy Brazilian bikinis and chic St. Barth goodies. There are beach sundries and souvenirs as well. ⊠ *Lower South Hill* ☎ *264/235–8878* ⊕ *www.anguillaluxurycollection.com.*

SPORTS AND ACTIVITIES

Anguilla's expanding sports options are enhanced by its beautiful first golf course, designed by Greg Norman, and part of the CuisinArt Resort, to accentuate the natural terrain and maximize the stunning ocean views over Rendezvous Bay. Players say the par-72 course is reminiscent of Pebble Beach. Personal experience says bring a lot of golf balls! The Anguilla Tennis Academy, designed by noted architect Myron Goldfinger, operates in the Blowing Point area. The 1,000-seat stadium, equipped with pro shop and seven lighted courts, was created to attract major international matches and to provide a first-class playing option for tourists and locals.

BOATING AND SAILING

Anguilla is the perfect place to try all kinds of water sports. The major resorts offer complimentary Windsurfers, paddleboats, and water skis to their guests.

FAMILY **Sandy Island Enterprises.** Take a day trip to the tiny island for a romantic barbecue lunch with your toes in the sand and a rum punch in your hand—*The Bachelor* did. The sea shuttle *Happiness* departs from the Sandy Ground Beach. The boat costs $10 per person round-trip. While reservations are preferred, you can come on a lark. ■TIP→ This is one of the best snorkeling spots on the island. ✉ *Sandy Ground* 🕾 *264/476–6534* ⊕ *www.mysandyisland.com* ⊘ *Closed after 4 pm; Aug. and Sept. by special arrangement.*

DIVING

Sunken wrecks; a long barrier reef; terrain encompassing walls, canyons, and hulking boulders; varied marine life, including greenback turtles and nurse sharks; and exceptionally clear water—all of these make for excellent diving. Prickly Pear Cay is a favorite spot. **Stoney Bay Marine Park**, off the northeast end of Anguilla, showcases the late-18th-century *El Buen Consejo*, a 960-ton Spanish galleon that sank here in 1772. Other good dive sites include **Grouper Bowl**, with exceptional hard-coral formations; **Ram's Head**, with caves, chutes, and tunnels; and **Upper Flats**, where you are sure to see stingrays.

Anguillian Divers. This is a full-service dive operator with a PADI five-star training center. The five-dive packages are a good deal, and they offer open-water certifications, too. ✉ *Meads Bay* 🕾 *264/497–4750* ⊕ *www.anguilliandiver.com.*

FAMILY **Shoal Bay Scuba and Watersports.** Single-tank dives start at $50 and two-tank dives at $90 at this highly rated Padi Dive Center. They run up to six different dives daily from their two locations, one at Sandy Ground at Roy's, and one in West End. Daily snorkeling trips at 1 pm are $25 per person. The shop sells a full range of masks, snorkels, fins, T-shirts, hats, shorts and SPF 50 water shirts. There are also private fishing charters, private dives, snorkel and sightseeing charters, and sunset cruises on offer. ✉ *West End, The Valley* 🕾 *264/235–1482* ⊕ *www.shoalbayscuba.com.*

FISHING

Johnno's Beach Stop. Albacore, wahoo, marlin, barracuda, and kingfish are among the fish found off Anguilla's shores. You can strike up a conversation with almost any fisherman you see on the beach, and chances are, you'll be a welcome addition on his next excursion. If you'd rather make more formal arrangements, Johnno's Beach Stop in

CLOSE UP

A Day at the Boat Races

If you want a different kind of trip to Anguilla, try for a visit during Carnival, which starts on the first Monday in August and continues for about 10 days. Colorful parades, beauty pageants, music, delicious food, arts-and-crafts shows, fireworks, and nonstop partying are just the beginning. The music starts with sunrise jam sessions—as early as 4 am—and continues well into the night. The high point? The boat races. They are the national passion and the official sport of Anguilla.

Anguillians from around the world return home to race old-fashioned, made-on-the-island wooden boats that have been in use on the island since the early 1800s. Similar to some of today's fastest sailboats, these are 15 to 28 feet in length and sport only a mainsail and jib on a single 25-foot mast. The sailboats have no deck, so heavy bags of sand, boulders, and sometimes even people are used as ballast. As the boats reach the finish line, the ballast—including some of the sailors—gets thrown into the water in a furious effort to win the race. Spectators line the beaches and follow the boats on foot, by car, and from even more boats. You'll have almost as much fun watching the fans as you will the races.

Sandy Ground has a boat and can help you plan a trip. ✉ *Sandy Ground Village* ☎ 264/497–2728.

GOLF

★ **Fodor's**Choice **CuisinArt Golf Club.** This Greg Norman course, a $50 million wonder, qualifies as one of the best golf courses in the Caribbean. Thirteen of its 18 holes are directly on the water. The course features sweeping sea vistas, elevation changes, and an ecologically responsible watering system of ponds and lagoons that snake through the grounds. Players including President Bill Clinton have thrilled to the spectacular vistas of St. Maarten and blue sea at the tee box of the 390-yard starting hole—the Caribbean's answer to Pebble Beach. There is an attractive Italian restaurant for lunch. Course typically closes for the second half of October for maintenance. Dress requirements include long shorts or slacks and a collared shirt. ✉ *Long Bay* ☎ 264/498–5602 ⊕ *www.cuisinartresort.com* ⚑ *$170 for 9 holes, $270 for 18 holes ($145/$225 for guests)* ⚑ *18 holes, 7200 yards, par 72.*

GUIDED TOURS

A round-the-island tour by taxi takes about 2½ hours and costs $55 for one or two people, $5 for each additional passenger.

Anguilla Access Tours. Take a three-hour tour of Anguilla for a comprehensive introduction to island heritage, food, nightlife, arts and crafts, or just beaches. Sign up online, get picked up at your hotel or villa. ✉ *Government Center, The Valley* ☎ *267/772–9827* ⊕ *www.anguillaaccess.com.*

Anguilla Tourist Office. Contact the Anguilla Tourist Office to arrange the tour by Sir Emile Gumbs, the island's former chief minister, of the Sandy Ground area. This tour, which highlights historic and ecological sites, is held Tuesday at 10 am. The $20 fee benefits the Anguilla Archaeological Historical Society. Gumbs also organizes bird-watching expeditions that show you everything from frigate birds to turtledoves. Other tours include a visit to Sea Turtle nesting sites, the Heritage Collection, and Wallblake House. ✉ *Coronation Ave., The Valley* ☎ *264/497–2759, 800/553–4939* ⊕ *www.ivisitanguilla.com.*

Bennie's Travel & Tours. This is one of the island's more reliable tour operators. ✉ *Blowing Point* ☎ *264/497–2788.*

HORSEBACK RIDING

Seaside Stables. If a sunset gallop (or slow clomp) has always been your fantasy, contact this company. Private rides on very gentle horses at any time of the day are $90 per hour, group rides in the morning or afternoon are $70; or try a bareback ocean romp or full-moon ride for $120; prior riding experience is not required. Choose from English, Western, or Australian saddles. ✉ *Paradise Dr., Cove Bay* ☎ *264/497–3667* ⊕ *www.seaside-stables.com.*

SEA EXCURSIONS

A number of boating options are available for airport transfers, day trips to offshore cays or neighboring islands, night trips to St. Martin, or just whipping through the waves en route to a picnic spot.

Chocolat. This 35-foot catamaran is available for private charter or scheduled excursions to nearby cays. Captain Rollins is a knowledgeable, affable guide. Rates for day sails with lunch (prepared by the captain's wife, Jacquie,

Little Bay, on Anguilla's northwest shore

of Ripples Restaurant) are about $80 per person. ✉ *Sandy Ground* ☎ *264/497–3394.*

Funtime Charters. This charter and shuttle service operates five powerboats ranging in size from 32 to 38 feet. They will arrange private boat transport to the airport ($65 per person), day trips to St. Barth, or other boat excursions. A new, fully air-conditioned 42-seat boat, *The Sunshine Express,* runs late-night and early morning direct to SXM, and also has inter-island excursions. ✉ *The Cove* ☎ *264/497–6511, 866/334–0047* ⊕ *www.funtimechartersanguilla.com.*

FAMILY **Junior's Glass Bottom Boat.** For an underwater peek at sea turtles and stingrays without getting wet, catch a ride ($20 per person) on Junior's Glass Bottom Boat. Snorkeling trips and instruction are available, too. Just show up at Shoal Bay Beach and look for the boat or ask for Junior at the Dive Shop. ✉ *Sandy Ground* ☎ *264/497–4456* ⊕ *www.junior.ai.*

No Fear Sea Tours. In addition to private airport transportation, day snorkeling trips, sunset cruises, and fishing trips on three 32-foot speedboats and a 19-foot ski boat, this charter service offers water-sports rentals (tubing, skiing, knee-boarding). ✉ *The Cove* ☎ *264/235–6354* ⊕ *www. nofearseatours.com.*

Sandy Island Enterprises. Picnic, swimming, and diving excursions to Prickly Pear Cay, Sandy Island, and Scilly Cay are available through Sandy Island Enterprises, which also rents Sunfish and Windsurfers and arranges fishing charters. Fans of TV's *The Bachelor* might recall the Valentine's Day picnic date here in 2011. You, too, can enjoy some rum punch and lobster. The Sandy Island sea shuttle leaves from the small pier in Sandy Ground daily November through July, and by reservation August through October. ✉ *The Valley* ☎ *264/476–6534* ⊕ *www. mysandyisland.com.*

4

TRAVEL SMART
ST. MAARTEN/
ST. MARTIN,
ST. BARTH &
ANGUILLA

GETTING HERE AND AROUND

St. Maarten/St. Martin, St. Barthélemy, and Anguilla are part of a cluster of islands in the Lesser Antilles that are fairly close together. In fact, the islands are linked by both frequent ferries and small-plane flights. St. Maarten/St. Martin, which has the only international airport among the three, is the international flight hub. Most travelers, regardless of which island they plan to visit, land in St. Maarten/St. Martin and make their way to their final destination.

▌ AIR TRAVEL

ST. MAARTEN/ST. MARTIN

There are nonstop flights from Atlanta (Delta, seasonal), Boston (JetBlue), Charlotte (US Airways), Miami (American), New York–JFK (American, Delta, JetBlue), Newark (United), and Philadelphia (US Airways). There are also some nonstop charter flights (including GWV/Apple Vacations from Boston). You can also connect in San Juan on JetBlue, LIAT, or Air Sunshine. Many smaller Caribbean-based airlines, including Air Caraïbes, Anguilla Air Services, Caribbean Airlines, Copa, Dutch Antilles Express, Insel, LIAT, and Winair (Windward Islands Airways), offer service from other islands in the Caribbean.

Airports Aéroport de L'Espérance. This airport, on the French side, is small and handles only island-hoppers. ✉ SFG Rte. l'Espérance, Grand Case, St. Martin ☎ 0590/27–11–00 ⊕ www.aeroport-saintmartin.com. **Princess Juliana International Airport.** This airport on the Dutch side handles all the large jets. ☎ 721/546–7542 ⊕ www.sxmairport.com.

Airline Contacts Air Caraïbes ☎ 0590/52–05–0 ⊕ www.aircaraibes-usa.com. **American Airlines** ☎ 721/545–2040, 800/433–7300 ⊕ www.aa.com. **Caribbean Airlines** ☎ 721/546–7660 ⊕ www.caribbean-airlines.com. **Delta Airlines** ☎ 721/546–7615 ⊕ www.delta.com. **Insel Air** ☎ 599/546–7621 ⊕ www.fly-inselair.com. **JetBlue** ☎ 721/546–7797, 877/306–4939 ⊕ www.jetblue.com. **LIAT** ☎ 888/844–5428 ⊕ www.liatairline.com. **St. Barths Commuter** ☎ 0590/87–80–73 ⊕ www.stbarthcommuter.com. **United Airlines** ☎ 721/546–7663 ⊕ www.united.com. **US Airways** ☎ 721/546–7680 ⊕ www.usairways.com. **Winair** ☎ 721/545–2568 ⊕ www.fly-winair.com.

ST. BARTHÉLEMY

There are no direct flights to St. Barth. Most North Americans fly first into St. Maarten's Queen Juliana International Airport, from which the island is 10 minutes by air. Winair, which celebrated its 50th anniversary of service to St. Barth in 2013, has regularly scheduled flights from St.

Maarten. Tradewind Aviation has regularly scheduled service from San Juan and also does V.I.P charters. Anguilla Air Services and St. Barth Commuter have scheduled flights and also do charters. You must reconfirm your return inter-island flight, even during off-peak seasons, or you may very well lose your reservations. Be certain to leave ample time between your scheduled flight and your connection in St. Maarten—three hours is the minimum recommended (and be aware that luggage frequently doesn't make the trip; your hotel or villa-rental company may be able to send someone to retrieve it). It's a good idea to pack a change of clothes, required medicines, and a bathing suit in your carry-on—or better yet, pack very light and don't check baggage at all.

Airports Gustaf III Airport (SBH) ⊠ *Rue de St. Jean, St-Jean* ☎ *0590/27–75–81.*

Local Airline Contacts An-guilla Air Services ⊠ *St. Barthé-lemy* ☎ *264/498–5922* ⊕ *www. anguillaairservices.com.* **St. Barth Commuter** ⊠ *St. Barthé-lemy* ☎ *0590/27–54–54* ⊕ *www. stbarthcommuter.com.* **Tradewind Aviation** ⊠ *St. Barthélemy* ☎ *800/ 376–7922, 203/267–3305 in Con-necticut* ⊕ *www.tradewindaviation. com.* **Winair** ⊠ *St. Barthélemy* ☎ *0590/27–61–01, 866/466–0410* ⊕ *www.fly-winair.com.*

ANGUILLA

There are no nonstop flights to Anguilla from the United States. TransAnguilla Airways offers daily flights from Antigua, St. Thomas, and St. Kitts. Windward Islands Airways flies several times a day from St. Maarten (SXM). Anguilla Air Services flies from St. Maarten (SXM) and St. Barth (SBH). LIAT comes in from Antigua, Nevis, St. Kitts, St. Thomas, and Tortola. Cape Air has two daily flights from San Juan (three on peak travel days).

Airport Clayton J. Lloyd Airport ☎ *264/497–3510.*

Local Airline Contacts An-guilla Air Services ☎ *264/498–5922, 264/235–7122* ⊕ *www. anguillaairservices.com.* **Cape Air** ☎ *866/227–3247, 508/771–6944* ⊕ *www.capeair.com.* **LIAT** ☎ *264/497–5002* ⊕ *www. liatairline.com.* **TransAnguilla Airways** ☎ *264/497–8690* ⊕ *www. transanguilla.com.* **Windward Is-lands Airways** ☎ *866/466–0410* ⊕ *www.fly-winair.com.*

▌ BOAT AND FERRY TRAVEL

ST. MAARTEN/ST. MARTIN

You can take ferries to St. Barth (45–80 minutes; €67–€93 from the Dutch or French side, though you can pay in dollars); to Anguilla (20 minutes; $25 from the French side); and to Saba (one to two hours; $90–$100 from the Dutch side). *Babou One,* a stabilized, air-conditioned boat run by West Indies Ferry Express, offers service between Marigot and Gustavia in only 70 minutes, timed to connect with international flights to and from St. Maarten's Princess Juliana Airport.

Contacts Dawn II. Ferry service to Saba. ✉ *Philipsburg, St. Maarten* ☎ *599/416–2299* ⊕ *www.sabactransport.com.* **Edge I and Edge II.** Day trips to Saba, St. Barth, and Anguilla. ✉ *Pelican Marina, Simpson Bay, St. Maarten* ☎ *721/544–2640, 721/544–2631* ⊕ *www.stmaarten-activities.com.* **Great Bay Express.** Service to St. Barth several times a day on a high-speed ferry. ✉ *Bobby's Marina Village, Phillipsburg, St. Maarten* ☎ *721/542–0032* ⊕ *www.greatbayferry.com.* **Link Ferries.** Ferry service to Anguilla from both Marigot and Princess Juliana Airport. ✉ *Marigot, St. Martin* ☎ *264/497–2231 in Anguilla, 264/497–3290 in Anguilla* ⊕ *www.link.ai.* **Shauna.** Service to Anguilla. ✉ *Simpson Bay, St. Maarten* ☎ *599/553–1820 in Anguilla.* **Voyager II.** Service to St. Barth from both Marigot and Oyster Pond. ✉ *Marigot, St. Martin* ☎ *0590/87–10–68* ⊕ *www.voy12.com.*

ST. BARTHÉLEMY

St Barth can be reached by sea via ferry service or charter boat. There are three companies that provide passenger ferry service between St. Maarten/St. Martin and St. Barth, so check each provider's timetable to determine the most convenient departure. All service is to and from Quai de la République in Gustavia. Voyager offers round trips for about $100 per person from either Marigot or Oyster Pond. Great Bay Express has several round trips a day from Bob-

by's Marina in St. Maarten for €55 if reserved in advance, or €60 for same-day departures. Private boat charters are also available, but they are very expensive; Master Ski Pilou is one of the companies that offer the service.

Boat and Ferry Contacts Great Bay Express Ferry. This express service provides quick ferry transportation between Phillipsburg and Gustavia two or three times daily. Online reservations are available on their website. Round-trip fares are €90 for adults and €45 for children, less if booked in advance. A same-day round trip is €56 for adults, €40 for kids. ✉ *Quai Gustavia, Gustavia* ☎ *690/71–83–01, 917/652–7346* ⊕ *www.sbhferry.com.* **Master Ski Pilou.** Private boat transfers from St. Maarten to St. Barth are available with Master Ski Pilou. ✉ *St. Barthélemy* ☎ *0590/27–91–79* ⊕ *www.masterski-pilou.com.* **Voyager.** This service offers several daily departures to Gustavia from Marigot or Oyster Pond in St. Martin. You can book online. ✉ *St. Barthélemy* ☎ *0590/87–10–68* ⊕ *www.voy12.com.*

ANGUILLA

Ferries run frequently between Anguilla and St. Martin. Boats leave from Blowing Point on Anguilla approximately every half hour from 7:30 am to 6:15 pm and from Marigot, St. Martin, every 45 minutes from 8 am to 7 pm. You pay a $20 departure tax before boarding ($5 for day-trippers—but be sure to make this clear at the window where you pay), in addition to the $15 one-way fare. Children under two years of age are free, children 2–5 are $10. On very windy days the 20-minute trip can be bouncy. The drive between the Marigot ferry terminal and the airport is vastly improved thanks to a new bridge across Simpson Bay. Transfers by speedboat to Anguilla are available from a new terminal right at the airport, at a cost of about $75 per person (arranged directly with a company, or through your Anguilla hotel). Private ferry companies listed below run six or more round-trips a day, coinciding with major flights, between Blowing Point and the airport in St. Maarten. On the St. Maarten side they will bring you right to the terminal in a van, or you can just walk across the parking lot. These trips are $35 one-way or $60 round-trip (cash only), and usually include departure taxes. There are also private charters available.

A late-night sea shuttle service leaves St. Maarten for Anguilla at 10:30 pm. This sea shuttle meets the daily American Airlines flight from Miami, which arrives at 9:55 pm. It then takes you directly to Blowing Point in Anguilla. The trip costs $85 per person. Another sea shuttle, which departs at 7 pm, also goes from St. Maarten to Anguilla. This connects with JetBlue and InselAir flights originating in San Juan. The cost is $65 per person.

Contacts Funtime Ferry ☎ 866/334-0047 ⊕ www.funtime-charters.com. **GB Express** ☎ 264/584-6205 ⊕ www.anguillaferryandcharter.com. **Link Ferries** ☎ 264/497-2231 ⊕ www.link.ai. **Shauna Ferries** ☎ 264/476-6275.

❙ CAR TRAVEL

ST. MAARTEN/ST. MARTIN

It's easy to get around the island by car. Most roads are paved and generally in good condition. However, they can be crowded, especially when the cruise ships are in port; you might experience traffic jams, particularly around Marigot and Philipsburg. Be alert for potholes and speed bumps, as well as the island tradition of stopping in the middle of the road to chat with a friend or yield to someone entering traffic. Few roads are identified by name or number, but most have signs indicating the destination. Driving is on the right. There are gas stations in Simpson Bay near the airport as well as in Cole Bay, and on the French side, in Sandy Ground and Marigot.

Car Rentals: You can book a car at Juliana International Airport, where all major rental companies have booths, but it is often much cheaper to reserve a car in advance from home. A shuttle to the rental-car lot is provided. Rates are among the best in the Caribbean, as little as $20–$35 per day. You can rent a car on the French side, but this rarely makes sense for Americans because of the unfavorable exchange rates.

Car-Rental Contacts Avis ✉ Simpson Bay, St. Maarten ☎ 721/545-2847 ⊕ www.avis.com. **Dollar/Thrifty Car Rental** ☎ 721/545-2393 ⊕ www.dollar.com. **Empress Rent-a-Car** ☎ 721/545-2062 ⊕ www.empressrentacar.com. **Golfe Car Rental** ✉ St. Martin ☎ 0590/51-94-81 ⊕ www.golfecarrental.com.

Hertz ☎ 721/545–4541 ⊕ www.
hertz.com. **Unity** ✉ Simpson Bay, St.
Maarten ☎ 721/520–5767 ⊕ www.
unitycarrental.com.

ST. BARTHÉLEMY

Roads are sometimes unmarked,
so get a map and look for
signs pointing to a destination.
These will be nailed to posts at
all crossroads. Roads are narrow and sometimes very steep,
but recent work has improved
roads all over the island; even
so, check the brakes and gears of
your rental car before you drive
away. ■TIP➜ Take a careful inven-
tory of existing dents and scrapes on
your rental vehicle with pictures on
your smartphone or digital camera.
Maximum speed on the island is
30 mph (50 kph). Driving is on
the right, as in the United States
and Europe. Parking is an additional challenge. There are two
gas stations on the island, one
near the airport and one in Lorient. They aren't open after 5 pm,
or on Sunday, but the station near
the airport has pumps that accept
automated payment by chip-and-
pin credit card (such as those used
throughout Europe), although at
this writing most U.S. credit cards
don't have the chip required for
credit payments. Considering the
short distances, a full tank of gas
should last you most of a week.

Car Rentals: You must have a valid
driver's license and be 25 or older
to rent, and in high season there
may be a three-day minimum.
During peak periods, such as
Christmas week and February, be
sure to arrange for your car rental
ahead of time. When you make

your hotel reservations, ask if the
hotel has its own cars available to
rent; some hotels provide 24-hour
emergency road service—something most rental companies don't
offer. A tiny but powerful Smart
car is a blast to buzz around in,
and also a lot easier to park than
larger cars. Expect to pay at least
$55 per day. A Mini Cooper con-
vertible makes the most of sunny
drives.

Car-Rental Contacts Avis ✉ Gustaf
III Airport (SBH), St Jean Rd., St-Jean
☎ 0590/27–71–43, 0590/27–71–52
⊕ www.avis-stbarth.com. **Budget**
✉ Gustaf III Airport, St. Jean Rd.,
St-Jean ☎ 0590/29–62–40 ⊕ www.
st-barths.com/budget/en/home.
html. **Cool Rental** ✉ Maison I, Flamands ☎ 0590/27–52–58 ⊕ www.
cool-rental.com. **Europcar** ✉ Gustaf
III Airport, St. Jean Rd., St-Jean
☎ 0590/27–74–34 ⊕ www.st-barths.
com/europcar/index.html. **Gumbs**
✉ Gustaf III Airport, St. Jean Rd.,
St-Jean ☎ 0590/27–75–32 ⊕ www.
gumbs-car-rental.com. **Hertz** ✉ Gustaf III Airport, St-Jean ☎ 0590/27–
71–14 ⊕ www.hertzstbarth.com.
Turbé ✉ Gustaf III Airport, St-Jean
☎ 0590/27–71–42 ⊕ www.turbe-car-
rental.com.

ANGUILLA

Although most of the rental cars
on-island have the driver's side
on the left as in North America,
Anguillian roads are like those in
the United Kingdom—driving is
on the left side of the road. It's
easy to get the hang of, but the
roads can be rough, so be cau-
tious, and observe the 30 mph
(48 kph) speed limit. Roundabouts are probably the biggest

driving obstacle for most. As you approach, give way to the vehicle on your right; once you're in, you have the right of way.

Car Rentals: A temporary Anguilla driver's license is required to rent a car—you can get into real trouble if you're caught driving without one. You get it for $20 (good for three months) at any of the car-rental agencies at the time you pick up your car; you'll also need your valid driver's license from home. Rental rates start at about $45–$55 per day, plus insurance.

Car-Rental Contacts Andy's Car Rental ☎ 264/235–7010 ⊕ www. andyrentals.com. **Apex/Avis** ⊠ Airport Rd. ☎ 264/497–2642 ⊕ www. avisanguilla.com. **Bryans Car Rental** ⊠ Blowing Point ☎ 264/497–6407 ⊕ www.bryanscarrentals.com. **Triple K Car Rental/Hertz** ⊠ Airport Rd. ☎ 264/497–2934.

▌ MOPED, SCOOTER, AND BIKE TRAVEL

ST. MAARTEN/ST. MARTIN
Though traffic can be heavy, speeds are generally slow, so a moped can be a good way to get around. Scooters rent for as low as €25 per day and motorbikes for €37 a day at Eugene Moto, on the French side. The Harley-Davidson dealer, on the Dutch side, rents hogs for $150 a day or $900 per week.

Contacts Eugene Moto ⊠ Sandy Ground Rd., Sandy Ground, St. Martin ☎ 0590/87–13–97. **Harley-Davidson** ⊠ 71 Union Rd., Cole Bay, St. Maarten ☎ 721/544–2704 ⊕ www.h-dstmartin.com.

ST. BARTH
Several companies rent motorbikes, scooters, mopeds, and mountain bikes. Motorbikes go for about $30 per day and require a $100 deposit. Helmets are required. Scooter and motorbike rental places are mostly along rue de France in Gustavia and around the airport in St-Jean.

Contacts Barthloc Rental ⊠ Rue de France, Gustavia ☎ 0590/27–52–81 ⊕ www.barthloc.com. **Chez Béranger** ⊠ 21 Rue du Général de Gaulle, Gustavia ☎ 0590/27–89–00 ⊕ www.beranger-rental.com.

▌ TAXI TRAVEL

ST. MAARTEN/ST. MARTIN
There is a government-sponsored taxi dispatcher at the airport and at the harbor. Posted fares are for one or two people. Add $5 for each additional person, $1 to $2 per bag. It costs about $18 from the airport to Philipsburg or Marigot, and about $30 to Dawn Beach. After 10 pm fares go up 25%, and after midnight 50%. Licensed drivers can be identified by the "taxi" license plate on the Dutch side and the window sticker on the French. You can hail cabs on the street or call the taxi dispatch to have one sent for you. Fixed fares apply from Juliana International Airport and the Marigot ferry to the various hotels around the island.

ST. BARTHÉLEMY
Taxis are expensive and not particularly easy to arrange, especially in the evening. There's a taxi station at the airport and another in Gustavia; from elsewhere you must

contact a dispatcher in Gustavia or St-Jean. Fares are regulated by the Collectivity, and drivers accept both dollars and euros. If you go out to dinner by taxi, let the restaurant know if you will need a taxi at the end of the meal, and they will call one for you. Limo-style private-car-and-driver service is also available through Taxi Prestige 24/7.

Contacts Gustavia taxi dispatcher ✉ *St. Barthélemy* ☎ *0590/27–66–31* ⊕ *www.stbarth-taxis.com.* **St-Jean taxi dispatcher** ✉ *Gustaf III Airport, St-Jean* ☎ *0590/27–75–81.* **Taxi Prestige** ✉ *St. Barthélemy* ☎ *0590/27–70–57* ⊕ *www.stbarts-limousine.com.*

ANGUILLA

Taxis are fairly expensive, so if you plan to explore the island's many beaches and restaurants, it may be more cost-effective to rent a car. Taxi rates are regulated by the government, and there are fixed fares from point to point, which are listed in brochures the drivers should have handy and are also published in the local guides. It's $26 from the airport or $22 from Blowing Point Ferry to West End hotels. Posted rates are for one or two people; each additional passenger adds $5 to the total, and there is a $1 charge for each piece of luggage beyond the allotted two. You can also hire a taxi for the hourly rate of $28. Surcharges of $4–$10 apply to trips after 6 pm. You'll always find taxis at the Blowing Point Ferry landing and at the airport. You'll need to call them to pick you up from hotels and restaurants, and arrange ahead with the driver who took you if you need a taxi late at night from one of the nightclubs or bars.

Taxi Contacts Blowing Point Ferry Taxi Stand ☎ *264/497–6089.* **Maurice & Sons Exquisite Taxi Services** ☎ *264/235–2676.*

ESSENTIALS

■ ACCOMMODATIONS

ST. MAARTEN/ST. MARTIN

St. Maarten/St. Martin has the widest array of accommodations of any of the three islands, with a range of large resort hotels, small resorts, time-shares, condos, private villas, and small B&Bs scattered across the island. Most of the larger resorts are concentrated in Dutch St. Maarten. Visitors find a wide range of choices in many different price ranges.

ST. BARTHÉLEMY

The vast majority of accommodations on St. Barth are in private villas in a wide variety of levels of luxury and price; villas are often priced in U.S. dollars. The island's small luxury hotels are exceedingly expensive, made more so for Americans because prices are in euros. A few modest and moderately priced hotels do exist on the island, but there's nothing on St. Barth that could be described as cheap, though there are now a few simple guest houses and inns that offer acceptable accommodations for what in St. Barth is a bargain price (under €100 per night in some cases).

ANGUILLA

Anguilla has several large luxury resorts, a few smaller resorts and guesthouses, and a rather large mix of private condos and villas. Lodging on Anguilla is generally fairly expensive, but there are a few more modestly priced choices.

■ COMMUNICATIONS

INTERNET

ST. MAARTEN/ST. MARTIN

Many hotels offer Internet service—some complimentary and some for a fee. There are free Wi-Fi hotspots (look for signs) all over the island, including on the Phillipsburg boardwalk, if you have your own laptop or tablet computer.

ST. BARTHÉLEMY

Most restaurants on the island now offer free Wi-Fi for customers, just ask your server for the password, and there is also a free hotspot at the port area.

Centre Alizes. Centre Alizes offers Internet service, fax, and secretarial services. They also rent phones. ✉ *Rue de la République, Gustavia* ☎ *0590/29-89-89.*

ANGUILLA

In Anguilla, Internet access is common at hotels, but Internet cafés are not. Many hotels offer only Wi-Fi access, so you may need to bring your own laptop or tablet computer to stay connected.

PHONES

ST. MAARTEN/ST. MARTIN

Calling from one side of the island to another is an international call. To phone from the Dutch side to the French, you first must dial 00–590–590 for local numbers (00–590–690 for cell phones), then the six digit number. To call from the French side to the Dutch, dial 00–721, then the local number. To call a local number on the French side, dial 0590 plus the six-digit number. On the Dutch side, just dial the seven-digit number with no prefix. Any of the local carriers—and most hotel concierges—can arrange for a prepaid rental phone for your use while you are on the island for about $5 a weekday plus a per-minute charge.

ST. BARTHÉLEMY

Many hotels will provide or rent you a cell phone to use during your stay. Some U.S. cell companies work in St. Barth, but ask your provider before you leave; you may need to have your phone authorized for international use. The country code for St. Barth is 590. Thus, to call St. Barth from the United States, dial 011 + 590 + 590 and the local six-digit number. Some cell phones use the prefix 690. For calls on St. Barth, you must dial 0590 plus the six-digit local number.

ANGUILLA

Most hotels will arrange with a local provider for a cell phone to use during your stay (or you can rent one). A prepaid, local cell gives you the best rates. Some U.S. GSM phones will work in Anguilla, some will not. To call Anguilla from the United States, dial 1 plus the area code 264, then the local seven-digit number. To call the United States and Canada, dial 1, the area code, and the seven-digit number.

▌EATING OUT

St. Maarten/St. Martin, Anguilla, and St. Barth are known for their fine restaurants. For more information on local cuisine and dining possibilities, see the individual island chapters. ⇨ *For information on food-related health issues, see Health below.*

PAYING

Credit cards are widely accepted on all three islands. For more information, see the individual island chapters.

▌ELECTRICITY

Generally, Dutch St. Maarten and Anguilla operate on 110 volts AC (60-cycle) and have outlets that accept flat-prong plugs—the same as in North America. You will need neither an adaptor nor a transformer in these islands.

French St. Martin and St. Barth operate on 220 volts AC (60-cycle), with round-prong plugs, as in Europe; you need an adapter and sometimes a converter for North American appliances. The French outlets have a safety mechanism— equal pressure must be applied to both prongs of the plug to connect to the socket. Most hotels have hair dryers, so you should not need to bring one (but ask your hotel to be sure), and some hotels have shaver outlets in the bathroom that accept North American electrical plugs.

▮ EMERGENCIES

ST. MAARTEN/ST. MARTIN
Emergency Services Dutch-side emergencies ☎ *911, 721/542–2222.* **French-side emergencies** ☎ *17.*

ST. BARTHÉLEMY
Emergency Services Ambulance and Fire ☎ *18, 0590/27–66–13.* **Hospital Emergency** ☎ *0590/27–60–35.* **Police** ☎ *11, 0590/27–11–70.*

ANGUILLA
As in the United States, dial 911 in any emergency.

▮ HEALTH

An increase in dengue fever has been reported across the Caribbean since early 2007. While Puerto Rico, Martinique, and Guadeloupe have been the islands most heavily affected, instances have been reported in other parts of the Caribbean as well, including St. Barth. Since there are no effective vaccines to prevent dengue fever, visitors to the region should protect themselves with mosquito repellent (particularly repellant containing DEET, which has been deemed the most effective) and keep arms and legs covered at sunset, when mosquitoes are particularly active.

There are no particular problems regarding food and water safety in St. Maarten/St. Martin, Anguilla, or St. Barth. If you have an especially sensitive stomach, you may wish to drink only bottled water; also be sure that food has been thoroughly cooked and is served to you fresh and hot. Peel fruit. If you have problems, mild cases of traveler's diarrhea may respond to Pepto-Bismol. Generally, Imodium (known generically as loperamide) just makes things worse, but it may be necessary if you have persistent problems. Be sure to drink plenty of fluids; if you can't keep fluids down, seek medical help immediately.

MEDICAL INSURANCE AND ASSISTANCE
Consider buying trip insurance with medical-only coverage. Neither Medicare nor some private insurers cover medical expenses anywhere outside the United States. Medical-only policies typically reimburse you for medical care (excluding that related to pre-existing conditions) and hospitalization abroad, as well as medical evacuation.

Another option is to sign up with a medical-evacuation assistance company. A membership in one of these companies provides doctor referrals, emergency evacuation or repatriation, 24-hour hotlines for medical consultation, and other assistance. International SOS Assistance Emergency and AirMed International provide evacuation services and medical referrals. MedjetAssist offers medical evacuation.

Medical Assistance Companies AirMed International ☎ *800/356–2161, 205/443–4840* ⊕ *www.airmed.com.* **International SOS** ☎ *215/942–8226* ⊕ *www.internationalsos.com.*

Medical-Only Insurers International Medical Group ☎ *800/628–4664, 317/655–4500* ⊕ *www.imglobal.com.*

▌HOURS OF OPERATION

ST. MAARTEN/ST. MARTIN

Banks on the Dutch side are open weekdays 8:30 to 4:30, Saturday 9 to noon. French banks are open weekdays 7:45 to 12:30 and 2:30 to 4; they're usually closed on Wednesday and Saturday afternoons and afternoons preceding public holidays. Dutch-side post offices are open weekdays 7:30 to 5. On the French side, post offices are open weekdays 7:30 to 4:45 and Saturday 7:30 to 11:30. Shops on the Dutch side are generally open Monday through Saturday 9 to 6; on the French side, Monday through Saturday from 9 to 12:30 and 3 to 7. In Grand Case and around the Sonesta Maho Beach, the shops generally stay open until 11 pm to cater to the dinner crowd. Increasingly, shops on both sides remain open during lunch. Some of the larger shops are open on Sunday and holidays when cruise ships are in port.

ST. BARTHÉLEMY

Banks are generally open weekdays from 8 to noon and 2 to 3:30, but most have 24-hour ATMs. The main post office on rue Jeanne d'Arc in Gustavia is open Monday, Tuesday, Thursday, and Friday from 8 to 3, on Wednesday and Saturday until noon. The branch in Lorient is open weekdays from 7 am to 11 am and Saturday from 8 am to 10 am. The post office in St-Jean is open on Monday and Tuesday from 8 to 2 and on Wednesday through Saturday from 8 to noon. Stores are generally open weekdays from 8:30 to noon and 2 to 5, Saturday from 8:30 to noon. Some of the shops across from the airport and in St-Jean stay open on Saturday afternoon and until 7 pm on weekdays. A few around St-Jean even stay open on Sunday afternoon during the busy season. Although some shops are closed on Wednesday afternoon, most are open from 8:30 to noon and 3 to 6.

ANGUILLA

Banks are open Monday through Thursday from 8 to 3 and Friday 8 to 5. Most shops are open from 10 to 5 on weekdays only. Most commercial establishments are closed weekends, although some small groceries open for a few hours on Sunday afternoon, but call first, or adopt the island way of doing things: if it's not open when you stop by, try again.

▌MAIL

ST. MAARTEN/ST. MARTIN

Letters from the Dutch side to North America and Europe cost ANG2.85; postcards to all destinations are ANG1.65. From the French side, letters up to 20 grams and postcards are €1 to North America. Postal codes are used only on the French side.

ST. BARTHÉLEMY

Mail is slow and can take up to three weeks to arrive. The main post office is in Gustavia, but smaller post offices are in St-Jean and Lorient. DHL, FedEx, and UPS all provide service to the island.

ANGUILLA

Airmail postcards and letters cost EC$1.50 (for the first ½ ounce) to the United States. The only post office is in The Valley; it's open weekdays 8 to 3:30. There's a FedEx office near the airport. It's open weekdays 8–5 and Saturday 9–1.

▮ MONEY

Prices throughout this guide are given for adults. Substantially reduced fees are almost always available for children, students, and senior citizens. Refrences to credit cards are made only in those cases where they are not accepted.

ST. MAARTEN/ST. MARTIN

Legal tender on the Dutch side is the Netherlands Antilles florin, but almost everyone accepts U.S. dollars. On the French side, the currency is the euro, but most establishments accept dollars. At this writing, quite a few restaurants continue to offer one-to-one euro-for-dollar exchanges in cash. ATMs dispense dollars or euros, depending on where you are.

ST. BARTHÉLEMY

Legal tender is the euro, but U.S. dollars are widely accepted. ATMs are common and dispense only euros.

ANGUILLA

Legal tender is the Eastern Caribbean (EC) dollar, but U.S. dollars are widely accepted. ATMs dispense both U.S. and EC dollars. All prices quoted in this chapter are in U.S. dollars.

▮ PASSPORTS

A valid passport and a return or ongoing ticket is required for travel to Anguilla, St. Barthélemy, and St. Maarten/St. Martin. There are no border controls whatsoever between the Dutch and French sides of St. Maarten/St. Martin. Passports must be valid for at least three months from the date of entry to the territory of St. Barthélemy.

▮ SAFETY

ST. MAARTEN/ST. MARTIN

Petty crime can be a problem on both sides of the island (though less so on the French side than on the Dutch side), and robberies (including armed robberies) have been on the upswing. Always lock your valuables and travel documents in your room safe or your hotel's front-desk safe. Don't ever leave anything in the car, even in the glove compartment. When driving, keep your seatbelt on and the car doors locked. Never leave anything unattended at the beach. Despite the romantic imagery of the Caribbean, it's not good policy to take long walks along the beach at night. You should be on guard even during the day. Don't flash cash or jewelry, carry your handbag securely and zipped, and park in the busier areas of parking lots in towns and at beaches.

Other suggestions include carrying only your driver's license and a photocopy of your passport with you for identification, leaving the original in your hotel safe. In general, use the same caution here as you would use at home.

ST. BARTHÉLEMY

There's relatively little crime on St. Barth. Visitors can travel anywhere on the island with confidence. Most hotel rooms have safes for your valuables. As anywhere, don't tempt loss by leaving cameras, laptops, or jewelry out in plain sight in your hotel room or villa or in your car. Don't walk barefoot at night. There are venomous centipedes that can inflict a remarkably painful sting. If you ask residents, they will tell you that they only drink bottled water, although most cook or make coffee with tap water.

ANGUILLA

Anguilla is a quiet, relatively safe island, but crime has been on the rise, and there's no sense in tempting fate by leaving your valuables unattended in your hotel room, on the beach, or in your car. Avoid remote beaches, and lock your car, hotel room, and villa. Most hotel rooms are equipped with a safe for stashing your valuables.

▌ TAXES AND SERVICE CHARGES

ST. MAARTEN/ST. MARTIN

Departure tax from Juliana Airport is $10 to destinations within the Netherlands Antilles and $30 to all other destinations. It is usually included in your air ticket. It will cost you €3 (usually included in the ticket price) to depart by plane from Aéroport de L'Espérance and $5 (the rate can change) by ferry to Anguilla from Marigot's pier. Hotels on the Dutch side add a 15% service charge to the bill as well as a 5% government tax. Hotels on the French side add 10%–15% and generally 5% tax.

ST. BARTHÉLEMY

The island charges a $5 departure tax when your next stop is another French island, $10 to anywhere else payable in cash only (dollars or euros). Some hotels add a 10% service charge. Sometimes it is included in the room rate, so check. There is a 5% room tax on hotels and villa rentals.

ANGUILLA

The departure tax is $20 for adults and $10 for children, payable in cash, at the airport at Blowing Point Ferry Terminal. If you are staying in Anguilla but daytripping to St. Martin, be sure to mention it, and the rate will be only $5. A 10% accommodations tax is added to hotel bills along with a $1-per-night marketing tax, plus whatever service charge the hotel adds (can be up to 10%).

▌ TIME

St. Maarten, Anguilla, and St. Barth are in the Atlantic Standard Time zone, which is one hour later than Eastern Standard and four hours earlier than GMT. Caribbean islands don't observe daylight saving time, so during the period when it's in effect, Atlantic Standard and Eastern Standard are the same.

■ TIPPING

ST. MAARTEN/ST. MARTIN

Service charges may be added to hotel and restaurant bills on the Dutch side (otherwise tip 15%–18%). Check bills carefully so you don't inadvertently tip twice. On the French side, a service charge is customary; on top of the included service it is customary to leave an extra 5%–10% *in cash* for the server. Taxi drivers, porters, and maids depend on tips. Give 10% to 15% to cabbies, $1 per bag for porters, and $2 to $5 per night per guest for chambermaids.

ST. BARTHÉLEMY

Restaurants include a 15% service charge in their published prices, but it's common French practice to leave 5% to 10% more in cash, even if you have paid by credit card. Most taxi drivers don't expect a tip.

ANGUILLA

Despite any service charge, it's usually expected that you will tip more—$5 per day for housekeeping, $20 for a helpful concierge, and $10 per day to beach attendants. Many restaurants include a service charge of 10% to 15% on the bill; if there's no surcharge, tip about 15%. Taxi drivers should receive 10% of the fare.

■ TRIP INSURANCE

Comprehensive trip insurance is valuable if you're booking a very expensive or complicated trip (particularly to an isolated region) or if you're booking far in advance. Comprehensive policies typically cover trip cancellation and interruption, letting you cancel or cut your trip short due to illness or, in some cases, acts of terrorism in your destination. Such policies might also cover evacuation and medical care. (For trips abroad you should have at least medical-only coverage. *See Medical Insurance and Assistance under Health.*) Some policies also cover you for trip delays due to bad weather or mechanical problems, as well as for lost or delayed luggage.

Another type of coverage to consider is financial default—that is, when your trip is disrupted because a tour operator, airline, or cruise line goes out of business. Generally, you must buy this when you book your trip or shortly thereafter; also, it's available only if your operator doesn't appear on a list of excluded companies.

Always read the fine print of your policy to make sure that you're covered for the risks that most concern you. Compare several policies to be sure you're getting the best price and range of coverage available.

Insurance Comparison Sites SquareMouth ☎ 800/240-0369 ⊕ *www.squaremouth.com.*

Comprehensive Travel Insurers Allianz Travel Insurance ☎ 866/884-3556 ⊕ *www.allianztravelinsurance.com.* **CSA Travel Protection** ☎ 800/711-1197 ⊕ *www.csatravelprotection.com.* **Travel Insured International** ☎ 800/243-3174 ⊕ *www.travelinsured.com.*

▌ VISITOR INFORMATION

ST. MAARTEN/ST. MARTIN
Contacts Dutch-side Tourist Information Bureau ✉ *Vineyard Park Bldg., 33 W. G. Buncamper Rd., Philipsburg, St. Maarten* ☎ *721/542-2337* ⊕ *www.vacationstmaarten.com.* French-side Office de Tourisme ✉ *Rte. de Sandy Ground, facing Marina Port la Royale, Marigot, St. Martin* ☎ *0590/87-57-21* ⊕ *www. iledesaintmartin.org.*

ST. BARTHÉLEMY
Contact Office du Tourisme ✉ *Quai du Général de Gaulle, Gustavia* ☎ *0590/27-87-27* ⊕ *www. saintbarth-tourisme.com.*

ANGUILLA
Contacts Anguilla Tourist Office ✉ *Coronation Ave., The Valley* ☎ *264/497-2759, 800/553-4939 from U.S.* ⊕ *ivisitanguilla.com.*

▌ WEDDINGS

ST. MAARTEN/ST. MARTIN
There's a three-day waiting period on the Dutch side. Getting married on the French side is not a viable option because of long wait times.

Information Chief Registrar ✉ *Census Office, Soualiga Rd., Philipsburg* ☎ *599/542-4267.*

ST. BARTHÉLEMY
Because of the long legal residency requirement, it's not really feasible to get married on St. Barth unless you're a French citizen.

ANGUILLA
Weddings are common, but there's a huge $241.80 (EC$650) fee for a license. Visit Anguilla's government website for more information:

Contacts Government of Anguilla Judicial Department ☎ *264/497-2377* ⊕ *www.gov.ai/marriage.php.*

INDEX

Photo Credits

Front cover: Chip Litherland Photography [Description: Maho Beach, St. Maarten] 1, Chris Caldicott / age fotostock. 2, James Schwabel / age fotostock. 3 (top), Loterie Farm. 3 (bottom): Walter Bibikow / age fotostock. 4 (top), Eden Rock. 4 (bottom), © thierrydehove.com/CuisinArt Resort & Spa. 5 (top left), Richie Diesterheft/Flickr Attribution-ShareAlike License. 5 (top right), Zach Stovall. 5 (bottom), DIDIER FORRAY / age fotostock. 6 (top), nik wheeler / Alamy. 6 (bottom), DIDIER FORRAY / age fotostock. 7 (top left), Joe Vaughn. 7 (top right), Slim Plantagenate / Alamy. 7 (bottom), Restaurant Le Gaiac. 8 (top), Olivier Goujon / age fotostock. 8 (bottom), M.Torres / Travel-Images. com. 10, Chris Caldicott/age fotostock. Chapter 1: Experience St. Maarten, St. Barth, and Anguilla: 12-13, Saint Barth Tourisme. 15 (left), Steve Geer/iStock-photo. 15 (right), St Maarten Tourist Bureau. 19, Lisa Gumbs. 20, Ku. 21, Foto Factory /Shutterstock. 22, Hotel Carl Gustaf. 23, Olivier Leroi. Chapter 2: St. Maarten/St. Martin: 25, Angelo Cavalli/age fotostock. 27, St Maarten Tourist Bureau. 36-37, alysta/Shutterstock. 40, liveo/istockphoto. 42, St Maarten Tourist Bureau. 45, St Maarten Tourist Bureau. 70, Chris Floyd. 82, Peter Phipp / age fotostock. 85, Kevin Gabbert/wikipedia.org. 88, Walter Hellebrand/wikipedia. org. 90, St Maarten Tourist Bureau. 92, Claude Cavalera. 94, Colin D. Young/ Shutterstock. Chapter 3: St. Barthélemy: 99, Christian Wheatley/shutterstock. 103, Karl Weatherly / age fotostock. 108, Christian Wheatley/iStockphoto. 130, Tibor Bognar / age fotostock. 136, Karl Weatherly / age fotostock. Chapter 4: Anguilla: 139, stevegeer/istockphoto. 143, Steve Geer/iStockphoto. 148-49, mag-gieandcharles/Flickr. 157, Straw Hat. 160, stevegeer/istockphoto. 169, Timothy O'Keefe / age fotostock. 172, stevegeer/istockphoto. Spine: rnfron/iStockphoto

About Our Writers: All photos are courtesy of the writers.

NOTES

NOTES

NOTES

NOTES

NOTES

NOTES

NOTES

NOTES

NOTES

NOTES

NOTES

Fodor's InFocus
ST. MAARTEN/ST. MARTIN, ST. BARTH & ANGUILLA

Publisher: Amanda D'Acierno, *Senior Vice President*

Editorial: Arabella Bowen, *Editor in Chief*; Linda Cabasin, *Editorial Director*

Design: Fabrizio La Rocca, *Vice President, Creative Director*; Tina Malaney, *Associate Art Director*; Chie Ushio, *Senior Designer*; Ann McBride, *Production Designer*

Photography: Jennifer Arnow, *Associate Director of Photography*; Jennifer Romains, *Researchers*

Maps: Rebecca Baer, *Senior Map Editor*; David Lindroth; *Cartographers*

Production: Linda Schmidt, *Managing Editor*; Evangelos Vasilakis, *Associate Managing Editor*; Angela L. McLean, *Senior Production Manager*

Sales: Jacqueline Lebow, *Sales Director*

Marketing & Publicity: Heather Dalton, *Marketing Director*; Katherine Punia, *Senior Publicist*

Business & Operations: Susan Livingston, *Vice President, Strategic Business Planning*; Sue Daulton, *Vice President, Operations*

Fodors.com: Megan Bell, *Executive Director, Revenue & Business Development*; Yasmin Marinaro, *Senior Director, Marketing & Partnerships*

Copyright © 2015 by Fodor's Travel, a division of Random House LLC

Editorial Contributor: Elise Meyer

Editors: Douglas Stallings, *series editor,* Perrie Hartz

Production Editor: Carrie Parker

4th Edition

ISBN 978-0-8041-4351-6

ISSN 1942-7344

All details in this book are based on information supplied to us at press time. Always confirm information when it matters, especially if you're making a detour to visit a specific place. Fodor's expressly disclaims any liability, loss, or risk, personal or otherwise, that is incurred as a consequence of the use of any of the contents of this book.

SPECIAL SALES

This book is available at special discounts for bulk purchases for sales promotions or premiums. For more information, e-mail specialmarkets@randomhouse.com

PRINTED IN THE UNITED STATES OF AMERICA

10 9 8 7 6 5 4 3 2 1

ABOUT OUR WRITER

Elise Meyer's friends insist that her middle name is "Let's Go." With an academic background in art history, she opened a gallery in SoHo in the 1970s, which was a great excuse to travel frequently to Europe. A life-long resident of New England, she believes that her regular trips to the Caribbean have always been a wintertime necessity, despite a passion for skiing. For 20 years, St. Barth and Anguilla have been frequent destinations, when she is not pursuing (and chronicling) interests in gardening, food, golf, the arts, and things that are funny. Now that the two kids are off on their own adventures, she's been enjoying longer and more exotic trips with a husband who shares her wanderlust, as well as a firm resolve never to check in luggage, and she's taken on St. Maarten/St. Martin as well. She's a long-time contributor to *Fodor's Caribbean*.

EUGENE FODOR

Hungarian-born Eugene Fodor (1905–91) began his travel career as an interpreter on a French cruise ship. The experience inspired him to write *On the Continent* (1936), the first guidebook to receive annual updates and discuss a country's way of life as well as its sights. Fodor later joined the U.S. Army and worked for the OSS in World War II. After the war, he kept up his intelligence work while expanding his guidebook series. During the Cold War, many guides were written by fellow agents who understood the value of insider information. Today's guides continue Fodor's legacy by providing travelers with timely coverage, insider tips, and cultural context.